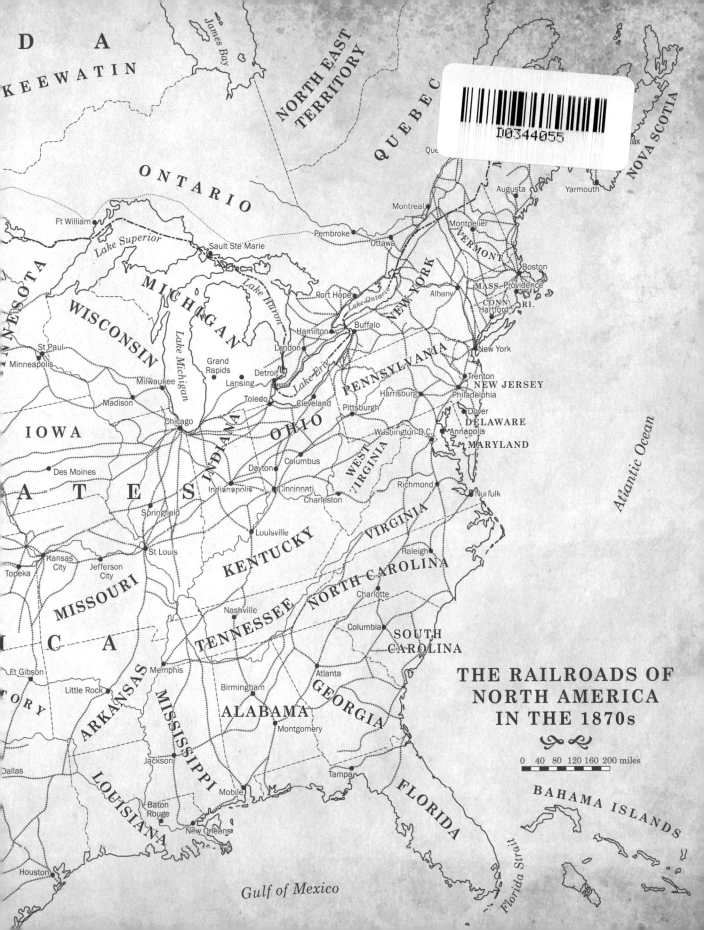

THE RAILROADS OF
NORTH AMERICA
IN THE 1870s

0 40 80 120 160 200 miles

GREAT AMERICAN RAILROAD JOURNEYS

GREAT AMERICAN RAILROAD JOURNEYS

HISTORICAL COMPANION TO THE BBC SERIES

Foreword by Michael Portillo

SIMON &
SCHUSTER

London · New York · Sydney · Toronto · New Delhi

A CBS COMPANY

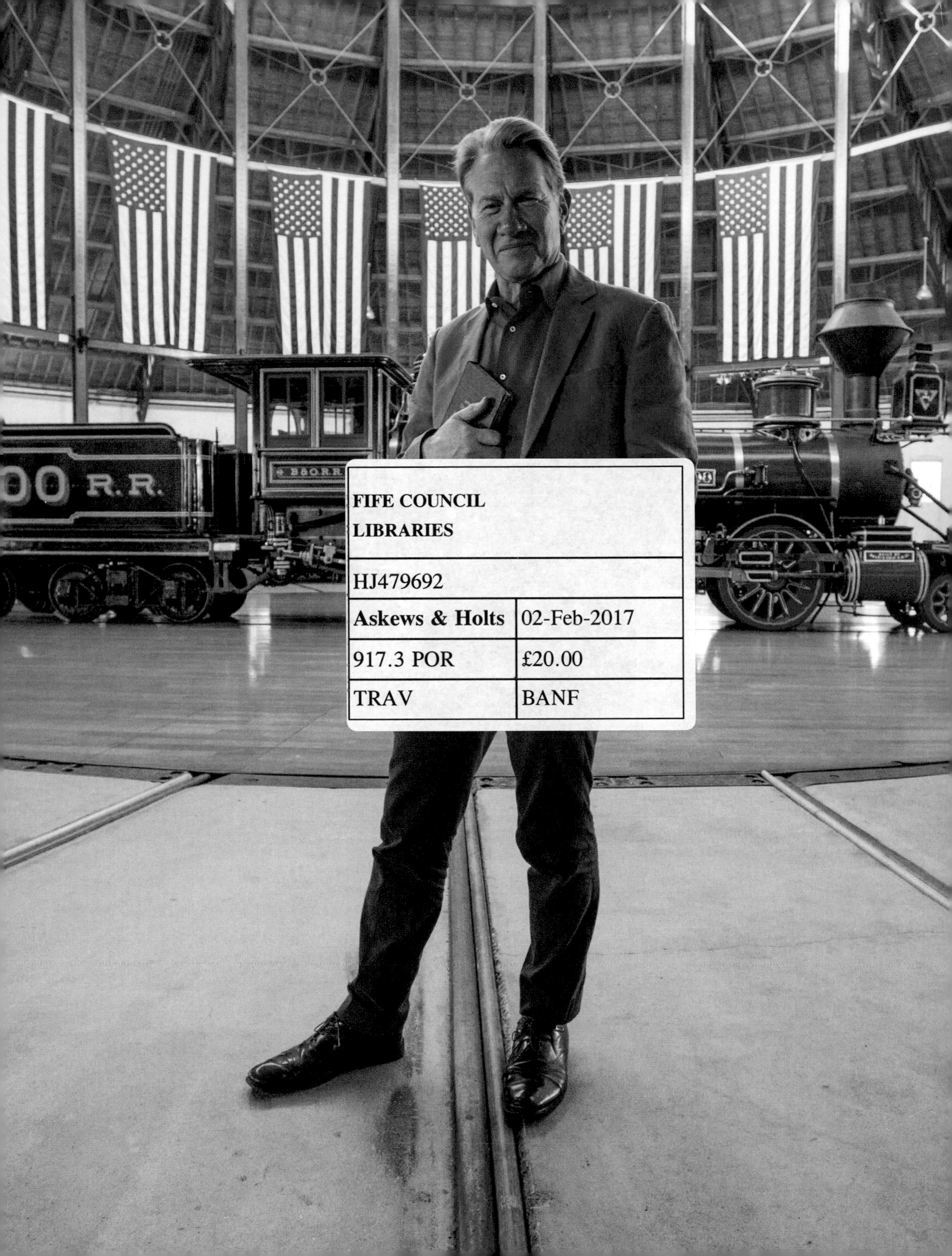

CONTENTS

FOREWORD

Throughout the years of making rail journeys for BBC television, first in the United Kingdom and then on the continent of Europe, I had dreamed of carrying the programme's concept to the United States. Although Britain was marginally ahead of the US with its first inter-city passenger railway, the Americans soon had a vastly greater network. Some Americans had worried that as their country pushed out rapidly to the west it would break up, becoming merely a collection of nations like Europe. The tracks and the locomotives may have arrived just in time to knit the expanding nation together.

Alas, there was no Bradshaw's handbook to steer me across the US, but a father and son called Appleton produced a *General Guide to the United States and Canada*, promising to illuminate all that is 'novel, picturesque, beautiful, memorable, striking or curious'; and I ventured forth with volumes published around 1879. Like Bradshaw's, they guided me to journey by train, opening up for me not just the continent but also the American state of mind little more than a decade after the end of the devastating Civil War.

As I soon discovered on my American rail journeys, it would be a mistake to forget the waterways and canals that preceded the tracks. The building of a canal in 1825 between Lake Erie and the Hudson River meant that grain from the Midwest – from as far afield as Minnesota – could pass via grain silos in Buffalo, New York down to New York City, and then across the Atlantic to feed Europe. The trade sealed the city's fortune, making it America's principal port.

The advent of the railroads speeded up everything, and the tracks were less susceptible than the canals to freezing. In a 'gilded age', they made great fortunes for tycoons, and in the second half of the nineteenth century they helped to unleash a revolution in heavy industries.

In the era of Rockefeller, Carnegie and Vanderbilt, the industrial success of the US and its expansion westward sucked in millions of European immigrants fleeing persecution or poverty, 'huddled masses yearning to breathe free', many passing through New York's Ellis Island.

As I explored New York State, I saw the Long Island mansions of the tycoons and the Manhattan tenements of the immigrants; and then I enjoyed the serene beauty of the mighty Hudson from my train seat, as it hugged the river bank mile after mile, before delivering me to witness the awe-inspiring power of Niagara Falls.

My rail journey south from Philadelphia confronted me with the political rather than the industrial history of the Americans. In 1607, three ships landed English colonists in continental America, where they constructed James Fort (near present-day Jamestown) in Virginia, the colony named after Queen Elizabeth. They soon came close to starvation and may have been saved by Native Americans (including Pocahontas) who thought it in their best interests to help the Europeans to survive.

Virginia became the pre-eminent colony by wealth and population. The revolution against British rule, preceded by skirmishing in Massachusetts, might not have occurred had

mighty Virginia not voted for rebellion. Certainly, it was a Virginian, Thomas Jefferson, who drafted the Declaration of Independence, and another, George Washington, who emerged as the hero of the war against the Crown, and the unanimous choice to be first president of the United States.

When I visited the Liberty Bell, cast in Whitechapel in London and already hanging in the Pennsylvania State House in Philadelphia when the Declaration was proclaimed, I was deeply impressed by the noble ambitions of the revolutionaries. 'All men are created equal' and entitled to 'life, liberty and the pursuit of happiness'.

However, back in 1619, Virginia had imported, for the first time, slaves from Africa. The slave population had then grown enormously. The agricultural economy, at least of the south, was thought to depend on slavery. The Founding Fathers perceived the contradiction that the United States was the land of the free and the home of the slave, but no political solution could be found at that time.

President Abraham Lincoln got off the train at Gettysburg, Pennsylvania on 18 November 1863 to attend the dedication of the cemetery where lay buried Union soldiers killed in the battle of the previous July. The north's aim (in what turned out to be the first American railroad war) had been to preserve the Union against secession by the Confederate states, rather than to abolish slavery; but in his Gettysburg address Lincoln, in a few brief remarks, recalled the words of the Declaration and committed the victors to a rebirth of freedom. Emancipation was to follow.

As always, my travels through history were punctuated by escapades. They helped me to understand the American cultures that have emerged from the country's diverse origins. At Nathan's on Coney Island, New York, there is a competition for how many hot dogs a person can consume in ten minutes! It is not for the faint-hearted. While on Long Island, I relived the era of F. Scott Fitzgerald's *The Great Gatsby* with a painfully incompetent attempt to dance the Charleston. In Philadelphia, I put on the shoulder pads and helmet of an American football player. In Virginia, in the elegant setting of the Richmond Woman's [sic] Club, I joined a cotillion, where the more refined sort of teenager (boys in bow ties, girls in pretty dresses) learns etiquette and the cha-cha-cha. In nearby Petersburg I was stirred by the rhythm and beat of the gospel choir of the First Baptist Church. Ploughing a furrow or two behind yoked oxen in Williamsburg, Virginia helped me to understand how proud colonials became independence-minded, as their own representative political institutions matured.

After the Civil War, new railroads helped to tie together the disunited states. But when I alighted from the train in Baltimore and then Washington, D.C., I met African Americans who believe that the progress towards equality, begun with the postwar emancipation of the slaves, still has far to go.

That does not make me cynical. To this day, the founding ideals of liberty and equality resonate with Americans. They provide them with clarity, unity and a sense of purpose, great strengths in a nation that is still filled with hope for its future.

Michael Portillo

INTRODUCTION

While the Europeans attribute America's bounty to the luck of her resources, Americans on the other hand like to ascribe it to nothing but character. It usually required a combination of both.

Alistair Cooke

Only partially formed, and burdened by domestic divisions, America nonetheless entered the nineteenth century feeling chipper.

After declaring independence in 1776, it had won the ensuing battle against British colonialists against all odds and was now flexing its economic muscle. Exports worth $20 million in 1790 rose more than three times in value by 1811. The population doubled in about the same period.

In 1803, Ohio became the seventeenth state of the Union, and an expedition by Meriwether Lewis and William Clark set off – the first to cross what is now the western portion of the US.

And, thanks to manoeuvrings by Napoleon Bonaparte in distant France, America doubled in size as a result of the Louisiana Purchase, when land previously held by Spain and France was relinquished. The deal encompassed 530 million acres (214 million hectares), the area of 15 modern states, bought by America for $15 million.

But this sheer abundance gave administrators plenty to ponder. Who would live in these vast tracts of land and how would they be governed?

Coastal and riverside communities were buoyed by the arrival of steamships, but these couldn't reach the continental interior, where communications were carried only as fast as a horse could gallop.

It seemed canals would provide a vital link. Colossal undertakings, their blueprints attracted funds and support. However, even with canals, national development would come at a snail's pace.

But before the middle of the century, both steamships and canals had been knocked from their high perches by the arrival of railroads. It would be the iron horse, as it was fondly dubbed, that took immigrant settlers to new cities, towns and homes.

At first, Americans were led by events unfolding in Britain, where steam technology had been born. Soon, they would be designing and building locomotives and railroads better suited to American terrain.

For decades, the new routes were focused on the east coast, where the fortunes of towns could be made or broken by the route of the railroad network. Southern states turned away from the invasive technology and paid the price.

It took 40 years for coast-to-coast tracks to finally unleash America's economic capabilities. At a century old, the country was a powerhouse for politics, industry and agriculture.

But there was a flip side that accompanied railroad expansion, extending far beyond the intrusion of the locomotive's rattle and smoke smuts.

America needed speculators from the get-go to build the foundations of the nation. But undue respect for those who put energy and capital into railroad schemes resulted in a management model that valued the dollar far above the lives of fellow men and women, putting in peril the notion of the Declaration of Independence that 'all men are created equal'.

Not everyone was so invested in rampant capitalism. When first inaugurated, President Lincoln pointed out: 'Capital is only the fruit of labour and could never have existed if labour had not first existed. Labour is the superior of capital and deserves much the higher consideration.'

For industrial cargo, when the power of one steam locomotive wasn't enough, others were lined up to help pull the heavy load.

The financial heft of the few affected all walks of life. Proof, if it is needed, comes in the form of the frequent 'panics' of the nineteenth century that wrecked the American financial markets and which were so closely intertwined with railroads.

Unconstrained capitalism was checked during the early twentieth century, by which time America had joined the international top tier.

In many respects, it was thanks to railroads that America could make the most of its attributes, uniting all-comers and making Federalism function.

THE EARLY YEARS

Before railroads, the vast American outdoors was pristine. The air was fragrant, the greenery unbroken and the loudest sounds to be heard were made by buffaloes and birds.

However, such tranquillity, so highly valued today, had its disadvantages, especially in terms of trade. Of course, people and goods did travel long distances, but journeys were unpredictable and often perilous.

Horses had primacy, hauling wagons and stagecoaches or being saddled up for riders. But whichever way people chose to use them, it was uncomfortable and slow, as the toll-charging turnpike roads were only roughly prepared.

Barges offered greater comfort and made swifter progress along the broad waterways that led inland from the coast. But routes were limited by the course and navigability of the rivers, and although canals were another feasible option, they took a long while to dig. Transport by water could also be badly affected by harsh winter weather.

And with such restricted options, the cost of using stagecoaches and barges was high.

Technological changes were afoot. Coarsely made rails were installed at mines at the inception of the industrial age, aping the Romans, who had used smooth grooves to help their carts make headway. Loaded mine wagons were sent downhill using gravity and hauled back up again with horses. Ridged or flanged wheels reduced the risk of derailments. After cast iron proved too brittle, wrought iron was used for more enduring rails.

Then the steam engine was invented, which would drive the industrial revolution worldwide. On land and at sea, new means of transport were rapidly developed. However, at first, steamboats appeared to have the edge, as unifying track and steam locomotive in a harmonious and safe partnership was not without its difficulties. For some years after locomotives were invented, horses were an integral part of the railroad story.

Precedents had already been set by Britain and in mainland Europe but, with such great distances and few people, the United States of America would have to write its own story. American networks grew from short, independent lines – although only a minority became more than a bold blueprint. American locomotives were initially slower than British ones, with smaller wheels that gave greater traction, better suited to the challenging tracks they were required to travel along.

In the US, railroads were the work of inspired individuals who could rally cash and expertise to their cause. Writing in 1835, French diplomat Alexis de Tocqueville noted that: 'In America, government never interferes, so to speak, and individuals do everything.'

The first locomotive built in America was The Best Friend of Charleston, *a prototype that was rapidly improved.*

DREAMS & REALITY

A few visionaries saw how the industrial age would shape up. But most people held fast to the familiar, and even where locomotives were embraced there was a gulf in science and skills that would take some time to bridge.

There were glitches to be ironed out, guesses that were wrongly made and gaffes, not least with the use of variously sized gauges. As ever, necessity led to invention, and improvements in the system ricocheted around the region where American locomotives were focused.

So, Jervis's truck or bogie was soon re-modelled into something superior by Henry R. Campbell (1781–1844) in 1836, by linking the four wheels that did the pulling into a single unit. Both were further enhanced by the equalizing beam introduced by Joseph Harrison (1810–74) in 1839. This allowed outside wheels to slip or spin on uneven track with greater safety, as the new link brought the point bearing the most weight into the middle.

Every new step changed trains inside and out. Slowly, locomotives evolved into a shape and spec that was recognizably American.

American steam locomotives soon adopted a familiar profile – from the cowcatcher on the front to the coal truck behind – although Western lines with no access to mines fuelled their locomotives with wood for much longer than those in the east.

BUNKER HILL MONUMENT

The front runner in America's race for commercial railroads is generally considered to be Boston, where tracks were laid to transport quarried stone for the nation's first memorial.

The Granite Railway in Quincy, Massachusetts was up and running by 1827. Admittedly, it was powered by horses rather than steam engines. But the use of iron-faced rails rather than wood for its trucks made it a cut above the wagonways that had been operating at other industrial sites, such as mines.

Quarry owner Gridley Bryant (1789–1867) was the man who built the railroad, to deliver granite blocks to the wharfside so they could be carried by boat up the Neponset River.

Their destination was Breed's Hill in Boston, where a monument to celebrate the Battle of Bunker Hill was being built. For some, this was a strange event to mark, for the newly fashioned colonial army was in fact defeated there in 1775 by the British Army during the American Revolution.

But, significantly, the well-equipped and highly trained Redcoats were repelled three times by their rag-tag opponents, inspiring confidence for future skirmishes. British casualties also far outnumbered those of the Americans.

It is best remembered for the order given to the patriots, allegedly by Colonel William Prescott: 'Don't fire until you see the whites of their eyes!', although it's not known for certain whether those stirring words did ring out.

The cornerstone of the monument was laid a half century later by General Lafayette (1757–1834), a Revolutionary War veteran. As an 18-year-old, Lafayette had left his native France to fight for the colonialist cause, and in 1826 he was touring the United States during its fiftieth anniversary year. Within 15 months the Granite Railway was hauling quarried stone at 50 cents a ton.

Financial difficulties dogged the memorial, which was finally funded when parts of the battlefield were sold off for housing, leaving only the summit of the hill where the fighting took place preserved.

After 17 years, the obelisk, standing 221 ft (67 m) high and composed of 6,700 tons of granite, was complete. Inside, 295 steps led to an observatory.

EARLY LINES

According to railroad historian Edward Hungerford (1875–1948), the Granite Railway was the best remembered of a clutch of early examples, including short lines in Richmond, Virginia, and at Bear Creek Furnace in Pennsylvania:

As early as 1807 Silas Whitney built a short line on Beacon Hill, Boston, which is accredited as being the first American railroad. It was a simple affair with an inclined plane which was used to handle brick ... Another early short length of railroad was built by Thomas Leiper at his quarry in Delaware County, Pennsylvania. It has its chief interest from the fact that it was designed by John Thomson, father of J. Edgar Thomson, who became at a much later day president of the Pennsylvania Railroad Company, and who is known as one of the masterminds in American transportation progress.

VIEW OF BUNKER HILL & MONUMENT. JUNE 17: 1843.

Pub. by J. Fisher, Boston.   N. Currier New York.

The Bunker Hill battle monument was completed in 1843, almost 70 years after the skirmish it commemorated. The monument's engineers achieved its epic scale thanks to an early railroad, which transported the necessary granite.

The Granite Railway wasn't Bryant's sole achievement. He designed a portable derrick (lifting device) for moving stone, and the snow plow, and honed railroad turntables, previously known as turn rails but generally used for major construction projects rather than vehicles.

He also had to defend his eight-wheeled carriage design, passed off by Ross Winans as his own. Bryant was reluctant to seek patents as he felt technological leaps should be available to all.

His son, also called Gridley, went on to be a noted architect.

NEW WORLD PROBLEMS

With railroads to serve its industrial cities, Britain powered further ahead in world dominance. For America, there was a host of domestic issues to address before it could enjoy a measure of that same greatness.

Its sheer size meant that America would not become laced with railroad tracks in the same way as England. Certainly, its northeastern corner was soon well connected, but vast swathes of the country would have to wait patiently for the arrival of the railroad.

There were other stark differences between the two countries that affected the spread of train and track, and for the enterprising souls tempted to build a railroad the difficulties were painfully apparent at the outset. The business of surveying for a track bed, for example, was more time consuming and altogether more hazardous than in England, given the potential presence of hostile Native Americans, ferocious wild animals or desperate outlaws.

In Britain, labour was cheap but land expensive. At the start of the railroad age, there was plenty of land available in America but manpower was at

Initially, there were too few railroad labourers in America to build far or fast, until immigrants and freed slaves were recruited.

SUNDRY STATIONS

In England, and particularly in Europe, stations were built with considerable grandeur, implying pride in the railroad service and an economic confidence linked to it. The same could not be said of early American stations, according to railroad historian Christian Wolmar:

Stations were an afterthought for the parsimonious rail companies who found it tough enough dealing with all the engineering problems such as track, tunnels and ties (sleepers) without having to consider providing for the wretched passengers.

a premium. That soon changed with the arrival of immigrant labour, although those who sought a new life in the US were not necessarily physically robust enough for the challenging conditions.

With great distances to tackle and a budget to keep within, the quality of the resulting railroad tracks was often poor. This led to numerous accidents and an unending cycle of repairs.

Nor were great efforts made to keep tracks level and straight. American railroads had a tendency to cling to the lie of the land, making for new hazards. As in England, the broad choice of gauges made links between lines impossible at the outset.

America also shared with Britain a period of mania that followed soon after the first railroads were up and running, when anybody with a spare dollar was investing in railroads. That led to economic turmoil, which had a direct impact on railroad provision.

For British visitors it was the differences that shone out. Writer Charles Dickens, a seasoned traveller on British trains, was largely horrified by his journeys by rail in America in 1842:

There is a great deal of jolting, a great deal of noise, a great deal of wall, not much window, a locomotive engine, a shriek and a bell ... Except when a branch road joins the main one there is seldom more than one track of rails so that the [rail]road is very narrow.

He was alarmed too by the routes chosen for locomotives:

It rushes across the turnpike road, where there is no gate, no policeman, no signal; nothing but a rough wooden arch on which is painted 'when the bell rings, look out for the locomotive'.

English politician John Delaware Lewis also found the close proximity of trains to centres of population unnerving. '[The train] rattles right up their main streets not infrequently stopping at the door of the hotel or in front of the church by way of a station.'

FULL STEAM AHEAD

According to railroad executive Charles Francis Adams Jr, 1835 marked 'an historical dividing line'. He was referring to the year when the advent of trains became more apparent to the American public. 'The world we live in came into existence then and humanly speaking it is in almost every essential respect a different world from that lived in by the preceding six generations.'

There followed a race to keep pace with the railroad needs of the nation. America was expanding all the while. After the arrival of railroads, seven states joined the Union before the end of 1850, making a total of 31. (The new additions were Arkansas, Michigan, Florida, Texas, Iowa, Wisconsin and California.) So the length of track required was increasing all the time.

Counterbalancing that was the risk that railroads to nowhere would be built, as the population remained sparse throughout the interior. Large tracts of land were still the domain of the explorer, the trapper and the cowboy, who initially had little interest in the advantages a railroad would bring.

RANDOM RAILROADS

America's system of administration meant that state governments were more involved than the Federal government with railroad building, although Washington did offer the assistance of West Point engineers, and reduced the tariff on imported iron and rails between 1830 and 1843. However, this didn't help with the creation of a planned and purposeful network.

Early passenger trains looked like stage coaches and even had supervising guards perched on the roof during trips.

The quest to milk every last cent from railroads came later. For now, the main aim was to lay tracks from A to B, as rapidly as possible.

Frenchman Michel Chevalier, who visited America in 1833, commented that: 'The Americans have railroads in the water, in the bowels of the earth, and in the air .... When they cannot construct a real, profitable railroad from river to river, from city to city or from state to state, [the Americans] get one up, at least as a plaything or until they can accomplish something better.'

The previous year, the first edition of the *American Railroad Journal* was published in recognition of the growing stature of the railroad industry. Stating its aims in the first edition, it wanted to 'diffuse a more general knowledge of this important mode of internal communication which at this time appears to engage the attention of almost every section of our country.'

The Panic of 1837, one of numerous financial crashes that stung American society in the nineteenth and twentieth centuries, sparked a recession that hindered railroad construction. It also opened the door to British investors with cash to spend on railroads, confident of their returns after witnessing bundles of money being made in the UK.

In 1838, when President Martin Van Buren signed a bill that made each railroad a carrier of the US mail, it seemed railroads had reached a high-water mark. In fact, the story was only just beginning to unfold.

At the end of the first decade that followed the arrival of railroads, more than 2,800 miles (4,500 km) of track was in use in America. Of 26 states in the Union in 1840 only four – Arkansas, Missouri, Tennessee and Vermont – had not laid down their first mile of track. New England and the Middle Atlantic states were romping ahead, with more than 60 per cent of rails.

COACH WORKS

At first, railroad passengers sat in carriages similar to the stagecoaches that were being usurped. The highly recognizable stagecoach body was cradled in a leather hammock then perched on four wheels without the benefit of further suspension.

Many were like the *Ohio*, which was built in 1830 by Baltimore carriage maker Richard Imlay and accommodated passengers both inside and outside. A canopy covered the row of seats fixed to the stagecoach roof, presumably intended for those paying a lower ticket price and wanting more of a view.

This double-decker style produced by a variety of manufacturers did not persist for long. While it was bearable when the coach was being hauled by horses at a rate of no more than 8 mph (13 km/h), the smoke and hot ash from locomotives rendered travelling on the top level unbearable.

There was an issue with stability too, it being so top heavy. Given the length of time some train journeys took, passengers also wanted to leave their seats and stretch their legs.

Thanks to Imlay and others, improvements were soon made in rolling stock, and from

Claims for being the first passenger service were made by several companies. The Mohawk & Hudson were among the forerunners.

The First Steam Railroad Passenger Train in America.

1831 America had adopted the bones of its now familiar wooden carriage design.

In effect, Imlay stretched the design of the stagecoach, putting four wheels at either end and doors at the centre. His hallmark was a raised roof for ventilation, called a clerestory roof, vital in an era before personal hygiene gained currency. After Imlay departed the carriage-building scene, his projecting roof was forgotten for 20 years, until it was rediscovered by a company called Webster Wagner, which recognized its benefits for sleepers.

Soon, the swollen body of the stagecoach was replaced with sleek lines more suited to railroad travel, and the doors were put either end of the carriage, to accommodate seats each side of a central corridor.

Another railroad carriage builder, James Goold (1790–1879), began with ideas similar to Imlay's, and built coaches for the Mohawk & Hudson Railroad in 1831 along the same lines. His Albany-based works was twice burned down in the 1830s, but nonetheless expanded with support from New York businessmen.

RUDIMENTARY REFRESHMENTS

On-board services were limited initially to water sellers who provided drinks out of kettles or

WHITE TICKETS

True to American principles of democracy, there was generally a single category of ticket rather than the rigid class system that was symptomatic of the British, where carriages were distinguished by compartments. However, African Americans and some immigrants were often confined to freight wagons.

pottery urns. All customers used the same glasses, which helps to explain the high rate of communicable diseases such as tuberculosis at the time.

At station stops passengers usually left their seats to get food and drink from nearby hotels and bars. As time wore on, a 'news butcher' became a familiar sight on trains, selling newspapers, tobacco and snacks.

Having pioneered an early sleeper, Imlay's coach-building days ended with the 1837 recession. Goold is thought to have continued until shortly before his death, although he remained best known for making the 'Albany Cutter', a horse-drawn sleigh.

THE PIONEERS

There was a host of 'firsts' associated with America's railroad past, which coalesce to tell the story.

The first locomotive that ran on American soil was *Stourbridge Lion*, unleashed in Pennsylvania. Charleston was the home of the first US-built locomotive, while most people caught their first glimpse of a track-borne steam wagon at Hoboken in New Jersey.

For some, like Col John Stevens in New Jersey, it was mechanical beauty and the promise of better things to come that kept him loyal to the notion of steam-driven travel. Others saw it as a route to future wealth.

Businessmen in Baltimore had been among the first to realize the opportunities that new railroads offered. For, while Washington had the Potomac River on which to ferry goods, and New York used the Hudson River linked to the Erie Canal, Baltimore had only the limited scope of the Patapsco River.

Those who endorsed locomotives early on had considerable courage. There was still little firm evidence that a technology used mostly in mines and quarries had such wide-ranging possibilities.

Opposite: With a strong faith in the power of steam, John Stevens devoted time and money to introducing the concept of locomotive travel into the US.

SOUTH CAROLINA RAILROAD COMPANY

Charleston felt a chill wind when foreign trade slumped in the 1820s. Cotton was the commodity projected to keep the economy afloat, but it needed to be transported swiftly and cheaply from inland fields to the port for shipment.

So the suggestion of a railroad – still in its infancy in distant Europe and an embryonic industry in America – soon found favour. And the soaring ambition of the South Carolina Canal & Railroad Company (SCCRRC) chief engineer Horatio Allen (1802–89) marked it for early significance.

An 1833 map of South Carolina shows early evidence of how tracks spider-webbed across the state.

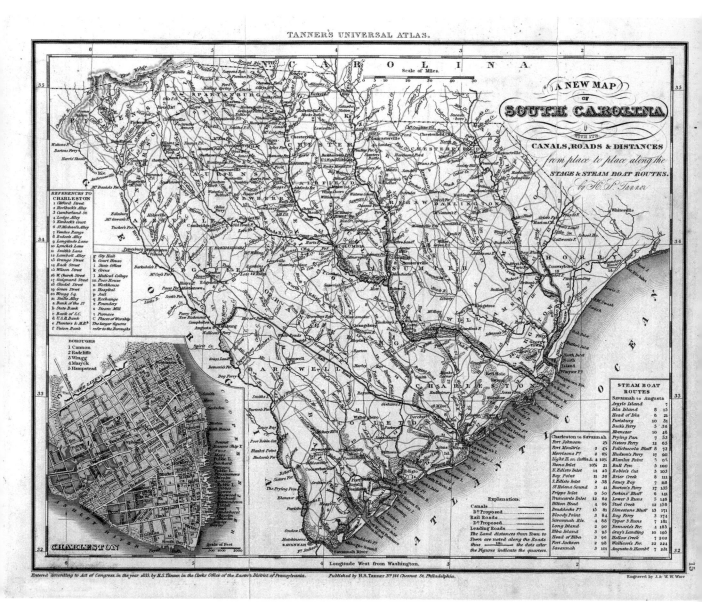

He was not content to have horse-drawn wagons on the newly installed wooden and iron rails, like other companies of the age, or even sails, which were fleetingly used in Charleston to drive carriages. Instead, he favoured locomotives, with their unbridled potential, declaring there was no reason to expect 'any material improvement' in the breed of horses but that no one yet knew where locomotive technology would end up.

HOME-GROWN LOCOS

His argument persuaded the railroad to purchase *The Best Friend of Charleston*, the first locomotive built in the US, for $4,000. It didn't resemble later engines, but had smoke escaping through openings in the side of the fire box and two cylinders in front of the boiler that worked the cranks.

It made its maiden journey on Christmas Day 1830 from Camden Depot, carrying 140 passengers for a 6-mile (10-km) journey at speeds not greater than 15 mph (24 km/h), which was as much as its wood-powered furnace would allow.

Despite the stately pace, the trip was exhilarating enough for one thrilled journalist to describe it as 'annihilating time and space, leaving all the world behind'. There was no time to be scared, he confessed, so swift was the journey. Nor was it just in use for holidays. Afterwards, the curious engine pulled a daily service.

The company was so taken with locomotives it bought a second, the *West Point*.

Its timing was fortuitous for no sooner had it arrived than the *Best Friend* exploded after a misguided fireman blocked the steam-pressure valve, apparently irritated by its constant hissing. The error cost him his life, while the engineer was badly scalded. Passenger confidence must have been dented, despite a wagon piled high with cotton bales being strategically placed between engine and carriage thereafter.

RIVAL ROUTES

Although Charleston flourished with the new railroad, rival port Savannah lost vital trade. In response, the city established the Central Railroad & Canal Company in 1833. Its aim – to construct another trade artery linking Macon with Savannah, a distance of some 190 miles (305 km) – was accomplished in October 1843, by which time the company was known as the Central Railroad & Banking Company of Georgia.

There followed a region-wide expansion programme that linked Savannah with Birmingham, Chattanooga and Montgomery among other places, although the initial rivalry with South Carolina continued.

By 1888 it had 2,600 miles (4,184 km) under its control but, despite linking with other companies, it went into receivership four years later, to re-emerge as the Central of Georgia.

But for Charleston there was no turning back, despite the tragedy. The track was continually extended, so that by October 1833 the 136-mile (219-km) route to Hamburg was completed, making it – briefly – the longest railroad in the world.

Parts from *Best Friend* were salvaged and co-mingled to make the appropriately named *Phoenix* locomotive, one of six operating on the line within just three years. Indeed, *Phoenix* was still at work at the outbreak of the Civil War. To mark its 100th anniversary, a replica of *Best Friend* was made in 1928 using original blueprints.

Today, the SCCRRC is seen as the ancestor of the Norfolk Southern Corporation, which operates 21,300 routes in 22 states and carries more cars and car parts than any other network.

HORATIO ALLEN

Few men had as much influence on the early history of railroads in America as Horatio Allen.

The son of a mathematics professor, Allen himself graduated from Columbia University in maths, determined to be an engineer. He gathered his earliest practical experience with canal companies and became a protégé of John B. Jervis, his manager at the Delaware & Hudson Canal Company. Both men were visionaries about the future of steam power, and Allen's outlook was cemented when he was sent by his employers, who wanted a railroad to link two stretches of canal, to England in 1828 to investigate the steam phenomenon.

He arrived in Liverpool on 15 February for a visit that would include Britain's newest railroads and its most advanced industrial sites.

Furthermore, he met the world's best engineers, discussing with them the most promising inventions of the day, including the merits of flanged wheels, the perils of fixed axles and the complexities of track beds.

The man who perhaps made most impression on Allen was George Stephenson, the father of steam.

In his diary Allen wrote: 'Mr Stephenson has nothing remarkable in his countenance. He has rather an ordinary appearance and face destitute of marks of the talent that he really possesses.'

As instructed by his employers, Allen bought several locomotives, including the *Stourbridge Lion*

The Stourbridge Lion *was made in England and imported into America for a tentative foray into the brave new world of passenger railroads.*

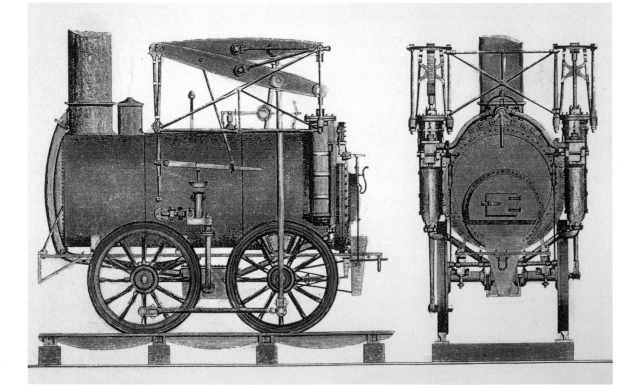

– designed by Jervis – which was duly shipped to America and re-assembled. It got its name after a locomotive painter added the likeness of a lion's head to the convex surface on the boiler end. According to railroad historian Edward Hungerford, it better resembled a 'giant grasshopper with its mass of exterior valves, and joints'.

AMERICAN STEAM FIRST

Displaying some personal courage, Allen chose to drive the locomotive himself on behalf of the Delaware & Hudson before crowds who gathered for its inaugural run at Honesdale, Pennsylvania. In doing so, he became the first person in America to move under steam power.

Despite extensive preparation, he did not realize the 11.2-ton locomotive would be too hefty for the newly laid hemlock timber rails. Later, he recalled: 'When the cheers of the onlookers died out as I left them on the memorable trip the only sound to greet my ears until my safe return, in addition to that of the exhaust steam, was that of the creaking of the timber structure.'

Still, he found room for optimism and took some personal pride in his achievement. In his reminiscences, published in 1885, he wrote:

I had never run a locomotive nor any other engine before; I have never run one since. But on that 9 August 1829 I ran that locomotive three miles and back to the place of starting and being without experience or a brakeman, I stopped the locomotive on its return at the place of starting.

NAMESAKE LOCOMOTIVE

In 1924, one of three high-pressure locomotives with watertube boilers built by the Delaware & Hudson Railroad was named for Horatio Allen. Tender and locomotive combined weighed in at a solid 273 tons and, although considered to require above-average levels of maintenance, it was known for its fuel economy.

Experience now assured him that the future lay in steam power and he brought that conviction with him to a new post in South Carolina.

The Delaware & Hudson Canal Company, which built America's first million-dollar enterprise in the shape of a 108-mile, 108-lock canal, imported the Stourbridge Lion. Its Coal and Iron Exchange, pictured here in 1850, reflected the wealth generated by canals and railroads.

NEWFOUND COURAGE

To Allen, the accomplishments of the South Carolina Canal & Railroad Company (SCCRRC) and the courage of its investors could not be understated. Here was a new breed of businessman, willing to part with vast sums of money to back the use of locomotives that were expensive and potentially unsafe. There was little verified proof that trains were the transport of tomorrow. Allen saw how the SCCRRC would be blazing a trail for the world to follow:

On this side of the water some 16 miles (26 km) of the B&O road had been constructed and was worked by horse power. On the other side of the Atlantic the Liverpool & Manchester Company was the only company that had the subject under consideration but as yet had not come to a decision although their chief engineer George Stephenson was the able and earnest advocate of the locomotive ... The resolution [for a steam locomotive] then passed and placed on record was the first act by a corporate body in the world to adopt the locomotive as the tractive power on a railroad for general passenger and freight transportation.

The inaugural trip of the *Best Friend* on the SCCRRC occurred just three months after the opening of Britain's Liverpool & Manchester Railway.

After this triumph, Allen continued to make significant contributions to America's railroad story. Soon, he initiated the first night-time rail journey, the locomotive illuminated with flaming pines set in sand on a flatbed wagon, which it pushed down the line. (Rail journeys after dark remained a rarity for a further decade until kerosene headlights were set against reflectors.)

His association with Jervis proved a particularly productive partnership, and between them they devised a 'swivelling bogie' to improve railroad comfort and safety. The bogie or truck is found beneath locomotives and carriages, with wheels attached. During his trip to England, Allen discussed whether fixed or rotating bogies were superior and decided that in America, where track curves were often sharper than in Britain, a more fluid movement was preferable.

TRAGEDY AND TRIUMPHS

In 1842, Allen joined a New York foundry called Novelty Works, although the link wasn't entirely

INDUSTRIAL BLIGHT

Despite considerable success, Allen remained concerned at the way industrial innovation led to the exploitation of hapless workers. When he visited Britain in his mid-twenties, his diary noted the stark contrast between the lives of rich and poor:

Frequently after passing through a village of 2,000 to 6,000 inhabitants all working for one establishment, receiving wages barely sufficient to keep body and soul together, and living in hovels that it was painful to consider the habitations of human beings, we would pass the princely residences of the proprietors, furnished and full with all that art could produce or money procure.

It was something he saw replicated in his native America before his death.

a happy one. The engines of the paddle steamer SS *Arctic* – which sank in 1854 – were made there. Among the passengers on that fateful voyage were Allen's brother George, who survived. But George's wife and infant son died, along with more than 300 others.

Otherwise, in a glittering career, he also became president of the Erie Railroad, was a consultant in the building of the Brooklyn Bridge, was an assistant engineer on the Croton Aqueduct and for two years he was president of the American Society of Civil Engineers.

His inventiveness didn't desert him, as American patents records reveal. An entry for 1843 shows that Allen registered 'a new and useful … machine for inserting stop-cocks'.

South Carolina's railroad was a trailblazer, with regular services underway before many tracks had been laid in Britain.

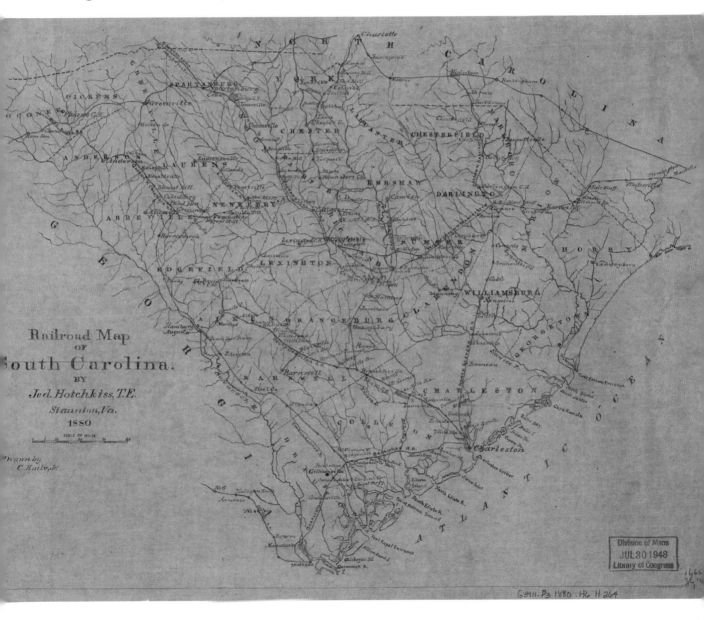

Railroad Map of South Carolina. BY Jed. Hotchkiss, T.E. Staunton, Va. 1880

Drawn by C. Hale, Jr.

BALTIMORE & OHIO

In 1828, the first stone of America's newest railroad was laid. Fittingly, the ceremony was carried out by Charles Carroll, the last surviving signatory of the Declaration of Independence, and the date was 4 July.

According to a local newspaper – rhapsodizing about how rails would enhance manufacturing industries – it was 'the most splendid civic procession perhaps ever exhibited in America'. All this for horse-drawn trains, rather than steam-driven ones.

At the time, Baltimore was the fourth biggest city in America, and was so prestigious it was the target of a British attack in 1812 after Washington had been overrun. A poetic description of Baltimore's defence was set to music to become The Star-Spangled Banner, finally adopted as America's national anthem in 1931.

Although the potential of the railroads was far from clear, there was a buoyancy about Baltimore at the time of the parade that thrilled everyone.

To the assembled dignitaries, Carroll (1737–1832), who was from a wealthy Catholic Irish immigrant background at a time of widespread discrimination, said: 'I consider this among the most important acts of my life.'

Although he was more than 90 years old, Carroll was sufficiently forward-thinking about this ambitious railroad project to become a shareholder in the newly wrought Baltimore & Ohio (B&O) company. Failing health meant it was his final public act after an illustrious career.

TOM THUMB

Inventor and manufacturer Peter Cooper (1791–1883) took on the challenge of building a locomotive that could cope with sharp curvatures like those on Baltimore's new line – something Stephenson declared could not be done.

Cooper described the difficulties. 'I had an iron foundry and had some manual skill in working in it. But I couldn't find any iron pipes. The fact was, there were none for sale in this country. So I took two muskets and broke off the wood part and used the barrels for tubing to the boiler.'

The result was Tom Thumb, an apparently capable 1 horse-power locomotive that, by the early 1830s, was covering the uphill journey to Ellicott's Mills in 1 hour and 12 minutes. When it made its first appearance on 28 August 1830, pulling a wagon with some 20 B&O passengers, it became the first locomotive on America's railroads.

Cooper's cobbled-together locomotive was soon challenged to a race with a grey mare pulling a wagon on a parallel track, owned by a rival haulier.

Initially, the locomotive had the better of the horse as it eased its way along the tracks. But a catastrophe with a drive belt slowed it down so much that the horse overtook it. Cooper risked injury to mend his locomotive but although it reached maximum speed again he faced the ignominy of coming second to horse power as the age of steam dawned.

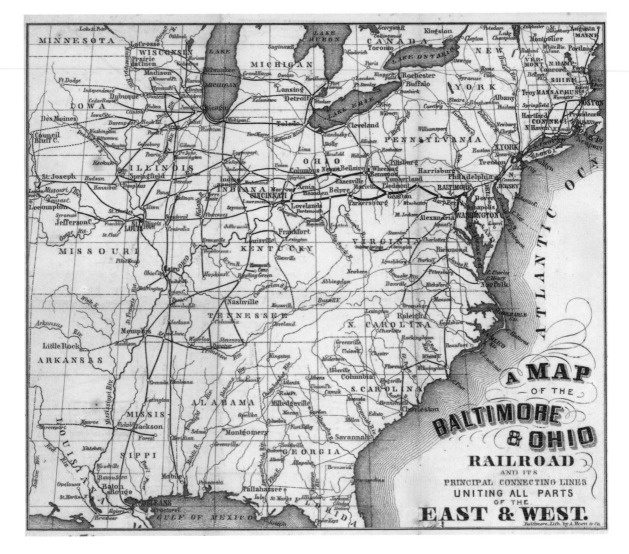

An 1860 map reveals the extent of B&O coverage prior to the outbreak of the Civil War.

But he lived long enough to see the opening of the Carrollton Viaduct, named in his honour, in December 1829.

With two railroad tracks across it, the impressive granite bridge was 312-ft (95-m) long, stood 52 ft (16 m) above the Gwynns Falls and is still in use today. (Similar in design, the Patterson viaduct built at the same time by the same builder and named for B&O director William Patterson was destroyed in a flood in 1866.) By

spring of the following year the railroad reached Ellicott's Mills, a modest 13-mile (21-km) distance but hailed as a triumph at the time. The first leg of America's railroad network had been laid.

Certainly, two of the B&O's representatives, Ross Winan (1796–1877) and George Brown, were inspired early on by the Rainhill Trials in England in 1829, at which George Stephenson's *Rocket* was crowned the best contender for work on the Liverpool & Manchester Railway. But there was a subsequent gap between dreams of steam and the reality, which was filled by horses.

DESIGN JUMPS AHEAD

Although Peter Cooper had come second to four-legged horse power with his 'tea kettle on a raft', as his makeshift locomotive was dubbed, a point about the potential of steam locomotives had been proved.

Yet, from a flying start into the brave new railroad age, the B&O quickly ground to a halt.

The B&O's Atlantic *was reminiscent of* Tom Thumb *in design although it was faster and smoother.*

The company had its sights set on a 40-mile (64-km) route to Washington, but a dispute with a competing canal-building company effectively ended construction for several years.

The row with the Chesapeake & Ohio Canal Company centred on level ground between Point of Rocks and Harper's Ferry along the Potomac River that appealed to the architects of both companies. At the time, canal building seemed the more promising business model, despite

well-known difficulties with elevation and a scarcity of water in the mountains.

America's courts sided with the canal company until the House of Delegates was drafted in to find a compromise.

In the meantime, the B&O tried to resolve the question mark that remained over steam locomotives. Taking its cue from the UK, it held a competition to encourage the best design that would exceed the limitations of the sluggish *Tom Thumb* and would cope with the twists and turns of the track. On offer was prize money of $4,000.

BIGGER AND BETTER

The winner was Phineas Davis (1792–1835), previously a clockmaker, who named his locomotive for his adopted hometown, York. During tests, his locomotive reached speeds of 35 mph (56 km/h) on the straight and 15 mph (24 km/h) on bends, fuelled by anthracite.

Davis went on to design the *Atlantic*, far bigger than *Tom Thumb*, but still featuring the vertical rods on the wheels that earned that class of locomotives the nickname 'grasshoppers'.

By August 1835, Washington had finally been reached and more Davis-designed locomotives were using the line.

In its first four months of operation, an average of 200 people travelled each day on the line between Baltimore and Washington. By the end of the year, it had seven locomotives, 44 passenger cars and 1,078 freight cars in service.

A SPIRITED DEFENCE

Completion of the route to Washington was hindered by riots among Irish labourers. High on their list of grievances was a ban on drink, imposed by the B&O at the suggestion of Caspar Wever, Superintendent of Construction.

Every contract made after 1829 for track laying or bridge building included a clause that outlawed spirits, which were considered destructive and demoralizing by bosses.

Mr Wever declared: 'It is believed that the work may be executed without the use of this dreadful poison, more advantageously to the interests of the company and certainly much more agreeably to its officers and contractors as well as beneficially to the labourers themselves.' That's not how his men saw it though. They were keen to finish their hard labour with a drink, not least to dull their senses to the appalling working conditions.

Unfortunately, Davis did not live to see the success he had helped to fashion. On 27 September that year, on a return trip along the Washington line, Davis was killed when one of his locomotives derailed.

HEADING WEST

While frantic railroad construction was underway after the 1830s, there was limited expansion towards the west. For the B&O's directors, intent on reaching the banks of the Ohio as the company founders had promised, there was the barrier of the Appalachian Mountains.

It was the Allegheny range, specifically, that barred the path. British railway builders might have blanched at such an obstacle, with only untried engineering at hand. But while the Baltimore railroad men were inspired by the rapidly expanding British railway system – in which straight lines and mild gradients dominated – they would not be dictated to by it. New problems required fresh thinking.

Massachusetts, the home of America's first railroad at Quincy, had three completed routes by 1835. More expansion followed the drawing of this 1853 map, and by 1870 it had one mile of railroad for every five and a half square miles of territory and per 954 inhabitants.

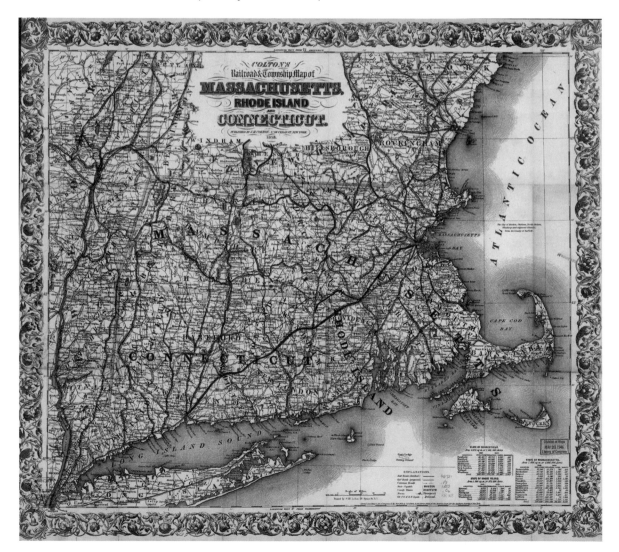

TO BOLDLY GO . . .

The work of Ross Winans was so admired in Europe that he was invited to kick-start the railroad age in Russia. In 1843 he sent sons Thomas and William, along with George W. Whistler, to Russia to help fashion the ambitious St Petersburg and Moscow railroad, Tsar Nicholas I's belated entry into the technological age. A career spent assiduously protecting his inventions by patents helped to ensure he amassed a $20 million fortune before his death, when one obituary called him 'a bold and original thinker'.

INNOVATIVE IDEAS

Ross Winans, who witnessed the world's first locomotive trials in England, designed a new so-called friction wheel with bearings on the outside of its radius, which set a benchmark in fundamental design that endured for a century.

After this breakthrough in 1828, he worked for B&O, further improving passenger comfort by refining axle and carriage design as well as tinkering with steam-engine efficiency. His name is also associated with distinctive camelback locomotives, produced from the 1840s, and steam-powered cigar-ships, although these failed to shape nautical fashion after their inception in 1858.

Safety standards took a leap forward in 1835 when Evan Thomas invented a braking system in which wooden brake shoes could be applied throughout the train at the tug of a chain. Primitive the design may have been, but it replaced a less reliable method and helped keep carriages on gradients under control. Thomas was the brother of B&O president Philip, for whom a viaduct was named.

Both innovations made for decent publicity in the *American Railroad Journal*, in its edition published on 5 December 1835:

The casting of the wheels has been brought to a perfection which removes all fear of accident from their breaking, even at the highest velocities ... The present brakes for passenger cars suggested by Evan Thomas have proved most efficient and durable. A new form of blowing apparatus combined with a contrivance for heating the water before it is pumped into the boilers has been invented by Ross Winans and produce increased efficiency.

Winans eventually parted company with the B&O but stayed a close neighbour for a while, developing rail manufacture and repair shops alongside Mount Clare – the extensive site run by the railroad company that included a foundry, ironworks, a roundhouse, a blacksmith and much more. The railroad was Winans's biggest customer.

But while the railroad and its leading figures were busy, their stated aim was still unfulfilled. The line extending to the banks of the Ohio – some 380 miles (612 km) distant – that so inspired the imaginations of those early Baltimore businessmen was still far from a reality.

To achieve a rail link with Wheeling, then classed as Virginia, meant the construction of 11 tunnels and 113 bridges, taking company finances to near breaking point. It wasn't until 1 January 1853 that the first B&O train arrived in Wheeling after a 16-hour trip.

It had taken time and not inconsiderable foresight – not to mention the encroachment of rival lines – but America's west could then be considered open for business.

CAMDEN & AMBOY

Although the Camden & Amboy (C&A) railroad was not the first or furthest in America, the man behind it stole a mighty march on competitors.

Col John Stevens (1749–1838) revealed uncanny foresight when it came to railroads, garnered from practical engineering experience

By 1826 Col Stevens was so confident in the power of steam that he established a track in the grounds of his home, to give the American public a taste for locomotive travel.

with steam ships and locomotive engines. He was such an early advocate of steam locomotives that in 1814 – more than a decade before the world's first authorized passenger railroad, the Stockton to Darlington line, was opened in England – he published a pamphlet regaling readers with its advantages.

In it he urged the government to investigate the potential of travel powered by steam by investing $3,000 in trials and to begin track surveys 'in all directions so as to embrace and unite every section of this extensive empire …. It might then

indeed be said that these states would then constitute one family, intimately connected and held together in bonds of indissoluble Union.'

As early as 1795 he had built a steam locomotive, but it proved too heavy to run on tracks in use at the time. A trained attorney, he'd also pioneered a patent system to protect the products in which he'd invested.

His powerful and patriotic words in the pamphlet were prompted by a feasibility study into the building of the Erie Canal but they failed to sway the prevailing view, entrenched in eighteenth-century technology.

As one observer later put it, the idea of tracks and trains was turned down 'on grounds which indicate very odd ideas of the nature of the work'. To Stevens' frustration, the canal project went ahead and the plans for railroad construction went nowhere.

But nothing dented Stevens' enthusiasm and persistence for the technology that he knew would change the world.

His outspoken support for steam may well have helped him win the country's first railroad charter in 1815, awarded by the New Jersey state legislature, and another in 1823, although neither came to fruition for want of finance. Still, in 1826 he publicly proved his point by running a steam locomotive on a circular track in the large garden of his home at Hoboken.

His 'steam waggon' was not the basis for future design but a bold attempt to win hearts and minds, and visitors flocked to see it in action. Thus it was, with some conviction, that

ONE STEP AT A TIME

Stevens wasn't a lone voice speaking out against a tried-and-trusted transport system. Oliver Evans (1755–1819), one of Stevens' rivals, was also a scientific visionary.

Before his death he wrote: 'I do verily believe that carriages propelled by steam will come into general use and travel at the rate of 300 miles a day.'

But ruefully he added: 'One step in a generation is all we can hope for. If the present generation shall adopt canals, the next may try the railroad with horses and the third generation use the steam carriage.'

Unlike Stevens, Evans – who built a steam-driven car in 1805 – became bitter with the derision he encountered and did not live long enough to see railroads come of age.

the wealthy Stevens, who won his rank fighting the British in the War of Independence, seized the opportunity to run what would be America's third national railroad in 1830. He was by now too old to run the Camden & Amboy, but he could at least hand it over to his sons.

Before Stevens died there was at last a palpable rise in railroad fever, validating the claims he had been making for more than a quarter of a century.

LIKE FATHER, LIKE SON

Following in the footsteps of a genius father is never easy. Fortunately, Col Stevens' sons shared his ardour for railroads and left legacies of their own.

Robert L. Stevens (1787–1856) was appointed president of the C&A in 1830, while his brother Edwin (1795–1868) was treasurer and general manager.

The most distinctive invention attributed to Robert L. Stevens, assisted in 1832 by his engineer Isaac Dripps (1810–92), was

John Bull, *which became a workhorse for the C&A, was officially re-named* Stevens *when it operated on American soil. But that name soon fell into disuse as its British origin was perpetually celebrated.*

the cowcatcher, which changed the profile of locomotives of the era. Properly called the 'pilot', it attached to the front of the locomotive to sweep livestock out of its path. Until then, a collision with a cow was enough to propel the locomotive into a ditch. As if that wasn't bad enough, railroad companies also had to pay for the unfortunate cow. It wasn't a feature of British locomotive design because tracks in the UK were generally fenced against livestock.

More significantly, but less obviously, Stevens had already changed the shape of the rails on which American trains would run.

Initially, tracks were iron strips fixed to wooden rails, laid on granite blocks. Problems arose when the weight of the train caused the length of iron (known as the strap) to rear up, forming what were known as 'snakeheads'. These posed a threat to the safety of the locomotive in general and passengers in particular when they suddenly forced themselves through the carriage floor. One woman was impaled through her thigh during a trip; another man was hit under the chin. On the look-out for these menaces, railroads crews always kept a spike hammer and spikes at hand to pin down the rogue iron coil.

To counter the issue, Stevens invented the T-rail, made entirely from iron. Shaped like an inverted T it was attached by its broad base to wooden sleepers with a special hooked spike that he also designed.

The idea for this robust rail came to him on a visit to England. He carved the first one out of wood then had tracks engineered in Wales before bringing them back to install on the C&A line. The first shipment arrived in Philadelphia in May 1831 and the line was

BOXING CLEVER

A curious difficulty prompted the C&A to introduce sandboxes into locomotive design. In 1836, New Jersey was plagued by grasshoppers, so prolific that they interfered with the safe running of trains. At first, the C&A employed men to walk the tracks, sweeping the insects aside, but as soon as the men had passed by the grasshoppers were back on the line in full force.

Engineers then tried installing scrapers on to some locomotives, and brushes to another, to resolve the problem. But both wore down on the rails, proving useless, and slowed the train to crawling speed.

Finally, an unknown employee used sand distributed in a stream in front of the wheels in a system that proved equally useful in wet, slippery conditions.

opened 17 months later, on 9 October 1932. With the enhanced safety record that followed the design of these new rails, they eventually became an industry standard.

Stevens failed to patent the design, which became known as the Camden & Amboy rail. Irish-born Charles Vignoles (1793–1875) is credited with a similar design that became popular in Europe.

With a third brother, John (1785–1857), Robert and Edwin were absorbed by maritime innovations as well as track-borne ones. Robert Stevens was working on the government's first iron-clad warship at the time of his death.

THE POWER & THE GLORY

Thanks to a pliant state government, the future for the Camden & Amboy was bright from the moment it was chartered in 1830.

In addition to track, the C&A had been planning to use waterways to link New York and Philadelphia. Investors were initially askance to see the creation of the Delaware & Raritan Canal Company, which proposed shifting freight along a similar corridor.

To counter what were perceived to be the negative effects of competition, the New Jersey legislature agreed that the two companies could merge. Moreover, no other companies were thereafter permitted to operate in the sphere of what was now officially known as 'the Joint Companies'. It was a monopoly fashioned by politicians of the day, keen to reap rewards in the form of transportation taxes that were thought to be worth about one-fifth of the state's income. The state also owned railroad stock.

Buoyed by the certainty of its future, the C&A opened its first 14 miles (23 km) of single track between Bordentown and Hightstown in September 1831, upon which carriages were pulled by horses. It wasn't until 1833 that steam locomotives were introduced. The following year, the planned 61-mile (98-km) section of railroad was opened, at a cost of $1.5 million, and travellers between New York and Philadelphia had a journey of just nine hours by rail and steamship to endure – a major improvement on the conventional horse-drawn vehicles used previously.

While the C&A was given the go-ahead to swallow up would-be competitors in the vicinity, no other company could battle for business on its turf. So, by 1839, all rail services between Philadelphia and New York were in its domain.

Predictably, its prices were high and investment levels low – and soon the company began flexing its political muscle. Before long, New Jersey became known as 'the state of Camden & Amboy'.

By 1877 the modified John Bull was a familiar sight on the Camden & Amboy Railroad.

LEGENDARY LOCO

King of its tracks was a locomotive called *John Bull*, bought by Robert Stevens during a trip to England from a factory belonging to George Stephenson.

Despite never having seen one before, Isaac Dripps re-assembled the 10-ton locomotive after it arrived in August 1831. He added a cowcatcher, bell and headlight in time for trials in October that

ACCUSATIONS OF FRAUD

In 1848 the *Burlington Gazette* published an article entitled 'Can the Monopoly Lawfully be Abolished?' that included a litany of charges against the C&A, claiming it was defrauding both public and state. The author was political economist Henry C. Carey (1793–1879). Two commissions were called to investigate the charges but the company was exonerated of all but the most trivial misdemeanours. However, Carey refused to end his crusade, calling for accounts to be published. Perhaps revealingly, company directors had the relevant records destroyed.

year. People who gathered to watch it in action were amazed to see it dashing by at 40 mph (64 km/h). The *John Bull* was 3.5 ft (1 m) in diameter, with a cylinder 9 inches (23 cm) wide and 20 inches (51 cm) long. Its fuel was pinewood. John Stevens senior hosted a celebration at the family's estate in Hoboken as his dream of steam locomotion was realized.

Like many at the forefront of the railroad revolution, the Stevens family still had an element of doubt about the new technology. So, for its first month of operation, a man on a fast horse rode ahead to clear the tracks. There was consternation, too, when the *John Bull* was derailed during an early trip. But faith in the railroad was quickly restored, despite registering the country's first fatal rail accident in 1833.

The *John Bull* would be the model for steam locomotives now being built in C&A workshops. Although it retired from service in 1866, it was an icon of American railroad history.

MOHAWK & HUDSON

When the Erie Canal opened in 1825, it was something of an economic miracle for mercantile interests on an increasingly busy east coast.

Although it took eight years to complete the 363-mile (584-km) canal at a cost of $8 million, it became the quickest and most direct route between New York City and the Great Lakes.

Horses or mules on the tow path hauled cargo in barges day and night, paying tolls for the privilege. They took passengers too, who could look forward to a relatively smooth – if damp – journey.

Instantly popular for its speed and ease, the canal was an inspiration and 'Erie fever' afflicted neighbouring states. By 1830, a further 1,250 miles (2,012 km) of canal had been completed and 10,000 miles (16,000 km) were planned.

When it came to railroads, some designers were rooted in the past rather than imagining any future potential for carrying more passengers.

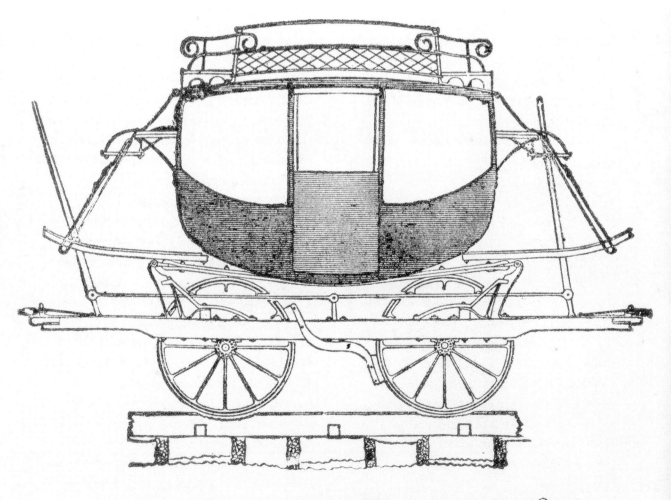

A MOHAWK & HUDSON CAR OF 1831.

For a while, canals developed a power base, which was duly abused – as observed in 1833 in his travels around America by Frenchman Michel Chevalier:

The Canal Commissioners establish administrative regulations, which they change at will, without previous notice. They fix and change the rate of tolls; they are surrounded by a large body of agents, entirely dependent upon them and removable at pleasure.

However, the rigidity of canals was highlighted almost immediately on the Erie. The 40-mile (66-km) water route between Albany and Schenectady included several locks and was notoriously slow going. It offered an opening to stagecoaches, which took advantage of a direct route between the cities amounting to just 17 miles (27 km).

But this desire to make the most of the shortcut led to the establishment of the Mohawk & Hudson Railroad (M&H), incorporated in 1825 just after the Granite Railway. During the four years it took to secure financing, numerous others were lined up for approval. However, finding the necessary cash for its construction wasn't the only issue it was facing.

There were political controversies to be resolved before any trains began operating in areas already committed to canals.

CANALS CALL THE SHOTS

Although successful, the Erie Canal and others like it were costly and had sucked up state money during construction. Keen to see a return on the investment, local authorities were less than enthusiastic about locomotives.

COMPARATIVE COSTS

By the time *Appleton's* was published, the average cost of rail travel was 2 to 3 cents per mile in New England and surrounding states and from 3 to 5 cents per mile in the south and west of the country, although through tickets for long journeys tended to be less expensive. 'Travel by steamboat is somewhat less expensive and less expeditious than by rail,' the guide warns, which advises investing in the cost of a state room 'for greater comfort and privacy'.

Vested interests – including those who made turnpike roads, ran stagecoaches, operated inns on canal stopping points and others – wanted to protect every canal's commercial future and did not welcome proposals for transport systems that would affect their success.

Among the measures suggested to protect canals and stagecoaches was a special tax for railroads that brought fares to parity with the competition, or restrictions on locomotive use to times when ice brought canal traffic to a standstill.

Bold canal investors even suggested that any profit from the railroad above 10 per cent be diverted to debt-ridden canal companies. In fact, it wasn't until 1851 that New York State freed railroads from an obligation to pay cash to the owners of the Erie Canal.

With such an array of hurdles in their path, the financing of numerous proposed lines failed.

FEAR & LOATHING

Piled on top of the opposition by supporters of and investors in canals were other, more obtuse, objections to the railroads, sometimes labelled 'the devil's work' by less far-sighted churches of the day.

In Ohio one school board branded them 'a device of Satan to lead immortal souls to hell'.

Farmers feared their livestock would take fright at the appearance of a tooting, steaming locomotive. The risk to passengers and passers-by posed by the railroads was often shamefully exaggerated to stir public feeling against proposed new lines.

The argument that rail travel at high speeds would never be possible because passengers would die of asphyxiation was a hardy chestnut.

Perhaps the last word in objections goes to a letter writer to the *Western Sun* in Indiana, whose words of dire warning about railroads were published on 24 July 1830:

It will have the whole world a-gadding. Twenty miles an hour sir! Why you will not be able to keep an apprentice boy at his work. Every Saturday evening he must take a trip to Ohio to spend the Sabbath with his sweetheart. Grave plodding citizens will be flying about like comets. All local attachments will be at an end. It will encourage flightiness of intellect ... Upon the whole sir, it is a pestilential, topsy-turvy, harum-scarum whirligig. Give me the old solemn, straightforward regular Dutch canal, three miles an hour for expresses and two for ordinary journeys with a yoke of oxen for a heavy load ... None of your hop-skip-and-jump whimsies for me.

Similar objections, not always so colourfully expressed, had been thrown up in Britain and around Europe when railways got started.

INEVITABLE ADVANCE

The changing face of industry ensured it was only a matter of time before railroad companies made headway. The M&H – designed and built by John B. Jervis (1795–1885) – was finally completed in 1832 at a cost of $640,000.

Terminal stations at Schenectady and Albany stood on the outskirts of town, ensuring that previously antagonistic stagecoach drivers still profited from fares to and from the centres. For a decade, carriages at Schenectady were lowered down a hill, called the inclined plane, by means of a stationary locomotive, balanced by a carriage filled with stone, before tracks were laid all the way to the destination. Services ran from both cities twice a day. Only after 1837 was the M&H permitted to carry freight.

Initially, attempts to link the successful M&H with other lines were continually frustrated by a combination of objections. In short bursts, new

SURVIVAL PLAN

Fears that the canal, as 'an expensive ditch', would become obsolete were unfounded. Although canals extended into only 14 states, they remained so popular for the transport of freight that the Erie Canal was substantially enlarged after 1837, even when the age of the train was underway. It ended up 70 ft (21 m) wide and 7 ft (2 m) deep and was used by 240-ton barges. In 1902 the Erie was better value still, after becoming toll-free.

lines finally linked the dots on the map, with most lines built by small, independently chartered railroad companies, which often merged after they were created, out of financial necessity.

A 78-mile (126-km) stretch between Utica and Schenectady opened in 1836, followed three years later by a 53-mile (85-km) connection between Syracuse and Utica. Rochester and Attica were linked by 1837, and the line was continued to Buffalo in 1843.

These weren't the only lines extending around the vicinity either, creating a confused mishmash for the travelling public. By 1847, the Mohawk & Hudson had changed its name to the Albany & Schenectady to reflect the cities it connected. Six years later it was among 10 companies to be consolidated into the New York Central Railroad Company.

Despite opposition, new legs of New York State's railroad network opened throughout the 1830s and 1840s.

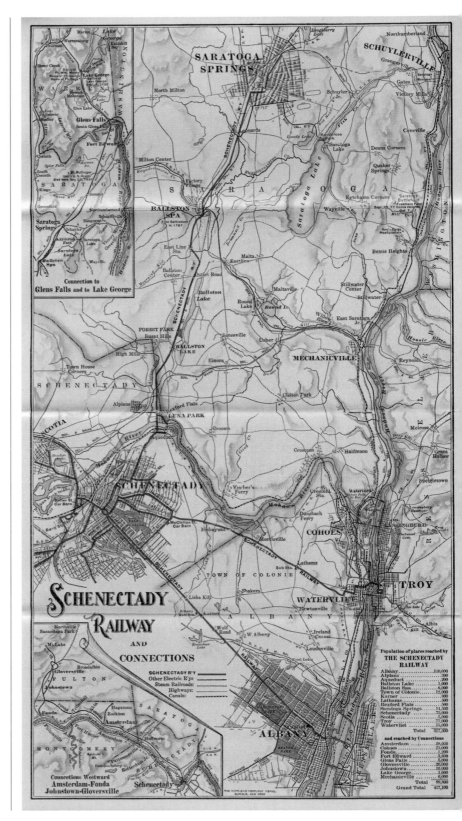

JOHN B. JERVIS

Although its population was mushrooming, America still felt like a blank canvas during the first half of the nineteenth century. There were frontiers to explore, settlements to build and fortunes to be made.

Engineer John Bloomfield Jervis made it his business to provide the nuts and bolts of the American dream.

Before working on railroads he was an engineer on the Erie Canal for $1.25 a day.

Large pipes sending fresh water into the heart of New York City, like this one being built in 1860, had a huge impact on public health.

Soon, his fascination with locomotives and the tracks they ran on brought him to the cutting edge of this new industry. He was involved in the building of the first five major lines in America.

When he became chief engineer of the Mohawk & Hudson Railroad, Jervis designed the *Experiment*, the first locomotive to have four of its six wheels mounted on a swivelling truck. His design in 1832 represented such fundamental progress, the *Experiment* was able to reach speeds of up to 60 mph (96 km/h). It was the fastest in the world at a time when American locomotives were famously slow.

Lith. of A Brown & Co. 47 Nassau St. N.Y.

For D. T. Valentine's Manual 1862.

HIGH BRIDGE DURING CONSTRUCTION OF THE LARGE MAIN
Viewed from the West Gate House looking East.

EMPIRE STANDARD

Appleton's describes a visit to the Croton Aqueduct's High Bridge as 'one suburban excursion which no visitor should fail to make… This magnificent structure by which the Croton Aqueduct is carried across Harlem River is of granite throughout and spans the entire width of valley and river, from cliff to cliff. It is 1,450 ft (442 m) long, 114 ft (35 m) high and supported on 14 massive piers and has been well called "a structure worthy of the Roman Empire".'

PLAYING IT SAFE

Yet although Jervis's nimble mind was embracing future possibilities, he wasn't at the front of every wave and, for a while, was wary of nineteenth-century technology.

When he was organizing the construction of the M&H line just a year before *Experiment* appeared, he insisted on including a passage for horses, which he felt would sometimes be needed to pull carriages. In a letter dated 20 July 1830 to the president and board of the Mohawk and Hudson Rail Road, he stated:

It will sometimes happen that a locomotive cannot be used in consequence of being out of order or from the slippery condition of the rails by reason of their being covered with frost, snow or sleet and the temporary use of horses will be necessary. The road will also be proved in firmness by this measure so that on the whole I believe it would not be prudent to neglect the construction of a horse path.

At least he insisted the path would be macadamized, following the principles used for the first time by Scottish engineer and road builder John Loudon McAdam just a decade previously.

Later in life, as he looked back on the technologies he'd helped evolve, he described railroads as 'a vast labour-saving machine diffusing its benefits to all classes and conditions of men, increasing the value of each of their own products and cheapening the cost of articles of necessity and comfort obtained from distant places.'

SERVICE TO PUBLIC HEALTH

But once again Jervis refused to be defined by a single engineering field. He left railroads for the sake of a project that, in terms of enhanced health and comfort, affected countless thousands of people.

The population of New York had ballooned, while public services were lacking. The Croton Aqueduct – designed by West Point's Major David Bates Douglass and built by Jervis, with help from Horatio Allen – brought fresh water by gravity from the Croton River in Westchester County to two above-ground reservoirs in Manhattan from 1842. With the arrival of fresh running water, health and hygiene improved accordingly, as it was coupled with a new sewer scheme.

Jervis was proud of the aqueduct's enormous capacity, supplying 35 million gallons (132 million litres) of water a day, which he thought would be ample for years to come.

Such was the expansion of New York a new system was being installed before the arrival of the twentieth century.

DEWITT CLINTON ENGINE

One locomotive soon earned itself a place in folklore history after colourful descriptions of its comical inaugural trip.

The *DeWitt Clinton*, built at the West Point Foundry, ran for the first time on the Mohawk & Hudson Railroad from Albany on a hot August morning in 1831. It was named for a politician firmly associated in the public eye with the Erie Canal. DeWitt Clinton (1769–1828), who ran for president in 1812 and lost to James Madison, steered the Erie project from the start.

Given the awkward relationship prevailing between canal and railroad it's thought the naming of the locomotive was deliberately provocative.

Anyway, the 12-ft (3.6-m) long locomotive, which weighed in at 6,758 lbs (3 tonnes), had been test-driven and was duly declared safe for the public's use. This was despite a lack of bell or whistle, headlight, proper brakes or a cab for the driver.

That day an excited public was separated from the locomotive by a flatbed wagon which carried a pile of wood and two barrels of water, linked to the engine's boiler by leather hose.

Engineer Dave Matthews, in charge of the DeWitt Clinton. *It reached speeds of up to 30 mph (48 km/h) after the locomotive entered regular service.*

Those who could not afford a seat in the three luxury stagecoach-style carriages that came next, each of which seated six people, or on the six flat carriages with wooden benches, were clustered along the tracks to watch the spectacle.

Conductor John T. Clark was among the first people in the US to issue the cry 'tickets, please' before blowing a tin horn to indicate the train was ready.

BAPTISM OF FIRE

With the jerky departure of the train, the scene descended into comedy. As the locomotive leapt into action so the coaches behind, which were linked by iron chains 3 ft (1 m) long, lurched forward, sending passengers sprawling from their seats. (Some of those who had crept on to the roof of the luxury accommodation were tossed to the ground.)

And they had little time to regain their composure before a new hazard became apparent. Smoke from the funnel, riddled with sparks, enveloped passengers, who were not only blinded but burned. Those in the open cars, who were particularly affected, patted down their clothes to put out smouldering patches caused by the ashes. Those who put up sunshades to shield themselves from the smoke soon had to discard them, as they too caught fire.

For those who had not experienced locomotion before, the speed must have seemed breathtaking, as the *DeWitt Clinton* bobbled along on four 48-inch (1.2-m) wooden wheels with iron treads. But as the first water station came into view, the engineer Dave Matthews braked. With only the locomotive in possession of brakes, the carriages once again cannoned into one another, dispatching everyone from their seats again.

This time, passengers rushed to the water point to put out the last patches of flame on their clothes. The most enterprising among them tore down some wooden fence posts, which were duly wedged between each carriage to prevent the domino crash from happening again.

AUDIENCE PARTICIPATION

Nor was the chaos restricted to those who'd thought themselves fortunate to get a ticket that day. There was mayhem among the crowds gathered along the route.

Artist William H. Brown who witnessed the scene described how horses 'attached to all sorts of vehicles' took fright:

After causing thus innumerable capsizes and smash-ups of the vehicles and the tumbling of the spectators in every direction [the train] arrived at the head of the inclined plane at Schenectady amid the cheers and welcomes of thousands.

NORTHERN CROSS

The railroads edged into the prairies early on, thanks to the Northern Cross Railroad. Illinois became America's 21st state only 20 years before the first tracks out of Meredosia in Morgan Country were built. Progress in the state was encouraged by the Internal Improvement Act of 1837, which brought forth financing where it was needed. For the Northern Cross, $1.8 million was earmarked for a line that would eventually extend to Springfield.

A newspaper advertisement that appeared on 10 August 1837 asked for 1,000 'good, sober and industrious' hands to build the new railroad, offering wages of $20 a month plus board. Reflecting a potential shortage of labour in areas like this, the advertisement went on to promise: 'This line runs through the most densely populated and healthiest portion of the state, abounding with all the comforts and conveniences of much older settled country.'

Sufficient manpower was found to install enough strap-iron rails (strips of thin metal nailed on to wood) to carry a locomotive called *Rogers* that had been shipped up from manufacturers in New Jersey for assembly at Meredosia. It was

From a slow start, the railroad infiltrated Chicago and surrounding states.

MAP OF THE CHICAGO & NORTH-WESTERN RAILWAY SYSTEM.

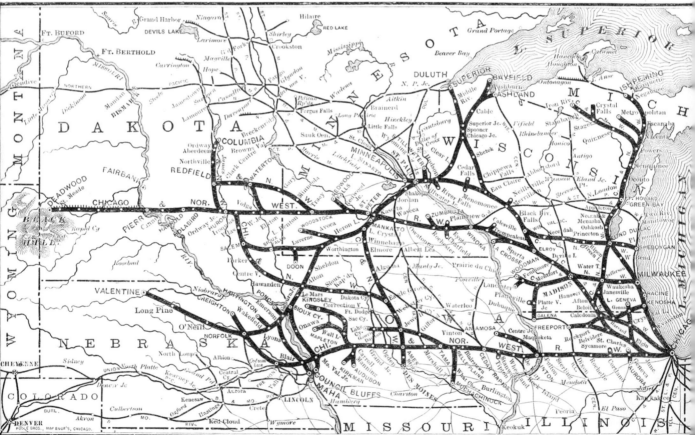

a modest machine, lacking a cab, a cowcatcher, a bell and a whistle – but it proved a great spectacle nonetheless.

'Crowds swarmed into town to view this new wonder and frequent trips were made to the end of the track, eight miles distant,' a report in the *Railway and Locomotive Historical Society Bulletin* of 1951 recalled. 'As the day wore on they became frequently delayed due to the "hospitality" offered the engineer and he had to be taken to a hotel to recover.'

By the following year, two services left daily between Meredosia and Morgan City, the 12 miles (19 km) being covered in two hours. In 1840 the line reached Jacksonville, and two years later it was in Springfield, the state capital.

PASSENGER PARTICIPATION

As delighted as the people of Illinois may have been by its arrival, the Northern Cross was not the sophisticated mode of transport they were anticipating. During stops made in the journey, passengers were expected to help collect wood to keep steam up. There were also too few water stations along the route. This meant that sometimes travellers had to set off from the stationary locomotive with buckets in hand, heading for the nearest water tank so that the service could get away once more. The service was also affected by adverse weather conditions, with the line quickly made impassable by the winter snow.

SNOW BLINDNESS

A severe prairie winter in 1855 left trains buried in snow up to their chimney stacks. One service, carrying members of Illinois' general assembly to Chicago, was trapped for three days, and passengers survived only because food and drink ordered prior to Lincoln's election victory celebrations by his wife formed part of the freight. Supplies for a different outcome ordered on behalf of the opposing candidate were also distributed among travellers, who finally broke up wooden seats for fuel. Two 'lost' freight trains went undetected until the blanket of snow thawed.

When state support ended and a buyer was sought the locomotive was worn out.

In 1847 the line was auctioned off for a fraction of the amount it had cost to build, to Nicholas Ridgley, who re-named it the Sangamon & Morgan Railroad. Initially, under his management, carriages were pulled by mules or oxen in the absence of a reliable locomotive. Its fortunes revived with fresh interest in railroad building across the state, and it eventually became part of the Wabash, which had tracks through Iowa, Missouri, Indiana, Ohio and Michigan, as well as Illinois.

GALENA & CHICAGO UNION RAILROAD

Today, Chicago is known as a railroad hub. For decades, the tangle of lines that led into the city represented growth and wealth.

Railroads transformed the region – which had been embroiled in a war with Native Americans in 1795 – at breathtaking speed. Yet the story of the city's first railroad is one of hitches and mishaps that led to a delay of a dozen years before a plume of locomotive smoke pierced its skyline.

Chicago was transformed by railroads, which first arrived in 1847 in response to a call by the farming community for better transport links.

A powerful incentive lay in the profitability of the lead mines at Galena, established in the 1820s when Chicago had just a few hundred residents. In 1829, it took 11 days for a consignment of lead to travel 160 miles (257 km) from Galena to Chicago, where it would continue onwards by ship.

At the start of 1836, when the population was an estimated 4,000, the Galena & Chicago Union Railroad (G&CURR) was incorporated by the state.

Chief engineer James Seymour didn't hesitate. He surveyed the line that same year and waited for the scheme's go-ahead.

TERMINALS OF THE CHICAGO AND NORTH-WESTERN RAILWAY AT CHICAGO.

WELCOME, IRON HORSE

On 21 November 1848 the *Chicago Daily Herald* reported: 'The Iron Horse is now fairly harnessed in the Prairie land and the freedom with which he travels betokens his satisfaction with the bounteous and almost unlimited pasture field.'

However, obstacles were lining up in the path of the juvenile company, being led by Elijah Hubbard (1812–39). First, there was the Panic of 1837, which sucked the life out of the infant economy. Then came Hubbard's untimely death from tuberculosis, which paralysed the project for no fewer than eight years.

It took rumblings of discontent from the people of Rockford, 90 miles (145 km) from Chicago, in 1846 to get the railroad back on course. Noticeably, farmers were joining the call for a railroad link to the bigger city to invigorate trade.

OGDEN THE VISIONARY

William B. Ogden (1805–77) took charge. He was mayor of Chicago in 1837 when it received city status. He'd arrived from New York a few years previously when his brother-in-law proposed buying land there – and advised against it. But when the land was drained and sectioned off into streets for houses, there was enough interest for Ogden to stay.

Ogden was tasked with raising the thousands necessary to get the railroad up and running, knowing there would be no state aid available. That railroads in Chicago would be a profitable venture wasn't necessarily a given, and he got short shrift from financier William F. Weld. 'When it breaks down as it surely will come and give it to us and we will take hold of it and complete it, as we are completing the Michigan Central,' the dour Weld responded.

Soon, Ogden had farmers in his sights as he pleaded the railroad's case. Riding on horseback between far-flung rural communities, he approached the task with missionary-like zeal. At the same time, he outlined the benefits of John Deere's steel plough that would replace the wooden ones still being used by farmers at the time. When those enlightened farmers began to share his vision, the money began to roll in.

The first tracks along a 10-mile (16-km) stretch between the Chicago River and Des Plaines were being laid in 1847. Next stop, when money would allow, was to be Elgin.

The G&CURR's first locomotive, the *Pioneer*, was purchased second hand and was already 11 years old. The track was also pre-used, discarded by another company investing in safer, solid rails. Still, Chicago permitted itself a feeling of triumph.

NEW TRACKS

In 1850, just one railroad existed to serve Chicago, that hardworking beacon of hope that was the Galena & Chicago Union Railroad. But one railroad track led to another, as small communities watched with dismay when it veered away from their homes and businesses towards more fortunate neighbourhood settlements.

When the tracks reached Elgin, the 40-mile (64-km) trip from Chicago took three hours. In contrast, a 44-mile (71-km) journey from Chicago to Sugar Grove took an eye-watering 16 hours over muddy roads. Accordingly, communities got together to organize railroads so they wouldn't be left out of the wealth-creation loop.

Many joined the track at West Chicago, later named for railroad president John B. Turner. As president of the G&CURR, his habit was to mount the stairs to a lofty observatory on the second floor of the depot to spot an incoming service using a maritime telescope. He believed he could see the smoke 6 miles (10 km) away.

And Chicago's first railroad company continued to flourish, with 60 per cent returns on investment in the first year. In 1852, there was enough money to install solid iron rails, with over half of Chicago's wheat using the line.

The following year, locomotives were arriving in Freeport. (Plans to reach Galena were abandoned. Mining wealth was now focused on California and the company could make use of Illinois Central lines already in place.)

CONVERGING ON CHICAGO

Railroad fever was soon sweeping Chicago, even though the trains were competing with the Great Lakes, the Illinois & Michigan Canal and the already existing G&CURR.

Close rivals, the Michigan Central from Detroit and the Michigan Southern both arrived in Chicago in 1852 – and soon a single-track railroad had increased to five. Four years later, Chicago had 10 different railroad companies operating a total of more than 3,000 miles (4,828 km) of track.

The effect on the city was immediate and extensive. In the early 1850s, Chicago had seven daily newspapers, plenty of five- and six-storey warehouses, numerous hotels and a series of depots for trains.

Its population was rising steeply, with English and Irish immigrants drawn to the area for its railroad boom, having begun work as track layers in New York a decade previously.

By 1860, Chicago was a city of 109,000, with 100 trains a day arriving or leaving the city.

WHEAT AND MEAT

Chicago's reputation as the greatest grain depot in the country was cemented by the 1850s, with a nine-fold increase achieved in just four years. It was also a centre for livestock. *Appleton's* recommends a visit to the Union Stockyards: 345 acres devoted to cattle and sheep trading, as well as the grain elevators. 'There are 19 of these buildings, all situated on the banks of the river and connected with the railroads by side tracks. They have an aggregate storage capacity of 15,600,000 bushels and receive and discharge grain with almost incredible dispatch.'

Previously called Alert*, this locomotive had been owned by two other railroad companies before starting service in Chicago on 25 October 1848.*

Four years later, the G&CURR became the core of a new, bigger corporation – the Chicago & North Western – in control of 600 miles (966 km) of railroad.

Despite Chicago being a boom town, the expanded railroad company tottered uncertainly. Initially, it was so desperately poor that it could not pay the interest on its bonds, and managers had to meet the pay-roll out of their own pockets. But soon it absorbed numerous short lines to emerge as a major corporation.

MARVELS & MACHINATIONS IN THE MID-CENTURY

With trains and the associated technologies, life was changing, fast. Some people were success stories, like Matthias Baldwin (1795–1866), who built *Old Ironsides* in 1831. He was disappointed when it failed to reached speeds greater than 1 mph (1.6 km/h) on the Philadelphia, Germantown & Norristown Railroad, but a few modifications quickly permitted the locomotive to reach 28 mph (45 km/h), although this was not possible in bad weather. Nonetheless, Baldwin found a new career building locomotives, producing five in 1834 and 14 the following year. By 1861 the annual figure stood at 1,000 and was still rising.

But railroads were not the only issue dominating the landscape. Division between north and south was deepening, and the tracks that some hoped would bind the country together seemed as if they might be a further cause for grief.

Opposite: Two men hang telegraph wire beside a railroad track, helping to forge a link between two technologies that changed the face and the pace of the nineteenth century.

WIRED FOR SOUND

With the new era of locomotives came dramatic progress in communications. Journeys that had previously taken days were now accomplished in hours.

When mail was legally permitted on the rails in 1938, letters similarly travelled at hitherto unknown speeds. Homing pigeons and the pony express were already looking dated.

However, instant communication was still the sought-after ideal. Geographically limited smoke signals or Semaphore provided it, but only for sections of society in the know.

During the 1830s and 1840s Samuel Morse (1791–1872) developed a way of transmitting electrical patterns and pulses along wires strung out for substantial distances that could be translated into a recognizable message down the line.

He wasn't the first to believe that electricity could be used for such a purpose, and a different system using the alphabet rather than a code

When Morse sent his first message, 'What hath God wrought', in 1844, he had no idea how it would change the way railroads operated.

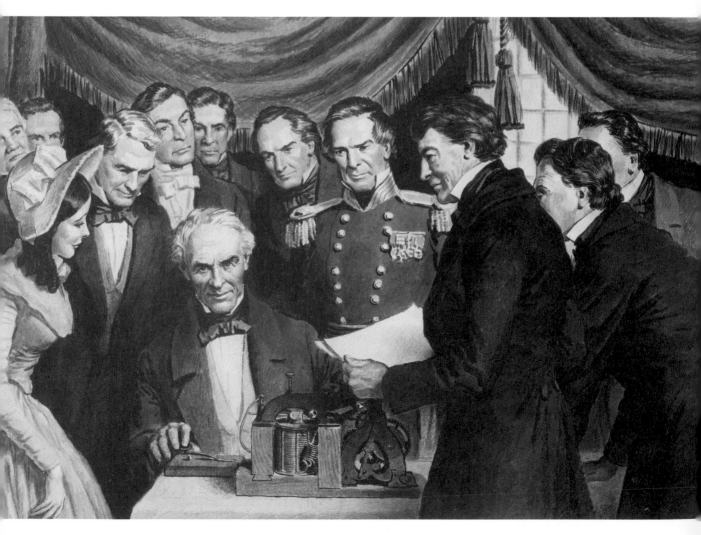

LIGHTBULB MOMENT

Years before he found fame as an inventor, Thomas Edison (1847–1931) won some local notoriety as a telegraph operator. Partially deaf, he found the mild disability helped rather than hindered. 'While I could hear unerringly the loud ticking of the instrument I could not hear other and perhaps distracting sounds ... I became rather well-known as a fast operator, especially at receiving.'

had been unveiled in London in 1837, the same year Morse patented his own design.

It was his assistant Alfred Vail who pioneered the code, a system of dots and dashes that corresponded to a letter of the alphabet. The code was tapped out with a key on what Morse called 'the Recording Telegraph' to interrupt the flow of electricity and make recognizable indents on a strip of paper at the receiving machine.

Morse found wires attached to poles more successful than those sunk into trenches.

A first showing of the new machinery before Congress wasn't entirely successful. One Senator later revealed: 'I watched [Morse's] countenance closely, to see if he was not deranged ... and I was assured by other senators after we left the room that they had no confidence in it.'

Still, Morse won some financial backing to further develop his machine's capacity.

On 24 May 1844, the religiously observant Morse, in Washington, successfully messaged Vail in Baltimore with the words 'What Hath God Wrought'.

Even then politicians felt the costs of the system too great, compared to postage. The following year, Morse helped the *Baltimore Sun* achieve a scoop by telegraphing the text of President James K. Polk's inauguration.

His was not the only system but it proved the most enduring. To cash in on his invention, he sold licences for its use until there was a plethora of companies vying for business.

RAILROADS PROVIDE THE LINK

In 1856, several companies consolidated to form the Western Union Telegraph Company, which typically used wires running alongside railroad tracks. Eventually, other companies followed suit to align into six businesses. Yet still there wasn't a system that spanned the US coast to coast.

Ultimately, Congress intervened with the Pacific Telegraph Act in 1860, which spurred the increasingly dominant Western Union into action. The task was completed the following year.

By 1866, a telegraph line had been laid across the Atlantic Ocean, linking the US and Europe. At the time, Western Union sent 5.8 million messages a year. By the turn of the century the annual figure had risen to 63.2 million.

Technology did not stand still, however, and soon the inventions of the telephone and radio with wireless telegraphy were threatening the primacy of the telegraph.

TELEGRAPHS, TRAINS & TIMETABLES

From 1851, the telegraph was used for routing trains, a valuable safety measure on the railroad system.

So far, mostly single tracks had been laid, leaving trains at risk of head-on crashes or same-direction shunts. It made station managers wary about dispatching trains, fearful of fatal consequences. This paralysed train services and timetables, adding unnecessary hours to the length of journeys.

An interval system was in place designed to prevent disasters. It meant a train from one

In 1848 New York's railroad arrangements were behind the times, as this silhouette reveals.

direction had priority over an oncoming train from the other, the second having to await the appearance of the first in a siding before setting off. If the 'ruling' train was delayed for more than an hour, the waiting service could proceed with a flag man walking ahead of the locomotive, keeping a look out for the missing timetabled train. Then one would have to reverse into the nearest siding so they could pass.

TELEGRAPHED TRAIN ORDER

It was Charles Minot (1810–66), superintendent of the Erie Railroad, who issued the first 'train order', a message that changed the meeting point between two trains heading towards one another on single tracks. The date is thought to have been 1851.

Harvard-educated Minot was an admirer of telegraph. Thanks to him, the Erie installed tell-tale telegraph trees alongside its line to link stations.

At the time the first train order was made he had been on a westbound train awaiting a late-running one from the east. Exasperated, he telegraphed the next station, Goshen, to discover the missing train hadn't yet been sighted.

Boldly, he decided to implement his long-held faith in the power of the telegraph. He ordered the late-running train to be held at Goshen and took the controls of the train he was on when the engineer Isaac Lewis was reluctant to buck the existing system of set intervals between trains. Lewis consequently sat on the last carriage, awaiting what he felt was an inevitable crash.

However, Minot's foresight meant there was no accident that day. He proceeded to two more stations before there was sight of the missing train, saving himself some three hours in journey time. His initiative was soon mimicked across the country.

Using the telegraph to communicate with each other, station managers knew the whereabouts

DEADLY BUSINESS

Safety was still a concern on railroads, as Minot's 1861 report reveals. In December 1860 alone, five people died on the Erie Railroad. He outlined the circumstances like this:

Dec 2 *Philip Lonegan*. Killed at Owego while coupling cars; did not raise draw bar high enough.

Dec 2 *John Colbert*. Had his leg broken at Paterson while attempting to jump off the cars; died Feb 16 1861.

Dec 5 *Henry Rosa*. Killed at Port Jervis; fell from cars and was run over while attempting to steal a ride.

Dec 16 *Thomas Torpy*. Killed at Lackawaxen; fell from cars and was run over.

Dec 25 *John Harrigan*. Was struck by engine while intoxicated at Cascade and died after a few days.

of trains under their supervision. Rail safety and efficiency improved substantially, at a far cheaper cost than laying double tracks throughout the country. Eventually, a two-letter code was developed for dispatching trains.

Minot's achievement was marked by a granite memorial unveiled in 1912 at Turner station, where he made the first 'train order'. Among those present at the dedication was Thomas Edison and Theodore Vail, cousin of code creator Alfred and first president of the Bell Telephone Company (later AT& T).

WEST POINT MILITARY ACADEMY

When America fought for its independence from 1776, the shortcomings in its defence networks were highlighted. Victory against Britain was thanks to verve and a dynamic campaign that overwhelmed any disadvantages brought about by lack of training and equipment.

As George Washington plotted to liberate his homeland he realized the strategic importance of the plateau where West Point Military Academy now stands, given its outlook on a crook in the Hudson River. Rudimentary fortifications were built long after he made it his headquarters in 1779.

It was this military prize that Benedict Arnold (1741–1801) promised the British in some double dealing that left his name a byword for treachery.

Arnold had been one of Washington's generals and was known for his courage on the battlefield against the British. However, he became disillusioned when he was overlooked for promotion and was also in debt. As a consequence, he offered to betray fellow Americans for cash during 1779. When the plan was uncovered, he fled for British lines and finally died in London, reviled by Americans and treated with ambivalence by his British hosts.

ENGINEERING EXPERTISE

West Point is the oldest continuously occupied military post in America. But its role in the early

West Point was a reputable military school. But its graduate engineers made important contributions in peace time, too.

history of railroads is less well known than its services to warfare.

At a time when there were no other engineering schools in America, it provided the expertise for numerous railroad schemes as well as harbours and bridges. So vital was the role of its cadets that the 1824 General Survey Act gave the green-light for them to assist with road and canal building.

The man who accelerated the status of engineers at West Point was Colonel Sylvanus Thayer (1785–1872), later known as the 'father of the Military Academy'. A veteran of the Revolutionary Wars in 1812, he was a graduate of Dartmouth College and West Point itself before being asked to take charge in 1817, following a spell spent studying in Europe. He put civil engineering at the core of the curriculum, which strengthened the US Army Corps of Engineers.

Punctual, particular, diligent and disciplined, Thayer was a popular figure among the young men he governed. He established a meritocracy, allowing entrants from poorer backgrounds to flourish.

Thayer is celebrated for the number of successful students he guided through West Point, many of whom left their mark on the development of the nation in the railroad networks they helped build. One acknowledged failure was writer and wit Edgar Allan Poe, who was court-martialled after seven months for failure to attend classes, disobedience and gross neglect of duties. Even so, in that short time he had published a volume of poems and Poe always spoke with admiration about Thayer.

In 1833, Thayer left West Point after political interference by President Andrew Jackson (1767–1845) – who, on 6 June that year, became the first White House incumbent to travel by rail.

OLD SCHOOL, NEW SCHOOL

Although he parted company with West Point, Thayer continued his interest in engineering, teaching its finer principles at eminent universities, and helping to install harbour defences in Boston. But he was acutely aware that the ranks of engineers in America were too thin. In 1867, he offered $30,000 to Dartmouth, his old college, to establish a school of engineering.

In 1871 Thayer School admitted its first three students. There was only one professor, West Point graduate Robert Fletcher, who taught every course. But for the next 47 years Fletcher directed Thayer School in much the same style Thayer would have done as it grew in eminence. Thayer – who never married – also left money for a library and a secondary school at Braintree, Massachusetts.

It's where his body was initially buried but, five years later In 1877, it was removed to West Point to be re-interred with honours.

WEST POINT FOUNDRY

While Britain rushed headlong into an industrial revolution, at the turn of the nineteenth century the Americans still maintained a predominantly agricultural economy. But during the 1812 war, in which hostilities between the two countries were renewed, the Americans realized they were being hobbled by a lack of industry, with only two cannon foundries producing the artillery needed for military engagement.

As a result, the West Point Foundry was planned, with a view to supplying the northern frontier, New York and the eastern states with arms in the event of another conflict.

At the time, the necessary metalwork techniques were largely untried, and early products emerging from the foundry after it opened in 1817 included bedsteads, ploughshares and sash weights.

A British law that prevented craftsmen from leaving the home country to practise skills elsewhere limited the scope for the recruitment of experienced workers. Nonetheless, Irishman William Young was recruited and, legend has it, brought foundry workers with him in a covert operation. It involved labourers who joined a ship bound for America at Liverpool disembarking at Queenstown, Ireland, to be replaced by the

West Point foundry was established in 1817, a dozen years before locomotives were first introduced to America.

skilled men needed at the foundry. When the ruse was discovered, the British Navy allegedly gave chase but weren't quick enough to catch them.

No doubt, then, that Irish talent went into the manufacture of the first three US-made locomotives in the West Point Foundry: *Best Friend*, *West Point* and *DeWitt Clinton*.

The foundry also began turning out stationary engines, mill machinery and hydraulic presses.

But it remained best known for the armaments it made, especially those churned out in the Civil War.

PARROTT POWER

For the manufacture of armaments, West Point Foundry was grateful for homegrown talent – in the form of a graduate from the military academy just across the Hudson River.

Captain Robert D. Parrott (1804–77) was a military inspector of ordnance before resigning his commission in 1836 and joining the Foundry. Among his first moves was to buy 7,000 acres of wooded land to ensure a charcoal supply, and he also purchased the nearby Greenwood Iron Furnace. For years he refined armaments, using the cliffs across the Hudson River for target practice.

In 1861, he patented the rifle cannon – with grooves cut inside its barrel to make the

BORN IN THE USA

When it took the order for the *DeWitt Clinton*, West Point Foundry agreed to furnish:

One locomotive engine and carriage complete with one boiler and two cylinders or sufficient capacity force to propel ten tons on the railroad at the rate of 15 mph on an elevation of one foot on two hundred and twenty five ft ... Strict attention in all the details of the plan to be paid to render the engine as conversant as practicable for the regular use for which it is intended, the weight of the engine and carriage complete not to exceed three tons and two hundreds weight and the whole to be delivered on or before the first day of July next in the city of New York.

projectile spin – and wrapped the breech of each gun with iron. Dubbed 'Parrott guns', the weapons he developed were lauded for being available, inexpensive and accurate, and helped the Union win the war.

During the war the Foundry produced 3,000 Parrott guns and 3 million projectiles.

BRIDGE OVER TROUBLED WATERS

In the 1850s, battle was joined for the very soul of the railroad. The early pioneers were keen to press ahead, connecting and settling vast swathes of the west, and talk of a transcontinental railroad was commonplace. But that meant hostility from steamboat operators fearful about lost trade. The showdown at Rock Island was inevitable.

Backers of a northern route for a transcontinental railroad saw Rock Island as the perfect spot for bridging the Mississippi. It lay in the centre of the river – the boundary between the cities of Rock Island, Illinois, and Davenport, Iowa – and would link the Chicago & Rock Island Railroad with the Mississippi & Missouri line. Supporters dangled the prospect of a journey from eastern Iowa to New York City in just 42 hours.

In 1853, the Illinois state legislature created a new corporation, the Railroad Bridge Company, to work in partnership with Iowa's M&M (owned by Thomas Doc Durant, see the Credit Mobilier scandal, pages 172–181). The founding charter required that the new bridge be built 'in such a manner as shall not materially obstruct or interfere with the free navigation of said river'.

This failed to impress steamboat operators, who argued it would do exactly that. They wanted a rail terminus on either bank with – unsurprisingly – a ferry link in between.

The boatmen had powerful allies, albeit with a cocktail of motives. The city of St Louis feared its commercial advantages as a river port would be seriously undermined, while southern states suspected the bridge was a plot to secure a northern – rather than southern route – for the transcontinental line. If successful, it would give the north a crucial head start in settling and exploiting an economic jackpot in the far west.

COMPETING INTERESTS

The most formidable bridge opponent of all was Jefferson Davis, a Mississippi politician who, in 1853, became President Franklin Pierce's secretary of war. Davis was set on securing a route deep south for the line, and favoured one along the Gadsden Purchase – 29,600 square miles (76,663 sq km) of territory bought from Mexico by the US government the same year. It covered parts of present-day Arizona and New Mexico.

When work on the Rock Island Bridge began on 16 July 1853, Davis initially appeared uninterested, so certain was he that his Gadsden route would be chosen. However, by the following spring it was clear political faction-fighting could delay his plans. In an attempt to fatally wound the bridge project, he claimed it interfered with a strategic (though disused) army fort on the island. He ordered a halt to work; construction carried on regardless.

Bridges like this one that took fast moving trains to their destinations were seen as a threat by angry paddle-steamer crews.

Davis then applied for a federal court injunction – *the United States vs Railroad Bridge Co* – and in July 1855 the suit came before Judge John MacLean of the Northern Illinois Circuit. His ruling proved a humiliation for Davis. Rock Island had been abandoned by the army, which had no right to claim it back. Besides, the bridge would be a useful public asset, promoting settlement and land values.

Judge MacLean concluded 'the state of Illinois has an undoubted right to authorize the construction of a bridge, provided that the same does not materially obstruct the free navigation of the river'. He said the central 'draw' or swing-bridge, sited above the usual steamboat channel, would cause no delay or hazard to river traffic. Within eight months the bridge had opened for business and Davis and his supporters were left licking their wounds.

But not for long. As dusk fell on 6 May 1856, the steamer *Effie Afton* headed slowly upriver from

A MIGHTY BRIDGE

The Rock Island Bridge – the first to span the Mississippi – was a superb piece of engineering. Its six spans covered 1,581 ft and included a swing-bridge rotating on a turntable. This moved on 20 wheels around a track 28 ft (8.5 m) in diameter, supported by a central pier 32 ft (10 m) wide. More than 190 miles (300 km) of timber and 600,000 lbs (272 tonnes) of cast and wrought iron went into its construction.

St Louis towards Rock Island. What happened next would define the battle between old and new technology – river versus rail.

Despite opposition, railroads would extend west relentlessly as locomotives superseded steamboats.

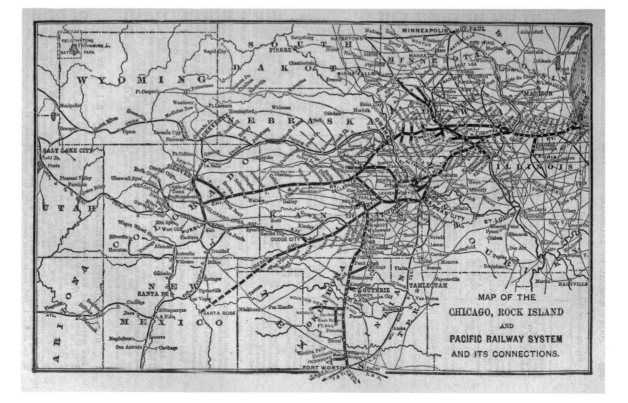

MAP OF THE
CHICAGO, ROCK ISLAND
AND
PACIFIC RAILWAY SYSTEM
AND ITS CONNECTIONS.

FIRE ON THE EFFIE AFTON

On the morning of 21 April 1856, cheering crowds gathered on the Mississippi shoreline to watch three steam locomotives pull coaches across Rock Island Bridge for the very first time. For supporters of the bridge it was a celebration of nation-building. But not everyone was cheering.

Steamboat operators had long been dreading this moment. They could see profits disappearing as fast as the steam spewing from those train funnels. But, whether by accident or design, they would soon find new hope.

As dusk fell on 6 May, the newly built $50,000 steamer *Effie Afton* was heading upriver from St Louis – her first trip so far north. She sounded her horn, indicating an intention to pass through the central swing bridge, and cleared the

A cabin stove which toppled over when the Effie Afton crashed into the Rock Island Bridge sparked an inferno. Although passengers were put at risk, the accident was hailed as a victory by steamship operators.

structure without difficulty. But then, just 200 ft (60 m) further on, her starboard engine stopped, while power increased on the port side. She heeled around, presenting her broadside to the flow of the river. Within seconds she was swept into a supporting pier alongside the still-open swing bridge.

The heavy impact damaged both bridge and boat but, more seriously, knocked over a cabin stove. The resulting fire spread with phenomenal speed, destroying the vessel inside five minutes and setting alight timber on the span above.

According to the *Chicago Democratic Press*:

…the upper works of the boat struck against the bridge with so much violence as to knock all in pieces; smoke pipes, stoves and the like were thrown down. The boat was set on fire in two or three places. The hull of the boat was in the meantime pressed under the bridge by the force of the current. The deck stood nearly at an angle of forty-five degrees. Boat and bridge were locked together.

All was confusion and yet several attempts were made to extinguish the fires. These were supposed for a time to be successful and yet soon after the flames broke out with such violence as to baffle all effort; but the connection with the bridge enabled the passengers to escape. They got themselves and their baggage on shore. The flames, however, were soon communicated to the bridge. The outer end burned off and fell upon the burning steamer; the other end of that span was cut away and bridge and steamer floated down together, a sheet of flame. In the meantime, the excitement had spread through the two adjacent cities and thousands from Rock Island and Davenport stood upon the shores watching the sublime spectacle.

HIGH STAKES IN COURT

The owner of the *Effie Afton*, Captain Jacob Hurd, wasted no time instructing lawyers. He sought $200,000 in damages, claiming his vessel 'was forcibly driven by the currents and eddies' created by the bridge piers. Hurd knew that if his suit was successful future bridge projects across the Mississippi would be mired in uncertainty – never mind potential maintenance and insurance costs. Trains would be obliged to transfer passengers and freight to river ferries and re-load on the opposite side. It would be a dagger to the heart of the burgeoning railroad industry.

But Hurd faced formidable opponents. Theories surfaced in newspapers suggesting the collision was deliberate and the *Effie Afton* had been loaded with flammable material. Difficult questions emerged. Why was the *Effie* operating so far north? Where was her cargo manifest? And why did the current not carry her back through, rather than against, the bridge? The Rock Island Railroad vigorously defended themselves against Hurd's claims – effectively accusing him of an intentional and pre-meditated act.

Incredibly, all 200-plus passengers and crew escaped, although the cargo of cattle, horses, machinery and merchandise was mostly lost. Now the sounds of celebration came not from the shores but the river itself. Steamboat skippers plying the route made their feelings clear by sounding horns and ringing bells.

ABRAHAM LINCOLN: SAVIOUR OF THE BRIDGE

The case of *Hurd vs Rock Island Railroad Company* was billed as the battle of the century between competing transport interests. It would become one of Abraham Lincoln's most celebrated legal triumphs and cement his blossoming reputation as a railroad advocate. Crucially, it established that bridging a river was not necessarily a public nuisance.

Lincoln was hired as lead defence counsel by his friend Norman B. Judd, general counsel of the Rock Island Railroad. Judd reportedly described the future president as 'one of the best men to state a case forcibly and convincingly

An engraving of Abraham Lincoln delivering a farewell address to his neighbours and friends at Springfield before departing for his inauguration, February, 1860.

that I have ever heard ... and his personality will appeal to any judge or jury.' Judd needed to be right. Steamboat owner Captain Jacob Hurd had engaged one of America's leading 'river lawyers' in Judge H. M. Wead.

Proceedings began in Chicago's Circuit Court on 8 September 1857 and lasted 14 days. They hinged on one key point: was the Rock Island Bridge a serious obstruction to steamboat traffic? Wead unleashed a battery of bridge engineers, pilots, river-men and boat owners to insist it was.

But Lincoln was nothing if not thorough. He'd researched the Mississippi's currents, speeds and eddies around the island, drawing on an 1837 survey by Robert E. Lee – later an icon of the Confederate Army. He'd factored in the angles of the bridge piers, the curvature of the river and the depth of the channel navigated by the *Effie Afton*. In his forensic examination of witnesses he delivered a devastating counter to Hurd's claims that the bridge was virtually impassable by night.

THE BOY WHO KNEW

When Lincoln was researching his case, the story goes that while walking across the bridge he spotted a local boy sitting on one of the spans. Lincoln asked what he knew of the river and discovered he was the son of B. B. Brayton, resident bridge engineer. Lincoln reportedly replied: 'I'm mighty glad I came out here where I can get a little less opinion and more fact. Tell me now, how fast does this water run under here?' Together, they worked out the speed of the current using logs dropped into the water.

The real ace in Lincoln's hand though was his oratory. His closing argument focused on the traditions and romance of river traffic. He also accepted that Hurd was justified bringing the case (while emphasizing it should not determine the future of other bridges). However, he accused the *Effie Afton's* crew of recklessness adding: 'If we are allowed by the Legislature to build a bridge, which will require them to do more than before, when a pilot comes along it is unreasonable for him to dash on heedless of the structure which has been legally put there.'

Lincoln insisted that citizens had as much right to cross a river as sail along it. The repaired bridge had proved crucial to colonization – in the year following the fire the railroad had hauled across 74,179 passengers and 12,586 freight carriages – and east-to-west traffic was 'building up new countries with a rapidity never before seen in the history of the world'. There was no alternative because tunnels and suspension bridges were too expensive. Without Rock Island and bridges like it, he concluded, the civilization of the west was at stake.

It was a cogent point, which cleverly tapped the jurors' desire for economic prosperity. They divided 9–3 in favour of the Rock Island Railroad, a decision hailed by the *Chicago Tribune* as 'virtually a triumph for the bridge', and although legal action rumbled on, it made little impact. In 1863 – under Lincoln's presidency – the US Supreme Court finally decided railroads had as much right to cross a river as boats had to sail on it. Without such an understanding, the Court ruled, 'no lawful bridge could be built across the Mississippi anywhere; nor could the great facilities of commerce, accomplished by the invention of the railroads, be made available where great rivers had to be crossed.'

Improved travelling times between major cities gave railroad companies plenty to crow about by the mid-nineteenth century.

THE AMERICAN CIVIL WAR

The American Civil War was a bloody conflict that stained the nation's history.

Although less than a century old, America had, for several decades, been diverging along geographical lines. In broad terms, the south was an agricultural economy especially dependent on cotton, while the north was rapidly industrializing and had a railroad network to match.

South Carolina was the first southern state to split from the Union, followed by Mississippi, Florida, Alabama, Georgia, Louisiana, Texas, Virginia, Arkansas, North Carolina and Tennessee.

After hostilities erupted, both the Union and the Confederate States claimed they were acting in the spirit of the Founding Fathers and the Declaration of Independence, while accusing the other side of sacrificing these sacred tenets.

Moreover, there were people in the north who had sympathies with the Confederates, and those in the south who were loyal to the Union.

Slavery is often cited as the cause of the war. Certainly, for the growing abolitionist movement in the north, it was the primary issue. The 13th Amendment, which abolished slavery, was agreed in 1865, just after the war had ended.

But others felt that the Union of states was the most vital aspect being risked by the actions of the Confederates. Without it, America would lose the strength of unity and, like Europe, would suffer perpetual divisions.

As for the Confederates, they felt their way of life was under attack, seeing little difference between the slaves they kept and the hordes of ill-paid industrial workers exploited by factory owners elsewhere.

At the time the war started there were 19 free and 15 slave states, eight of which did not immediately sign up to the Confederate cause. Indeed, Maryland, Delaware, Kentucky and Missouri never joined the fight.

Still, victory for the north was by no means guaranteed, despite this numerical advantage.

Soldiers in the south, prepared passionately to defend what they believed in, initially chose to fight on home ground. So, for Union troops there was the difficulty of mounting an invasion in an unfamiliar landscape.

There was a real fear in the north that either Britain or France would come to the aid of the south. While Britain was loud in its condemnation of slavery, it depended on southern cotton to keep its mills turning, and was notoriously expedient in its decision-making. Although Lincoln ensured southern ports were blockaded, the British navy would have made short work of his ships.

Also, early Confederate victories might well have tempted defeatists in the north to withdraw support for the war. In reality, foreign powers would only step in after seeing a clear winner emerge and this failed to occur.

Despite fervently held hopes, it was clearly not going to be a short war, and the pain of attrition would be felt by both sides.

As Lincoln observed: 'America will never be destroyed from the outside. If we falter and lose our freedoms, it will be because we destroyed ourselves.'

MODERN WARFARE

The American Civil War has the dubious distinction of being considered the first 'modern' war for the use of railroads and other advanced weaponry.

In fact, it wasn't the first conflict in which railroads proved pivotal. During the Crimean War in 1853–56, a 7-mile long railroad, built by the British and the French, helped to supply the armies laying siege to Sebastopol in 1855.

Long before this, theorist Friedrich List (1789–1846), who first saw railroads when he lived in America, had pondered the use of railroads for the purposes of defence.

Until the Crimean War, battles were big set pieces that invariably ended with an emphatic victory, as only a finite number of men, horses and ammunition could be brought into play. In short, it took fewer battles for the outcome of the war became clear.

In the second half of the nineteenth century, investment in infrastructure began to count for something, providing not only an economic advantage but a military one.

Dumpy but high powered, artillery like this played a destructive role throughout the conflict.

LOCOMOTIVE LOGISTICS

As hostilities began in 1861, railroads played a central logistical role. Trains took recruits, horses, ammunition, food and mail to the front line. On the return trip, they carried the wounded and the dead.

An aerial observation post was established by the Union side with the hot air balloon Intrepid, *here in Virginia before the Battle of Fair Oaks.*

In the Revolutionary War (1775–83), soldiers had marched into battle – and were exhausted before the fighting had even begun. On their backs they carried heavy packs containing their weapons and several days' rations.

Of course, there were horses for the officers, and mules to haul supplies. But the animals needed to be fed, as well as the fighting men. That served to increase an army's heavy load and further slow its pace.

But the arrival of trains changed all that.

SUPPLY LINES

Armies supplied by a freely running rail service were at least in theory – better fed. This was good news for soldiers, and for the populations surrounding army camps and battlefields too. They were largely left alone when previously their homes and harvests might have been pillaged to feed the troops.

Medical supplies, such as they were, could also now be distributed at speed.

Behind the lines, regular railroad services meant that secret messages – carried either by military personnel or spies – could be delivered with far greater speed and security. This was especially vital as telegraph wires were frequently cut.

For generals plotting the course of campaigns, there was potential for more fluid troop movement to consider, and the lull between armed clashes diminished as troops were ferried swiftly and in quantity between different sections of the front line.

So, for the first time in history, no battle need be lost for lack of numbers, as railroads introduced the element of industrial scale to warfare.

As a result, there were 400 skirmishes that could properly be called battles during the American Civil War, an average of one every four days. As a consequence, more American lives were lost in this conflict than in the rest of the wars involving the US to the present day, combined.

FLYING HIGH

Ingenuity and innovation tend to follow in the wake of warfare, and the inspired use of trains was not the only military advance to take place in the American Civil War. The Union Army had a height advantage after it established the Balloon Corps in 1861. Scientist Thaddeus Lowe (1832–1913) was appointed by President Lincoln to lead the reconnaissance unit, sending the first dispatch by telegraph straight to the White House, claiming observation of some 50 miles (80 km) around.

LEGACY OF WAR

The war was something of a wake-up call to railroad companies who, until now, had fiercely guarded their fiefdoms. In both north and south, many lines deliberately avoided interlinking with others, for fear of offering an advantage to a perceived rival.

That meant that two lines might arrive in the same town at different points. Before the war, passengers took a carriage to the next station to overcome the mildly irritating hiccough in the journey. But during the war entire armies and their supplies had to cross town, losing precious momentum and more than doubling workloads.

After the war, there would be more joined-up thinking by railroad planners to eliminate track-free gaps. But that wrinkle wasn't immediately clear to the participants of the Civil War, as they got to grips with railroad warfare.

Their first instinct was to remain in the vicinity of a railhead to reap all the newly realized logistical benefits it could offer.

STRATEGIES & TACTICS

If one side hailed a particular railroad for the logistical support it offered, the other saw it as a target. Thus, lifting railroad tracks to cause derailments became a dark art practised by both sides.

There were other ways of putting a train out of commission, too. Sharp shooters were sometimes used to pierce locomotive boilers. If the crew survived stray bullets, they were still at risk from an eruption of scalding steam.

Collaborating with the military, railroad companies were keen to put armour on locomotives for added protection. However, this was finally restricted, as liberal use of heavy plating made the cab intolerably hot and cramped.

Destroying train and track at the same time was an even better option. Accordingly, explosives were put on the rail bed to be detonated by passing trains.

Channels on bullet cases like these enhanced distance and accuracy.

The forerunner of today's explosive mines, the most effective were artillery shells with specially built detonators triggered by the pressure of the oncoming train. Many were powerful enough to lift locomotives and carriages or wagons off the rails.

ENGINES OF WAR

As the conflict continued to unfold, new and hitherto unknown uses for the railroad locomotive were established.

It could be used for reconnaissance, especially given the habit of both armies to congregate around railroad lines. While it might seem reckless to bring a locomotive within sight of the enemy it could, of course, go forwards or in reverse at full throttle and outrun any pursuing cavalry.

Shunting blazing wagons towards the enemy became another ruse to disperse soldiers, or towards wooden bridges and covered tunnels in order to wreck the track.

Sometimes, empty trains were dispatched into enemy-controlled territory under close scrutiny. When there was welcoming gunfire, the observers knew the enemy's precise location.

Haphazard train movements might also send the wrong message to watchful scouts, implying that reinforcements were being made when in fact a retreat was taking place.

A locomotive could tow heavy artillery into position. Advances in the technology surrounding heavy weaponry meant the railroad only had to be near, not next to, the area coming under siege.

For example, 'the Dictator' was a coastal mortar with a 13-inch (33-cm) bore and a range of about 2.5 miles (4 km), initially designed to fling explosives towards ships at sea. But mounted on a specially strengthened flatbed railroad truck, it was moved by the Union army with ease to where it was needed. At the siege of Petersburg, it was fired 218 times in less than three months. The gun's recoil pushed the wagon some 15 ft (5 m) along the rails.

Soldiers on both sides soon learned to loathe the shrill whining that accompanied an incoming artillery shell, quickly followed by an earth-shaking explosion.

Sometimes, weapons were mounted on larger handcars, which nimbly scooted along rails, avoiding any deluge of shells issued by way of response.

A new breed of soldiers, known as sharp shooters, wreaked havoc among opposition ranks.

NEW WEAPONRY

Technology also leapt ahead with a new bullet – known by soldiers as 'the minnie' – that increased accuracy over greater distances. The Minié ball had been developed in France a few years previously, with grooves along the bullet casing that helped stabilize it in flight.

Iron-clad ships were used for the first time, in turn leading to the development of submarines. Also, guerrilla tactics, especially suitable in the destruction of railroad lines, came of age.

THE ARMY OF THE POTOMAC—SHARP-SHOOTER IMPROVISING A REST FOR HIS RIFLE.—Sketched by A. R. Waud.

RAILROADS IN THE SOUTH

For its part, the Confederacy had some significant disadvantages to counter as it braced for war.

Although Charleston had been host to the country's first railroad, the south had only about one-third of railroads in America under its control. Virginia boasted the best network, extending to some 1,770 miles (2,848 km), while Arkansas – although well away from the front line – had just 38 miles (61 km) of track. There were no railroad bridges across the Ohio or Potomac rivers.

Railroads there had been built for economic purposes rather than military, so the majority tended to be short and unconsolidated, as the first priority had been to get 'king cotton' to ports for trading purposes, along with tobacco harvests.

The Confederates started off on the front foot, though. Unaligned Maryland was a slave state with southern sympathies that stayed loyal to the government thanks to the presence of numerous Federal troops. However, partisans made their feelings known by destroying railroads leading to Washington in a well-intentioned but ultimately fruitless quest to isolate the Union capital.

THE FEDERAL TROOPS UNDER GENERALS BRANNAN AND TERRY DRIVING THE CONFEDERATES UNDER BEAUREGARD ACROSS THE POCOTALIGO BRIDGE, NEAR THE CHARLESTON AND SAVANNAH RAILROAD, OCTOBER 22D, 1862.—FROM A SKETCH BY OUR SPECIAL ARTIST.

Above: When they had the opportunity, Union soldiers disabled the Confederate network. This incident occurred at Pocotaligo Bridge on 22 October 1862.

Opposite: Only at the end of the conflict did railroads begin to proliferate in the south.

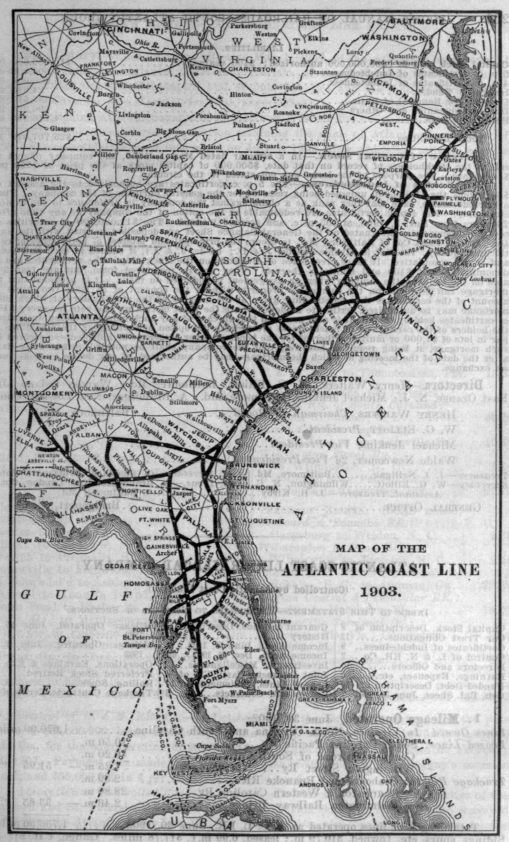

MAP OF THE
ATLANTIC COAST LINE
1903.

A CONFEDERATE PREDICAMENT

If the war had been fuelled by passion, then the south would have stood more than a fighting chance. Unfortunately, industrial hardware played its part.

In the south, production of rails stood at about one-ninth of the north's capacity. Little iron was produced in the south, and it was difficult for the Confederacy to import, given the port blockade. At the time, the major producers were Britain and the Union. The Confederates were left having to rip up inconsequential branch lines to secure important routes.

There were also fewer locomotive manufacturers in the south, which meant the Confederacy was unable to keep up with the production levels necessary during war time.

Union soldiers relished the opportunity to wreck Confederate railroads, thus hobbling the south's capacity to fight on.

Typically, men from the south had been less inclined to work as engineers on railroads than those from the industrialized north. This wasn't a problem before the conflict, as plenty of men from the northern states moved south to operate the lines. But they quickly left when war broke out, to save their skins.

In their absence, there was a shortage of skilled workers. That meant services could not be properly run and rolling stock was not maintained.

Reflecting this, John Lewis, superintendent of the Western & Atlantic, commented in his 1861 report about the suitability of staff at his disposal:

There are some of these who have been on the Road for a long time, and steady, competent sober-minded, faithful men. These, in my opinion, deserve and ought to receive, more pay than untried men.

There are some itinerating runners for whom I have (to say the least of it) a feeling amounting to horror – *incompatible, reckless, and devoid of the feeling of moral responsibility; they are unfit to be put in charge of life and property.*

Spare parts became increasingly difficult to secure. As trains became more dilapidated, their speeds slowed, sometimes to as little as 10 mph (16 km/h).

THE BATTLE FOR THE B&O

There must have been hopes that the significant resources of the B&O would be put at the disposal of the Confederates.

Baltimore was a divided city, where southern sympathizers pledged to take action. B&O's

GAUGE THE DIFFERENCE

Typically, railroad companies had preferred gauges that jarred with neighbouring lines in the hope that it forced traffic their way. This proved a hindrance to military movement of railroads. Initially, there were at least 11 different gauges in the north of the country, but by 1860 the standard gauge was the most commonly used. However, in the south a variety of broad gauges was still favoured, presenting difficulties to an army tasked with taking men and artillery across country.

president John Garrett received an anonymous note from someone who purported to represent 100 Marylanders who would 'destroy every bridge and tear up your track' if another Union soldier was transported in its trains.

But Union soldiers soon moved into the city, arresting suspected Confederate supporters, including rail innovator Ross Winans, while railroad executives became frustrated with Confederates being cavalier with rolling stock.

Southern hopes that the states in the northwest would side with the south, or at least stay neutral, in any civil conflict were also dashed. Part of the reason, at least, was that trade between the northeast and northwest by train was vibrant.

The south was also more affected by inflation caused by the war, with the cost of lubricating oil rising from $1 to $50 a gallon, while carriage wheels, once an attainable $15 each, were hiked to $500.

THE FIRST BATTLE OF BULL RUN

Swift movement of troops proved decisive for the south in the first major clash of the war.

Confederate soldiers in the Army of the Potomac under the command of Brigadier General Pierre Beauregard were massing at Manassas Junction in July 1861 to protect the key railroad interchange.

Lincoln was eyeing that with concern, as it lay just 25 miles (40 km) from his capital, Washington.

The crucial railroad in the vicinity was the Manassas Gap Railroad (MGRR), incorporated in 1850 by merchants and farmers anxious to win back a share of the wheat, corn, butter and apple trade that had been swept up in the region by the powerful B&O, and effectively linking the fertile Shenandoah Valley to the rest of Virginia.

Completed in three years, it linked to the recently opened Orange & Alexandria line at Manassas Junction. According to one newspaper,

SPECTATOR SPORT

The rout of the Union army was further confused by fleeing bystanders drawn to the scene, believing it would be a knock-out blow by the Union. Alongside reporters there were spectators, most with picnic baskets, who had travelled from Washington to witness the goings-on.

From their vantage point, they watched acrid smoke rise from the battlefield. 'On to Richmond,' they cried, believing the Union army to be in the ascendancy. This is exactly what happened to unfortunate New York congressman Alfred Ely, who strayed too close to Confederate lines and was taken prisoner.

a ride on it 'affords one of the most lovely and picturesque scenes which nature and rural industry have combined anywhere to create.'

But at Manassas Junction, freight wagons had to use the O&A lines to complete the journey, at a hefty cost of $30,000 a year. So, investors led by Edward Marshall (1805–82) planned another line, some 34 miles (55 km) long, to Alexandria, thereby cutting costs and securing profits.

'I warrant that in less than 18 months the Iron Horse will be seen prancing in your midst,' Marshall told the people of Fairfax, as he sought new stockholders.

Work on the Independent Line, as it was called, got underway with alacrity, and the landscape was duly fashioned to receive rails. But difficulties stacked up against the MGRR, which was dogged by poor harvests, a national financial crisis and growing tensions between north and south.

The company's declining fortunes meant that work was suspended in 1858 without a single rail being laid. Preparatory earthworks for the project eventually became battle sites.

But for the first Battle of Bull Run in July 1861 it was the transportation of troops along the Manassas Gap Railroad that proved crucial.

MGRR PROVIDES REINFORCEMENTS

Untried Union troops had been sent by Lincoln, against the advice of his senior commander Winfield Scott, to answer the criticism of inaction levied at him from some quarters in Washington. Back in April he had asked for 75,000 volunteers to serve for three months, hoping this would be sufficient time to quell the rebellion. Now their allotted time was nearly up, and the raw force hadn't seen action.

ON THE MARCH TO BULL RUN.

At Bull Run, the Union force, some 28,400 strong, were in the majority – as long as Confederate armies were prevented from uniting at Manassas Junction.

However, General Joe Johnston for the south, in charge of 21,800 men, used the railroad to bring in reinforcements, who arrived in time to turn the tide of the battle.

Union soldiers fled in disarray in the face of an apparently inexhaustible supply of enemy fighters. Hundreds were taken prisoner.

Movement of troops was always a factor in the outcome of a battle. When they could be moved swiftly by rail to where they were needed, it was enough to secure victory.

For the South, this was a welcome lesson in warfare. The Confederates could not afford to cede territory to the north. By using railroads they could spread men across the vulnerable approaches, directing them to battles as necessary.

THE SECOND BULL RUN BATTLE

Little more than a year after the Confederate victory, Bull Run was the scene of a second battle.

This time, the railroad had a different part to play, as men sank seamlessly into the 'cut and fills' that had been made for the Manassas Gap Railroad's extension. Precisely carved contours, left by engineers four years previously, were now blurred by undergrowth, although the excavated track bed was still accessible.

Taking up this uncharacteristically defensive position, General Thomas Jackson (1824–63) was content with the rudimentary camouflage.

Devastation marked Manassas Junction as early as 1862.

Jackson had made a name for himself when he led reinforcements at the First Battle of Bull Run, in more ways than one. Leading exhausted men, Brigadier General Barnard Bee shouted: 'Look at Jackson standing like a stonewall … Rally behind the Virginians.' The name 'Stonewall' stuck.

A staunch Presbyterian, who died after a friendly fire incident, he once professed his religious beliefs made him feel as safe in battle as in bed.

Before settling in at Bull Run, he and his men had rifled through a Union supply depot at Manassas Junction. What was left uneaten was burned.

Suitably fortified, they survived numerous attacks by General John Pope's forces until the Union army was finally outflanked by Confederate reinforcements and forced into a retreat.

THE MANGLING OF THE MGRR

The Second Bull Run was another victory for the southerners but, with the wholesale destruction of the neighbourhood, there was little to celebrate for those linked to the MGRR.

The engine house, machine shop, locomotive servicing facilities and yard tracks at Manassas Junction were wrecked. The turntable, like the track bed, was strangled with weeds. Those few rails and wagons that remained were targeted by both sides throughout the rest of the war, and the company never recovered to fulfil its intention of completing the Independent Line to Alexandria.

In 1866, Marshall reported that the railroad infrastructure had been devastated to the point where normal operations were impossible.

Nor was it the only victim, in terms of railroads in the vicinity. The O&A was likewise obliterated and in 1867 the two companies merged to become the Orange, Alexandria & Manassas

MASON–DIXON LINE

Defining the border between north and south was a perpetual challenge, although the Mason–Dixon line was considered significant. That frontier, marked with boundary stones, had been completed in 1768 by Englishmen Charles Mason (1728–86) and Jeremiah Dixon (1733–79), astronomers and surveyors who were tasked with marking the disputed border between Pennsylvania and Maryland. Territory issues aside, it became vital after 1781, when Pennsylvania abolished slavery, as the 'finish line' for escaped slaves from the south, along with the Ohio River. Today, it's considered more of a cultural frontier.

The Mason-Dixon line established a border between two states and a finish line for escaped slaves before and during the Civil War.

Railroad – which would eventually become part of the Southern Railroad System. The route of the Independent Line, once owned by one of the few men in the locality who had voted against secession, reverted to farm land.

Unfinished railroad lines featured in three other Civil War battles, including Gettysburg.

RAILROADS IN THE NORTH

With their importance underscored early on, war inevitably brought prosperity to railroad companies in the north.

For example, the Illinois Central, built with government land grants, still made a profit and paid healthy dividends throughout the war, despite being compelled to reduce its rates for the government, and finding its capacity and income affected as a result. In 1863, investors received an 8 per cent dividend. Two years later the figure rose to 10 per cent.

It wasn't alone in reaping rewards. The Wilmington & Weldon Railroad paid a staggering 31 per cent dividend in 1863.

Indeed, the *American Railroad Journal* branded that year 'the most prosperous ever known to American railroads'.

One of the key advantages wielded by the Union was the extent that railroads covered its territory. The valuable trade it generated kept other northwestern states loyal during the conflict.

G3711 P3 1865 .C6 RR 91

93

RAILROAD COMPANY SUPPORT

O n paper it seemed the Union was blessed with key numerical advantages.

Two-thirds of the nation's tracks were in the north – the Pennsylvania and Erie railroads together had nearly as many locomotives as the entire Confederacy – and networks were bigger and better organized than those of the south.

But, initially, railroad company bosses were only happy to support the Union at a price. Leading from the front in this was secretary of war Simon

Cameron (1799–1889) from Pennsylvania, who had invested heavily in the railroad industry.

When it was discovered he was manipulating rates to the advantage of big business and the detriment of government, he was sacked by

Union soldiers besieged at Chattanooga were relieved by rail on what was known as 'the Cracker Line', which led to victory against the Confederates and further access to the southern states.

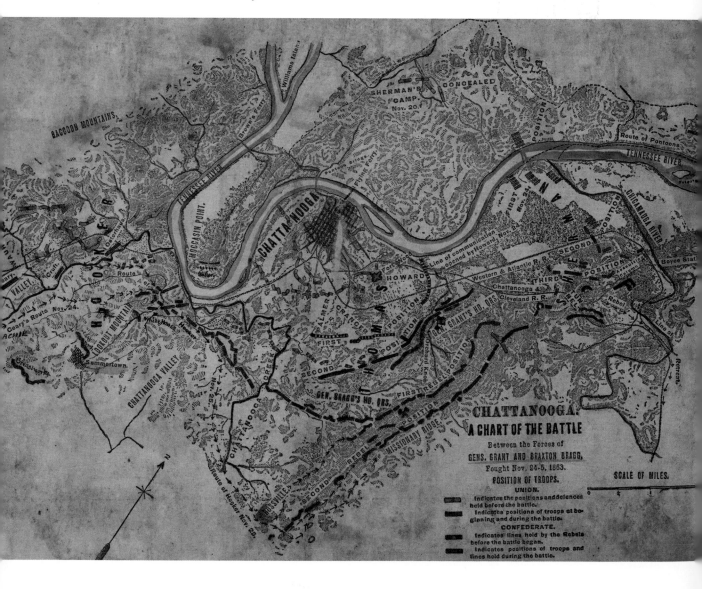

Lincoln, who promptly passed the Railroad and Telegraph Act of 1862. This led to the creation of the United States Military Railroads (USMRR), which empowered the Union to use privately run operations when it needed to for the army's best tactical advantage.

Corruption and profiteering lessened when Lincoln made it clear that lines owned by transgressors might be seized. Ultimately, 16 lines in the east and 19 in the west were pressed into service by the USMRR, led by Daniel C. McCallum, during the war.

Yet it wasn't necessarily possession of locomotives, but how they were used, that would count.

The theory of using trains to aid a war effort was still evolving. One story handed down from the era tells of a Union commander who held a supply train for 24 hours while he decided whether he needed it to move his men. He was apparently blissfully unaware of the shortages he was creating at the front, and the traffic jam building up down the line.

CHATTANOOGA CHOO CHOO

Even Lincoln didn't necessarily grasp the crucial element that locomotives and rail networks now played in times of war.

In September 1863, secretary of war Edwin Stanton proposed to lift the siege of Chattanooga by dispatching 30,000 men to its environs by train. He felt five days would be sufficient time to do it. Lincoln responded incredulously, 'I will bet that if the order is given tonight the troops could not be got to Washington in five days.'

Stanton was indeed being over-optimistic, but within 12 days nearly 25,000 men, horses and artillery were in position, having travelled

TRACK CARNAGE

The north was not immune from Confederate action, and damage to the B&O was chronicled in its annual company reports. In 1861, the company said 26 bridges, 102 miles (164 km) of telegraph lines and two water stations had been destroyed, along with rolling stock. The following year, news of how the Monocacy iron suspension bridge had been blown up was related. In 1863, there was more bad news, this time from Martinsburg:

The polygonal engine house, the half-round engine house, the large and costly machine shops, warehouse, ticket and telegraph officers, the company's hotel and dining and wash house, coalbins, sand houses, blacksmith shop and tool houses, pumping engine for water station and connecting pipes were all destroyed.

1,200 miles (1,931 km) to Tennessee in 30 trains comprising some 600 carriages and wagons. On the route, they passed through Harper's Ferry, Columbus, Indianapolis, Louisville and Nashville.

The Union benefitted from the support of numerous railroad workers, as well as railroad company presidents such as John Garrett of the B&O. Thomas A. Scott, vice president of the Pennsylvania Railroad, served a year as assistant secretary of war. This accumulated wisdom helped formulate ways of putting military strategy into railroad operation.

BRIDGE BUILDING

Sabotaging train lines became a strategic aspect of the Civil War's fight and flight.

Remedying it for the Union was Herman Haupt (1817–1905), a West Point graduate who became known for throwing up railroad bridges that had been torn down by retreating Confederates.

His work made a lasting impression on Lincoln after the president witnessed one of Haupt's constructions on the Richmond, Fredericksburg & Potomac Railroad in May 1862. 'I have seen the most remarkable structure that human eyes ever rested upon,' exclaimed Lincoln. 'That man Haupt has built a bridge across the Potomac Creek about 400 ft long and nearly 100 ft high over which loaded trains are running every hour and upon my word ... there is nothing in it but beanpoles and cornstalks.'

Equally remarkable was the fact that the job – containing over 6,000 cubic yards (4,700 cubic metres) of lumber cut in nearby woods – had been completed in less than two weeks. His specially chosen workforce consisted of frontier woodsmen, craftsmen and freed slaves. This became the model for military railroads of the era.

HAUPT IN CHARGE

Haupt had already accumulated long experience on railroads before the outbreak of the conflict, initially as an assistant engineer. Aged 22, he patented a wooden design for a truss bridge.

As chief engineer on the Pennsylvania Railroad he supervised construction of the Alleghany Tunnel, opening a vital artery to Pittsburgh. Just prior to the war, he worked on the problematic Hoosac Tunnel in Massachusetts, the first major rock tunnel built in the US.

A skilled administrator, he co-ordinated services on the web of railroads at critical points with a rigid timetable, and objected to any military interference in it, no matter how compelling the reason.

Haupt wasn't completely inflexible. At the Second Bull Run campaign, he pulled out all the stops to transport reinforcements to Major General John Pope's army stranded at Manassas Junction.

However, Brigadier General Samuel D. Sturgis seized the opportunity to transport his own men by rail to the front. Just outside Alexandria, he took charge of four trains already earmarked by Haupt and running to a strict schedule.

Nor was the embarkation achieved swiftly. Before Sturgis had finished, nearly a day had been lost, hours that had been carefully pre-planned by Haupt. When Sturgis was finally confronted by an outraged Haupt, he was far from contrite. 'Why, I don't care for John Pope one pinch of owl dung.'

Crucially, Haupt formed a Construction Corps which was responsible for making lines fit for the military. Working at speed, the men repaired and rebuilt track, tunnels and bridges, often using prefabricated parts. By the end of the war, this corps numbered 10,000 men.

He also organized a Transportation Corps to manage train operations, mostly using ex-railroad employees.

RAILROAD HERO

Perhaps Herman Haupt's greatest achievement was linked to the Battle of Gettysburg in 1863. Before the armies clashed, he had transformed the small-scale Western Maryland railroad so it could carry five times its previous capacity. And his men had repaired the ruined Gettysburg lines in time to transport 16,000 wounded soldiers in the wake of the fighting.

An apparently flimsy trestle bridge quickly constructed by army engineers is robust enough for the locomotive Firefly.

GOLDEN RULES OF MILITARY RAILROADS

At the start of his tenure, Edwin M. Stanton, secretary of war, told Herman Haupt: 'Be as patient as possible with generals. Some of them will trouble you more than they will the enemy.' However, it was often a case of Haupt troubling other generals.

Haupt was talented, forceful and honest but tended to fall out with those conducting campaigns in the field. It was partly linked to the way he operated.

To maintain the slick operation of Union railroads Haupt developed five golden rules that he single-mindedly sought to impose:

1. Supplies were to be sent forward only when needed. Otherwise valuable capacity was devoted to sending them back down the line during a retreat.

2. If telegraph lines were down, trains adhered to a strict timetable and left on time, whether they were full or not.

3. On single-track lines with few sidings, trains were to travel in convoys, to return before the next batch of trains set out. This saved waiting time and lessened the chances of accidents.

4. Newly arrived trains had to be unloaded by everyone in the vicinity to speed their progress to the next destination. Officers who refused to help should be disciplined, he insisted.

5. No military officers were to interfere with the running of the railroads.

It was the last two of these rules that grated with senior officers. Haupt also made it his business to be at the front line at times of crisis. When General George Meade refused to pursue the defeated Lee after the Battle of Gettysburg, Haupt immediately boarded a train to Washington to report back to Lincoln.

On this issue Lincoln, Stanton and Haupt thought as one, that Lee should be chased down. But Meade chose instead to rest his exhausted soldiers, and was later reprimanded for doing so. The tale-telling cannot have endeared Haupt to others in the military.

BUILDING BRIDGES

Perhaps it was no surprise then that he left the army the same year, unwilling to submit to further army discipline. However, he did commit the knowledge he had accrued to paper, publishing a book in 1864 called *Military Bridges*.

In it he accepted that in peacetime, railroad bridges should be built for permanence but that

PIPELINE PIONEER

After leaving the army, Haupt returned not to the unfinished Hoosac tunnel, despite the money he had invested in the project, but to various railroad companies, including the Piedmont Air-Line Railroad, the Northern Pacific Railway and the Dakota & Great Southern Railroad. But perhaps his most celebrated post-war achievement was building an oil pipeline in Pennsylvania, despite opposition from Rockefeller's Standard Oil Company when it was at the height of its monopolistic powers (see pages 154–157).

during conflict 'time of construction and simplicity of detail are far more important than durability'.

Military bridges should also not require immense skill to build, given the inexperienced uniformed labour inevitably being used.

The bridge's parts should be few and simple: the plan should be such as to accommodate

An official portrait of Herman Haupt, who kept Union trains running on time.

itself to any length of span so that material for any extent of bridging could be prepared in advance and would answer for any span or any locality.

MARCH TO THE SEA

Just as a new rulebook had been written about railroads in warfare, so it was ripped up even before the Civil War had ended.

The author of the next chapter was Union General William Tecumseh Sherman (1820–91), who devised a controversial strategy for ending the conflict. From Atlanta, which he'd taken from the Confederates in September 1864, he proposed to head for Savannah to crush the last vestiges of Confederate opposition.

But he wasn't planning to take Georgia's Central Railroad, incorporated in 1833, for ease and speed. Rather, he and his men were going on foot in what was dubbed 'The March to the Sea'.

RIPPING UP THE RAILROAD

On the way, they ripped up the very railroad line that might have taken them to Savannah. The rails were then put on a bonfire and heated until they could be bent around trees in what were known as 'Sherman's neckties'. This was to ensure that they could not be salvaged and used again. It is estimated that 300 miles (480 km) of track were destroyed in this way.

Because Sherman's men could not now rely on the railroad for supplies, they foraged for food – and loot – in houses and farms en route. Rumours about their brutality spread like wildfire.

It was all part of Sherman's plan to break the Confederacy economically and psychologically. For years, he was remembered as a monster for the destruction that accompanied the march. But just 3,000 people died in the five-week trek, compared with the countless thousands who had been lost in battles.

Union soldiers liberated slaves when they could, but left them in limbo afterwards. Columns of slaves followed the army because they had nowhere else to go, but were often treated harshly and sometimes perished.

After he received the surrender, Sherman gave the city of Savannah to Lincoln as a Christmas gift.

In a telegraphed reply Lincoln admitted:

When you were leaving Atlanta for the Atlantic coast, I was anxious, if not fearful; but feeling that you were the better judge, and remembering that 'nothing risked, nothing gained' I did not interfere. Now, the undertaking being a success, the honor is all yours.

Sherman's brutal march helped secure a resounding victory for the Union.

Sherman had succeeded in annihilating all meaningful opposition.

By its end, the war had proved to be a catastrophe for railroads in the south. Splintered lines were pock-marked with burnt-out stations, twisted rails and wrecked locomotives. The losses for the railroad companies involved ran into millions.

When Chief Justice Salmon P. Chase visited North Carolina a month after the war ended, one newspaper report told how he was taken there by 'a wheezy little locomotive and an old mail agent's car with all the windows smashed out and half the seats gone'.

But the Confederacy took some consolation in having caused some $2.5 million of damage to northern railroad lines, some $35 million by today's standards.

SCARRED LANDSCAPE

At the time *Appleton's* was written in the 1870s, travellers on the Western & Atlantic Railroad could still see ample evidence of civil war in the landscape. 'Mementoes of the struggle may be seen by the traveller on the crests of nearly every one of the huge ranges of hills which mark the topography of the country in the shape of massive breastworks and battlements which time and the elements are fast obliterating.'

African Americans helped to twist Confederate rails to assist the victors.

ENGINE EXPLOITS

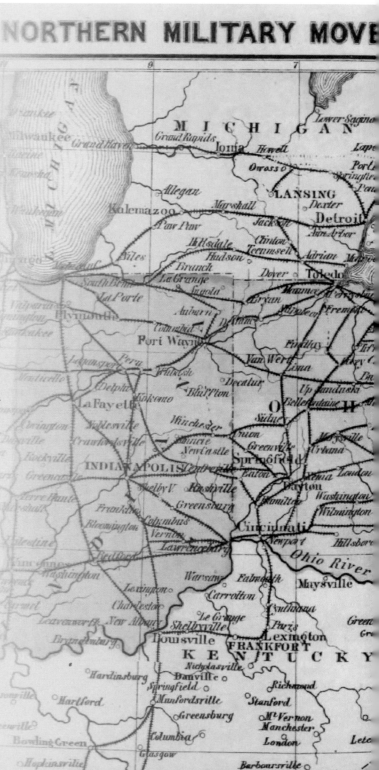

The significance of railroads during conflict was immediately apparent to a number of adventurers, who weren't afraid of using locomotives to their advantage.

Even before the war began, abolitionist John Brown was ready to hold up a train, knowing that the act of doing so would bring extra weight to his cause (although even he was reluctant to compromise the passage of the US mail).

Those involved in the Great Locomotive Chase of 1862 were aware of the tactical uses of a retreating locomotive, destroying tracks and burning bridges to leave the network behind in chaos. Their sound strategy was compromised by the determination of patriotic southerners, the absence of track-lifting tools – and the late running of trains.

History has them down as brave adventurers for their bold use of steam technology – although they failed to substantially change the course of the war and some lost their lives in the process.

Railroad dominance ultimately led to victory for the north.

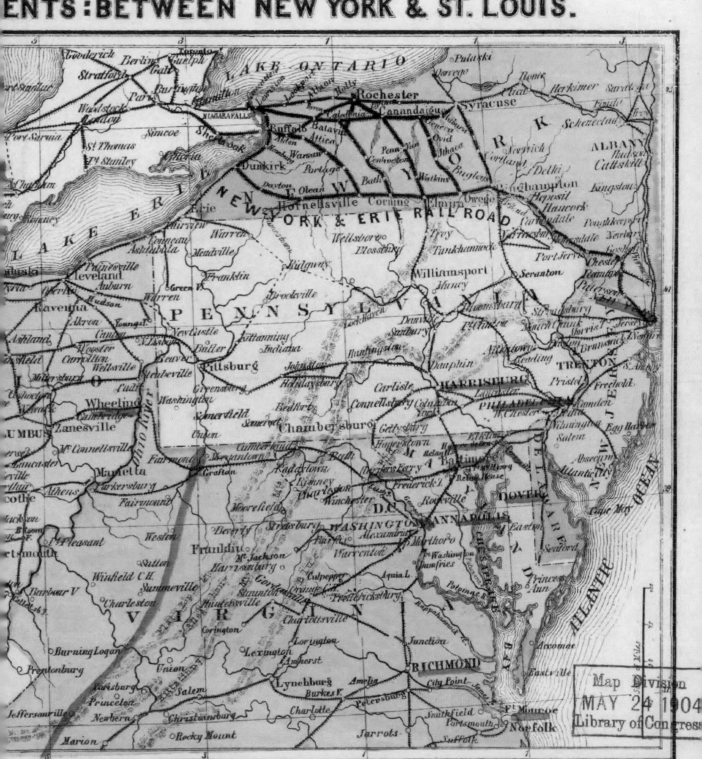

ns. in the Clerks Office of the district Court for the Southern District of New York.

JOHN BROWN

One ill-fated pre-war attempt to instigate rebellion among slaves put the differences between north and south into sharp focus. On 16 October 1859, abolitionist John Brown (1800–59), backed by a small force, seized guns from a Federal arsenal at Harper's Ferry, to arm slaves and overturn the prevailing system.

The following day, Brown and his newly armed men stopped a Baltimore & Ohio express bound for Wheeling, Virginia, in the early morning, swinging lanterns to bring the train to a halt.

Shots were fired, hitting the porter Hayward Sheppard. Darkness might well have disguised the fact he was African American. Eventually, Brown, using the pseudonym Captain Anderson, explained the purpose of the hold-up to the conductor, A. J. Phelps.

In a telegraph sent to William Prescott Smith, master of transportation, Phelps explained:

They have possession of the bridge and of the arms and armoury of the United States. Myself and baggage master have been fired at and Hayward, the coloured porter, is wounded very severely ... They are headed by a man who calls himself Anderson and number about 150 strong. They say they have come to free the slaves and intend to do it at all hazards. The leader of these men requested me to say to you that this is the last train that shall pass the bridge, either east or west. It has been suggested that you had better notifying the secretary of war at once.

Telegraph wires had already been cut, which explains why the message was delayed. Phelps bravely parried the demands of 'Captain Anderson', on the grounds that the train was carrying the US mail and could not be meddled with.

After being accused of exaggeration and over-excitement, Phelps responded sharply, saying: 'I have not made it half as bad as it is.'

In fact, this poorly planned insurrection, involving fewer than 20 men, was over in less than 48 hours, having received scant support from bemused slaves, but not before the deaths of seven people, including the railroad porter. For this, Brown was arrested and later hanged.

By curious irony, it was Robert E. Lee, who led the US Marines who recaptured the arsenal and Thomas 'Stonewall' Jackson, who was in charge at Brown's execution.

TAKING CONTROL OF THE B&O

According to *Appleton's*: 'During the Civil War Harper's Ferry was alternately in the hands of the Federals and Confederates and a detailed narrative of its changing fortunes would reflect with fidelity the vicissitudes of the war itself.'

Eighteen months after Brown's assault, General Jackson took over the Harper's Ferry arsenal with

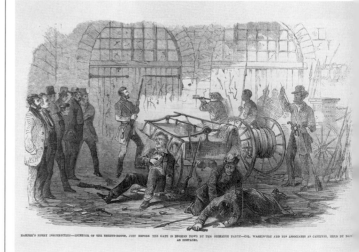

HARPER'S FERRY INSURRECTION—INTERIOR OF THE ENGINE-HOUSE, JUST BEFORE THE GATE IS BROKEN DOWN BY THE STORMING PARTY—COL. WASHINGTON AND HIS ASSOCIATES AS CAPTIVES, HELD BY BROWN AS HOSTAGES.

John Brown organised an armed revolt to end slavery but the event was soon over.

some Virginia militiamen, although it had already been burned out by retreating Union forces. He then set about improving the locomotive stocks available to the south.

He ordered B&O president Garrett to stop running heavy coal trains through Harper's Ferry at night on the grounds that it was disturbing his men's sleep. Later, he imposed a restriction on trains, giving them a two-hour window between 11 am and 1 pm. There was little the railroad could do to oppose him.

As traffic piled through, Jackson ordered Confederate soldiers to block the line in the near distance and captured the queuing locomotives, some of which were moved by road to different lines heading south. An estimated 56 locomotives and 300 freight wagons were included in the haul, many of which were later burned to stop them being retrieved by the Union.

The following month, he destroyed a seven-span road and railroad bridge, effectively preventing any chance of their return. His actions shut the main B&O line for nearly a year and confirmed in railroad president Garrett's mind that his loyalty was to the north.

Harper's Ferry became a flashpoint for action before and during the Civil War. Here, John Brown chose to begin his anti-slavery rebellion prior to the conflict, and later Confederate leaders commandeered locomotives.

JOHN BROWN – TERRORIST OR HERO?

Supporters of slavery in the south were outraged that they were exposed to such violence as John Brown's attempted rebellion, and were suspicious of other such plots being hatched.

In the north, John Brown's principled stand against slavery was admired – so much so that his exploits were later the subject of a Yankee army marching song.

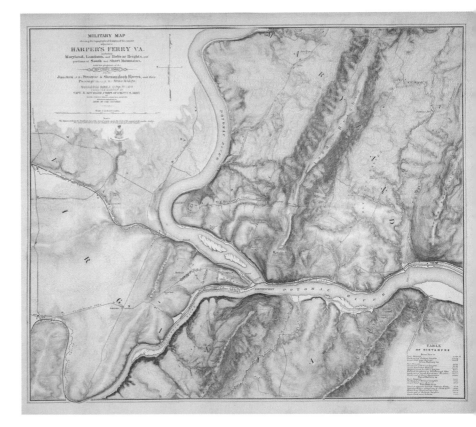

THE GREAT LOCOMOTIVE CHASE

Runaway trains tend to be the stuff of legend. But a train that made a dash from behind enemy lines during the Civil War has proved a more enduring story than any fictional account.

The Andrews Raid of 1862, better known as the Great Locomotive Chase, has been the subject of two films and numerous books.

Its chief instigator was James J. Andrews (1829–62), a Kentucky-born opportunist who worked as a spy for the Union Army during the Civil War.

While smuggling contraband from the south, he conceived the idea of stealing a train from the heart of Confederate territory and then heading north, wrecking telegraph lines, train tracks and bridges as he went.

It was planned to chime with an attack on Chattanooga by a Union army led by General Ormsby Mitchel, already in Huntsville, Alabama. Here was an opportunity to assist the proposed assault, crippling the rail network to prevent reinforcements and supplies reaching the southern town.

With southerners in hot pursuit, the raiders tried vainly to block the line.

Chattanooga was considered a prize by the Union as it was a communications and rail hub. The Western & Atlantic line, which had opened in 1850, was the valuable spur targeted by the Union this time.

Two dozen soldiers from three Ohio regiments volunteered for the mission, which they were warned was top secret and highly perilous. When the plan was outlined to them in a field at twilight by the personable Andrews, it seemed credible enough.

Together with Andrews and another civilian, Bill Campbell, they would slip into southern-held territory in plain clothes – dividing into threes and fours so as not to attract attention – then rendezvous to steal a train. But from the start the plan began to unravel.

PUTTING PLAN INTO ACTION

During the 200-mile (322-km) journey into enemy territory, the raiders were hampered by swollen streams and muddy byways until they boarded a train heading to their initial destination, Marietta. Although Andrews delayed the plan by a day, one man still failed to make the meeting point. Two more were captured by southern forces, unconvinced by their cover stories of being Kentuckians hoping to join the Confederate army. Another overslept, reducing the group to 20.

And, in delaying the operation, Andrews inadvertently put the venture in jeopardy, because of changes in the railroad timetable he knew nothing about.

This wasn't immediately apparent when the men gathered on the train heading out of Marietta on 12 April 1862 – the first anniversary of the start of the war.

BIG SHANTY

The memorably named station at which the raiders struck had previously been a construction camp for labourers building the state-run Western & Atlantic Railroad between 1838 and 1841. The men, whose shacks were known as shanties, were responsible for establishing a gradient of 18 ft per mile (5.5 m per 1.6 km), so this section became known as 'the big grade to the shanties', finally truncated to Big Shanty. The name was changed to Kennesaw in about 1870.

When the train reached the next stop, Big Shanty, the legitimate crew and most of the passengers got off for breakfast. None of the infiltrators had expected to see so many soldiers in the vicinity, as a Confederate camp had only recently been established there.

Even so, no one noticed as one of the commandoes discreetly uncoupled the passenger carriages.

At a nod from Andrews, who'd taken up position on the footplate, the engineers and firemen previously posing as travellers sprang into action and fired up the locomotive, called *The General*.

With a jerk the locomotive steamed out of the station – chosen by the raiders because it had no telegraph – leaving crew, passengers and soldiers in Big Shanty open mouthed and with no opportunity to warn stations ahead.

THE CHASE IS ON

Timetable in hand, Andrews knew his train had been due to meet two scheduled services further down the single-track line, as well as a freight service. His best hope was initially keeping to the timetable before speeding towards two target bridges that would be destroyed before meeting with Mitchel at Chattanooga.

Water and wood were hastily produced at the first stopping points, when Andrews told station staff the train was running gunpowder at the behest of General Beauregard. Soon, though, luck began to run out.

Having escaped Confederate clutches, *The General* and its new crew stopped to rip up lines behind it and cut telegraph wires.

It wasn't long before progress of the locomotive was slowed. At Kingston, Georgia – some 30 miles (48 km) into the journey and the junction with the Rome Railroad – it pulled into a siding to let a freight train pass. Unexpectedly, the freight

Two men pitched against one another in the Great Locomotive Chase. Andrews was the instigator while train conductor Fuller was determined to halt his progress north.

JAMES J. ANDREWS

WILLIAM A. FULLER

train bore a red flag indicating another was close behind. This, too, had a red flag, warning that a third was on its way. Ironically, the unscheduled services were caused by an evacuation started by Mitchel's threatened attack. After a delay of more than an hour *The General* got underway again.

FULLER IN PURSUIT

What those aboard didn't know was that chase was being given by the train's rightful conductor, William Fuller (1836–1905) and Anthony Murphy, foreman of the Atlanta railroad machine shops.

Although they were initially on foot, their pursuit wasn't a lost cause. This was hilly terrain and they knew the train could not take the gradients at speed.

Soon, the pair mounted a hand-car, powered by two men using a see-saw action, along the same rails taken by *The General*, until the first unseen rupture of the line propelled them down an embankment. At the next station, they commandeered a locomotive themselves, the *William R. Smith*, and headed for Kingston.

Fuller and Murphy arrived there just minutes after *The General* had departed. But now they too were held up by the lengthy freight trains.

They switched to another, more fortuitously positioned, locomotive and gave chase. But torn-up lines once again hindered their progress and they began to give chase once more on foot.

As it happened, they encountered another locomotive, *The Texas*, which had halted *The General* again further up the line. She was hastily thrust into reverse and ditched her freight wagons in sidings. Another, *The Catoosa*, which narrowly missed a collision with the fast-moving *General*, also reversed into the chase. People watched in astonishment as the locomotives dashed through stations – one heading forwards, two in reverse – just minutes apart.

Soon, the dogged Fuller and his crew were within sight of *The General*, at a halt while men tried to crowbar up the lines.

EYE-WITNESS

William Pittenger, a private who had joined the raiders, later re-told the tale:

Not far behind we heard the scream of a locomotive bearing down upon us at lightning speed! The men on board were in plain sight and well-armed. Two minutes – perhaps one – would have removed the rail at which we were toiling then the game would have been in our own hands, for there was no other locomotive beyond that could be turned back after us. But the most desperate efforts were in vain. The rail was simply bent and we hurried to our engine and darted away while remorselessly after us thundered the enemy.

RETRIBUTION

There was, of course, no opportunity for the pursuing trains to overtake *The General* on the single track. But the fleeing locomotive no longer had time to sabotage rails and bridges as its crew had planned.

Remarkably, *The General* did have the opportunity to take on water and wood twice more, the men having deposited obstructions on the line as they went. But none barred the progress of the chasing engines for long.

Said Pittenger:

Thus we sped on, mile after mile, in this fearful chase, around curves and past stations in seemingly endless perspective ... The time could not have been so very long, for the terrible speed was rapidly devouring the distance, but with our nerves strained to the highest tension each minute seemed an hour.

As a last throw of the dice, the raiders set light to, and unhitched, a wagon inside a covered bridge over the Oostanaula, hoping a conflagration would ensue. But the barely blazing wagon, damp from spring rain, was simply shunted along by the pursuing train. And now, at Ringgold, a mere 18 miles (29 km) from their destination, *The General* was running out of steam.

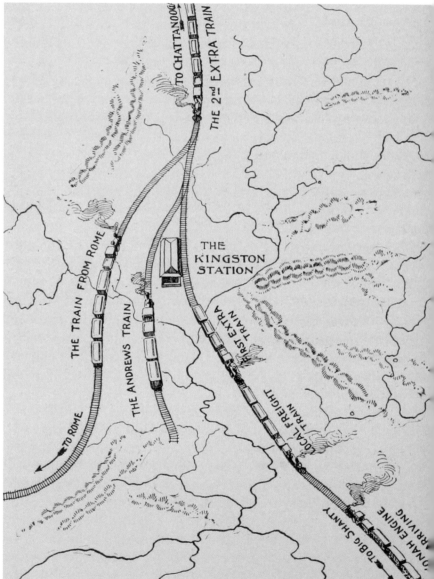

A map revealing the route of the Great Locomotive Chase in 1862.

Andrews ordered his men to leap from the cab and make their way as best they could through woods to nearby Union lines.

All were captured. Wearing civilian clothes they were tried as spies and eight, including Andrews, were executed.

MEETING THEIR FATE

Each case was heard individually in a court that was by now being shelled by General Mitchel's forces. They were then evacuated to Atlanta, where Andrews was hanged on 7 June.

According to Pittenger, who later became a clergyman, the execution of others, 11 days later, came out of the blue, after the surprise arrival of some cavalrymen, who called seven of the men outside the shared cell:

A moment after the door opened and George D. Wilson entered, his step firm and his form erect but his countenance pale as death. Someone asked a solution of the dreadful mystery, in a whisper, for his face silenced everyone.

'We are to be executed immediately', was the awful reply ... Our comrades ... were ready if need be to die for their country but to die on the scaffold – to die as murderers die – seemed almost too hard for human nature to bear.

The rest attempted a jail break within a matter of weeks. Eight escaped to distant Union lines while six, including Pittenger, were recaptured and became the subject of a prison exchange the following year. No lasting damage was done to the Confederate railroad system as a result of the raid. However, the survivors were given the first Congressional Medals of Honour ever awarded by the Union government. It was also awarded posthumously to the soldiers who had been hanged.

Andrews was not a recipient, as they were restricted to military personnel only.

HONOURS EVEN

As for William Fuller, who had led the chase, he was made a captain in the newly created Independent State Roads Guards, dedicated to ensuring better security on the railroads. In 1950, the state of Georgia commissioned a special medal to mark his contribution to the Confederate cause, which was presented to his surviving family.

THE GENERAL

Today, *The General* is a gleaming locomotive that epitomizes the power and charm of the age of steam.

She must have looked something similar to this when she emerged from the foundry in Paterson, New Jersey, in 1855, making the journey to Georgia by ship to a new home on the Western & Atlantic Railroad. *The Texas*, another locomotive involved in the Great Locomotive Chase, came from the same makers and looked similar.

They were among 46 locomotives that ran

The General – one of the Western and Atlantic Railroad trains – led a high speed chase after it was hijacked but ground to a halt when it ran out of steam.

A KEATON CLASSIC

In 1926, Buster Keaton made a film called *The General*, loosely based on Pittenger's account, featuring a real steam locomotive, from which the comedian does daredevil stunts. A black and white silent movie, it has recently been hailed as one of the best films of all time. Critic Gary Giddins said: 'If the film begins as a contest between man and machine, it ultimately depicts a triumphant collusion between the two.'

out of Atlanta on the 138-mile (222-km), 5-ft gauge route that was initially chartered in 1836.

However, the chase was only one incident in an eventful existence for *The General*. As Confederate fortunes nosedived, she pulled the last train out of Atlanta on 1 September 1864, but was forced back by Union artillery fire. Almost immediately, the locomotive was dispatched into 81 wagons filled with ammunition, causing an explosion that engulfed the railyard.

Deserted by General John Hood's Tennessee Army, the battered locomotive was put to use by the United States Military Railroad Service on the same line. Instead of a name, she was known as No. 39. And, as just one of many workhorses in the region, she didn't stand out for special care and attention.

Advancing age and years of service began to take their toll, as did a crash at Kingston. In 1886, she and the line were re-gauged to the standard 4 ft 8½ inches (1,435 mm). But by now *The General* was relegated to pulling excursions, and by 1891 she was taken out of regular service.

A LIFE BEYOND SERVICE

The fame of *The General* was assured by the construction of a monument in Chattanooga National Cemetery, dedicated to the eight raiders buried there, which was topped by a model of her. And the Nashville, Chattanooga & St Louis Railroad, which now owned the W&A lease, was persuaded to refurbish *The General* in time for the Chicago World's Fair in 1893.

There followed a number of celebrity appearances, and she was even offered a part in *Gone with the Wind*, but the cost of transporting her to the set proved prohibitive. Still, her notoriety saved her from the scrapyard.

During the 1960s, there was another renovation project in time for the Civil War centenary, and now she could move under her own steam again. An early 'nose job' was reversed, so her distinctive profile once again resembled a classic American-style wood-fuelled train.

Curiously, the locomotive then became the subject of a legal battle that went all the way to the Supreme Court, as Tennessee and Georgia fought over where the museum piece should be sited.

Eventually, it was agreed *The General* would return to Kennesaw, Georgia, where she was positioned about 100 yards from where she was first stolen by Andrews' doomed raiders.

ABRAHAM LINCOLN

As a farm worker and store assistant, Abraham Lincoln (1809–65) didn't at first glance have the makings of a national icon.

A fond nickname for him was 'railsplitter', not for any work carried out on locomotive tracks but because he once regularly spliced wood used as fence rails. The moniker underscored his humble beginnings.

But Lincoln dreamt of better things and joined the legal profession, where his law partner noted: 'His ambition was a little engine that knew no rest.'

During his tenure, however, Lincoln did forge links with the nation's burgeoning railroad system that are recalled to this day.

It was by rail that Lincoln chose to enter Washington from his distant Illinois home after he was elected. As president, he signed the legal paperwork that kick-started the route that finally linked the east and west coasts.

And, mournfully, the rail journey that took his body home after he was assassinated was talked about in hushed tones for years afterwards, as the country came together in a sense of shared grief.

Opposite: This rare photo shows Lincoln (circled) in the crowd at Gettysburg, Pennsylvania, before his 1863 address.

SECESSION

In 1861, when Abraham Lincoln became America's 16th president, loud rumblings of discontent had long sounded in the south and were now erupting even before he'd taken his oath of office.

Lincoln, a Republican, knew very well that his support lay solely in the north, but felt that secession, already mooted by the south, was illegal, and that his task was to keep the country together.

'In your hands, my dissatisfied fellow countrymen, and not in mine, is the momentous issue of civil war,' he told southerners during his inaugural address, adding that for his part he would 'preserve, protect and defend' the government.

At this stage, he did not particularly seek to outlaw slavery, one of the key issues in the north–south conflict, believing it to be a matter for individual states to decide. What he wanted was unity.

He had already outlined his stance on the subject during election debates held earlier in Illinois, as he fought for a Senate seat against Southern Democrat Stephen Douglas, with these prescient words:

I believe this government cannot endure, permanently, half slave and half free. I do not expect the Union to be dissolved; I do not expect the house to fall; but I do expect it will cease to be divided. It will become all one thing, or all the other. Either the opponents of slavery will arrest the further spread of it and place it where the public mind shall rest in the belief that it is in the course of ultimate extinction, or its advocates will push it forward till it shall become alike lawful in all the states, old as well as new, north as well as south.

TOUR OF DUTY

In February 1861, Lincoln embarked on a meet-and-greet railroad tour, taking in eight states in 12 days, as he made his way to Washington, D.C. from his home in Springfield, Illinois. Although it was prior to the outbreak of war, plans to publicly pass through Baltimore on the final leg of the trip were scrapped when it was rumoured that pro-southern sympathizers were ready to protest. Instead, Lincoln travelled to the city under cover of darkness. A team of horses pulled his sleeper carriage through the quiet streets to the B&O Camden station, from where he was taken on to Washington.

THE SPLIT OCCURS

Unconvinced by his rhetoric, South Carolina decided to secede as soon as it became clear Lincoln would get the presidency. This inspired Mississippi, Florida, Alabama, Georgia, Louisiana, and Texas, who had all left the Union by February 1861 – prior to Lincoln's official inauguration. At a meeting that month, held in Montgomery, Alabama, Jefferson Davis (1808–89) was elected as president of the Confederacy, with a capital being declared at Richmond, Virginia.

There was a natural reluctance on both sides to resort to arms. After all, many of those in the armies that were now set to face each other had trained together at West Point and, in some cases, were veterans of the Mexican War, which had ended a dozen years before. In fact, Lincoln and Davis fought as comrades in the Black Hawk War of 1832, against Native Americans.

And there was a fervent hope that the war would be short, with those in the south confident victory would be theirs 'without a thimbleful of blood' being spilled.

THE OUTBREAK OF WAR

However, the war began at 4.30 am on 12 April 1861, after Confederate artillery opened fire on 68 Federal troops who had been holed up at Fort Sumter since secession. More than 3,000 shells were dispatched towards the poorly supplied troops behind the fort walls in Charleston before

the men, under Major Robert Anderson, a former slave owner who was nonetheless loyal to the Union, surrendered.

With an inspiring victory already notched up, the Confederacy was joined by Virginia, Arkansas, North Carolina and Tennessee.

An 1861 map detailing the infrastructure and transport routes in the Union portion of the continent, where most of the nation's industry and railroad lines were focused.

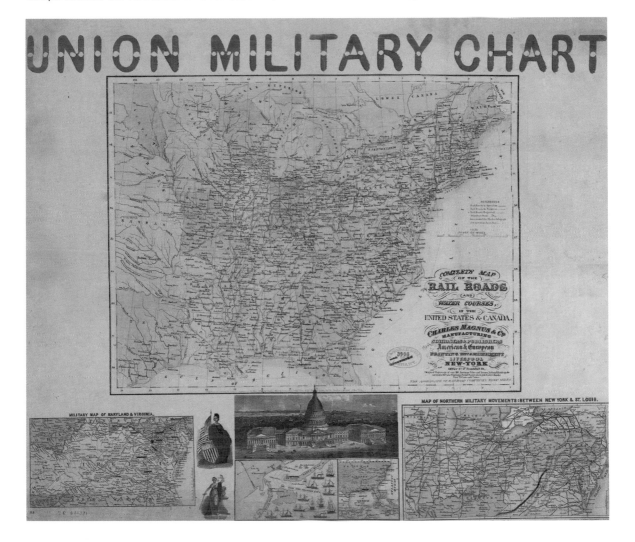

'FOREVER FREE'

From 1863, the abolition of slavery became a central plank of Lincoln's policy.

The year started with the enactment of the Emancipation Proclamation, pledged by Lincoln four months previously and now seen as pivotal in the story of how America began unpicking its history of slavery.

In fact, the finely worded document amounted to more style than substance. Yes, it promised that slaves held in states that had rebelled against the government would be 'forever free' and that the government, army and navy 'will recognize and maintain the freedom of such persons, and will do no act or acts to repress such persons, or any of them, in any efforts they may make for their actual freedom.'

However, it was specifically restricted to states that were still fighting for the Confederacy. Those that had already fallen to the Union, and the border states that supported slavery, did not come within the remit of the proclamation. Thus, not a single slave was freed that day.

A BEACON OF HOPE

The efficacy of the proclamation also turned on a Union victory. Clearly, Lincoln's words had no bearing on what went on in the south at that time. But it did give vital clarification to African Americans in the southern states, who set about securing their own freedom, and offered a glimpse of a brighter future in the wake of a Union victory. Much later, civil rights campaigner Martin Luther King called it 'a great beacon light of hope' for African Americans.

Abolitionists celebrated a qualified victory when news of the proclamation arrived by telegraph. At Plymouth Church in Brooklyn, campaigner Henry Ward Beecher (1813–87) preached a persuasive sermon to a capacity crowd. 'The Proclamation may not free a single slave,' he acknowledged, 'but it gives liberty a moral recognition.'

The proclamation also sent out a message that slavery would no longer be tolerated, with Lincoln branding the proclamation 'an act of justice'.

Perhaps in real terms the proclamation was key because it paved the way for African American soldiers and sailors to join the Union cause, strengthening the ranks of an army weakened by grievous loss of life. About 185,000 freed slaves took up arms.

It was, however, not a cynical manoeuvre on Lincoln's part. Before flourishing his pen on 1 January he said: 'I never, in my life, felt more certain that I was doing right than I do in signing this paper.'

UNDERGROUND RAILROAD

Despite its name, the underground railroad had nothing to do with subterranean trains.

From the 1830s, slaves who fled from masters and plantations in the south were smuggled through to 14 northern states or Canada, where they could live freely.

The routes used were described as 'underground' because they were secret. Slave owners sent out men to bring back escaped captives still in state jurisdiction. Fugitive slaves who made their escape still risked being captured by ruthless bounty hunters.

And those who helped the escaped slaves adopted railroad terminology to disguise their activities, as helping slaves to escape was illegal. So, stopping places were known as stations or depots, guides were called conductors or engineers, and the slaves themselves became 'packages', 'freight' or 'cargo'.

Although abolitionists and some members of church communities helped, the Underground Railroad mostly functioned among the community of freed slaves, who developed a network of safe houses.

One such was Harriet Tubman, who once declared: 'I never ran my train off the track and I never lost a passenger.'

Tubman and others would act as guides through tricky journeys, made under cover of darkness, usually covering fewer than 20 miles (32 km) a night.

Vigilance committees sprang up in large northern cities to provide shelter, jobs and letters of recommendation to those who successfully made the trek.

It's impossible to assess how many escapes were made, but some estimates put the figure as high as 100,000. It's probably been inflated in a desire to add a measure of romance to a sordid chapter of American history.

Harriet Tubman was proud of her unblemished record in helping slaves escape.

BRAVE MEN & CONSECRATION

A three-day battle in Gettysburg in July 1863 left an estimated 50,000 men dead, dying, injured or missing.

It erupted after General Robert E. Lee took his Confederate troops north to secure a victory for the south on enemy territory. Against the odds, the smaller Union army he found there held out, and it proved a pivotal point of the conflict.

In reality, there were no winners. A raft of American youth had been lost, the bereaved could not bury their dead and the local townspeople were overwhelmed by the number of corpses and dead horses left fermenting in the summer sun.

From this came the notion of the Soldiers' National Cemetery where, initially, the Union dead would receive a proper burial, albeit miles from home. And here, to show respect to those who had perished, President Lincoln gave a succinct address that has since been held up as a masterclass in politics and diplomacy.

For years it was rumoured that Lincoln wrote the 272-word speech as he undertook the six-hour train journey from Washington to Gettysburg, making train changes at Baltimore and Hanover Junction.

But the task in hand was momentous. Mindful of the scale of loss without resolution, he wanted to keep up morale in the Union and steady the nerve of those who had doubts. Yet he also hoped to reach out to those in the south who were also mourning their dead and feeling disillusioned by the war.

Instinctively, he knew he needed to reference the lofty ideals of the Declaration of Independence, to recall how courageously Americans had freed themselves from colonial rule less than a century previously. Crucially, he wanted to remind people

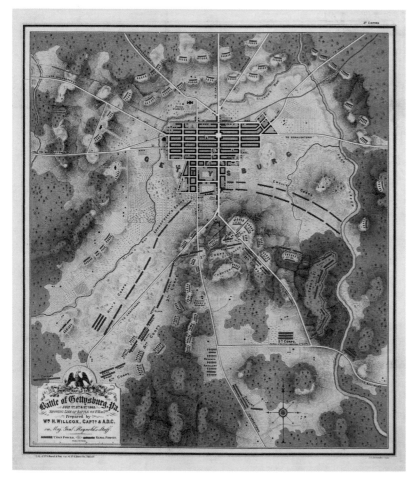

The battle at Gettysburg left thousands dead and was the most costly confrontation of the war in human terms. It compares with fewer than 5,000 fallen soldiers at the first Battle of Bull Run.

that liberty and equality were at the heart of those actions.

Moreover, he hoped to evoke a vision of what America would be when the war was over. If there were religious overtones to the speech, it was to chime with a largely devout population on both sides of the divide. The resonance of the final lines was not diminished, even if similar inspirational expressions had already been uttered in Europe.

Lincoln was known for his precise approach to text, so it seems unlikely that he wrote his famous words on the back of an envelope in a rolling train carriage, despite several independent claims that he did.

THE MOMENT OF DELIVERY

Lincoln wasn't the main orator billed at the dedication on 19 November 1863. Politician and pastor Edward Everett (1794–1865) delivered a two-hour speech, detailing what happened in the battle, before Lincoln got to his feet.

Even though the President spoke slowly to the hushed crowd gathered closely around him, it took just a matter of minutes to complete the speech.

Behind the politician's veneer, there was a deep anxiety too. Lincoln had left at home his wife Mary tending to son Tad, who showed symptoms similar to typhoid, just a year after losing another son, Willie.

His spare and artful prose has since been lauded. Yet at the time it wasn't universally praised, with the *Chicago Times* branding it 'silly, flat and dishwatery'. Critics were primarily split along political lines.

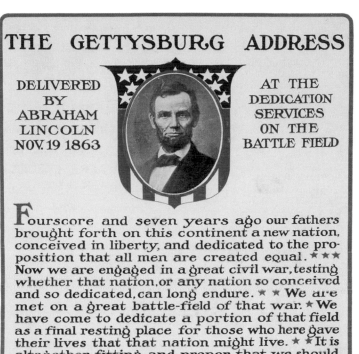

The text of Lincoln's famous address given at Gettysburg.

THE FINAL JOURNEY

When President Lincoln set off for a theatre trip on Good Friday 1865, he must have been in good spirits.

He had been re-elected the previous year in the face of an obnoxious campaign by the Democrats, and was newly sworn into office. More importantly, the war against the south had been won five days previously, with General Robert E. Lee's surrender at Appomattox.

Accompanied by his wife Mary, he went to the Ford's Theatre in Washington to see *Our American Cousin* from a private box. Seizing his opportunity, a bodyguard slipped away for a drink.

It was then that actor and assassin John Wilkes Booth struck, firing a pistol at point-blank range. Lincoln died nine hours later at a nearby boarding house, where he'd been taken for treatment. Although he hadn't joined the Confederate army, Booth supported the south and was apparently outraged at Lincoln's recent suggestion that freed African American slaves would receive a vote.

Booth went on the run, being tracked down and shot dead 12 days later. The onward journey for Lincoln was altogether more dignified and stately.

FUNERAL TRAIN

A week after his death, a train carrying the president left Washington, D.C., heading for Illinois to embark on a memorial trip on the network of railroads that Lincoln had seen being etched on the northeastern landscape. Before arriving in his hometown of Springfield, it visited 180 cities in seven states so that millions could pay their respects.

Two dozen different locomotives drew the train that held his body – with that of his son Willie,

Despite his proximity, gunman John Wilkes Booth failed to killed Lincoln outright.

Maj. Rathbone. Miss Harris. Mrs Lincoln. President. Assassin.

THE ASSASSINATION OF PRESIDENT LINCOLN.

AT FORD'S THEATRE WASHINGTON. D.C. APRIL 14TH 1865.

previously buried in Washington – and some 300 people, including the President's eldest son Robert.

Each of the locomotives was marked by the President's portrait, fixed above the cowcatcher, and the train's route was published in local newspapers.

At points along the journey, the coffin was unloaded from the train and became the focus for large-scale memorial services. In the wake of the war's bloodshed, his murder seemed especially poignant and wasteful.

But even by night there was evidence of his singular popularity in the north. Bonfires were lit by the tracks, around which thousands of people gathered. At some, town bands played suitably sombre music. At others, a parson led prayers or a local dignitary read Lincoln's significant speeches. Farmers and their families sat with heads bowed in their buggies, travelling for miles to the trackside, despite the darkness. It was particularly affecting African Americans, who viewed Lincoln as a saviour. People wept as the locomotive, draped in black bunting, sounded its mournful whistle as it passed by.

The Lincoln Special, as it was called, completed its circuitous 1,654-mile (2,661-km) trip on 4 May, to be greeted by Old Bob, the president's favourite horse, who joined a procession to the cemetery.

Although the coffin has been moved a number of times, his body has remained in Springfield.

In 1911, a prairie fire near Minneapolis, Minnesota, consumed the carriage that had transported Lincoln from the national capital to his hometown.

STATESMAN'S STATUE

Although he was the first American president to be assassinated, he wasn't instantly catapulted to the status of political idol. At the time of Lincoln's death, George Washington was generally considered more of a national hero. Only later was the distinctively gaunt president seen as an adept politician with a deft diplomatic touch. He became more revered nationally in 1909, during celebrations to mark the centenary of his birth.

In 1914, construction of the famous Lincoln Memorial began, with a 19 ft (5.8 m) tall, 175-ton statue of the seated president encased in a classical temple with 36 pillars, to represent each of the Union's 36 states at the time of Lincoln's death. The Memorial, designed by the prolific sculptor Daniel Chester French (1850–1931), was finally opened in 1922, and bears the words of the Gettysburg Address and the Second Inaugural Address on its inner walls.

The Lincoln Memorial, featuring his most memorable speeches, is now a symbol of American liberty.

ROBBER BARONS

As the nineteenth century unfolded, America seemed a land of plenty. There was empty territory to be tamed and an influx of people ready to put in the hard graft necessary to fashion a bright future.

But with this American dream there was an implicit pledge of financial reward. Soon, pursuit of riches through unfettered capitalism usurped initial noble aspirations. It paid off for a privileged few, largely at the expense of workers.

The talked-about tycoons of the era were legendary figures, prepared to battle with government and each other to carve out an ever-greater stake in American society.

These were highly driven men, whose appetite for wealth knew no bounds. When the sums are translated to modern values, it's clear they made far greater fortunes than the industrial rich of today.

Eventually, their names would be synonymous with oil, steel, electricity and cars. But first came railroads, the ground-floor industry that proved a gateway to the rest.

All of them maintained an interest in the flourishing railroad networks that began appearing on the landscape like fractures in porcelain, not least to get their goods to new domestic markets.

But as men like Cornelius Vanderbilt, Jay Gould, John D. Rockefeller and Andrew Carnegie quested for bigger slices of the national pie, they had little time for legislative or moral rules that would tie down their vaulting ambitions.

After buying one line, the temptation was to snap up the competition. Scruples that guided others in an enlightened age were cast aside as their empires expanded. National monopolies were their aim as these represented a golden ticket with apparently endless potential to bring in vast quantities of cash.

Government intervention was sparing. With politicians bought and paid for, there was little hope for statutory improvements in working conditions for the people they employed.

As a consequence, the members of this elite group were branded 'robber barons', a term that put their public conduct on a par with detested feudal lords from the medieval era who likewise knew no boundaries when it came to achieving their goals.

Even railroad bosses who weren't tainted by allegations of corruption operated in ways that would not be tolerated today.

Wealthy industrialists clashed when it came to controlling railroads like the Erie, which both Vanderbilt and Fisk targeted as an acquisition.

CORNELIUS VANDERBILT

One of the first to be elevated to the ranks of the super-rich was Cornelius Vanderbilt. Although initially poor and ill-educated, he refused to allow these two issues to define him and, following his success, he came to characterize the self-made man so beloved by American folk lore.

During an extraordinarily long and busy life Vanderbilt displayed fruitful acumen that underpinned his golden touch. The lives of everyone in America were touched by his wide-ranging business activities, not always positively. According to biographer T. J. Stiles, there is 'probably no other individual [who] made an equal impact over such an extended period on America's economy and society.'

Perhaps his hard-edged, clear-eyed and markedly unsentimental approach to making money set the tenor for a generation of capitalists who shared his 'dollar first' objective.

Yet, he insisted, it was not making money but making his point and coming out ahead that counted for him.

Opponents were crushed, often with a brinkmanship more appropriate to a game of poker than a nationally significant industry. For anyone who crossed him, he had these sinister words: 'I won't sue you, for the law is too slow. I'll ruin you.'

Opposite: In 1854, when this portrait was commissioned, Cornelius Vanderbilt's business activities were restricted to steamships.

m a Daguerreotype   Eng.d by L.S. Pun.

STEAMSHIP KING

At his death, Cornelius Vanderbilt (1794–1877) was worth $100 million. One estimate says that by then he possessed one-ninth of all US currency in circulation.

His name is indelibly associated with railroads, and he was the first to be dubbed a 'robber baron' for his unsavoury business practices.

But Vanderbilt didn't make his initial millions in railroads. He had already established himself as a much-feared operator of steamships, and it wasn't until he was in his seventies that he unleashed his shrewd, aggressive and ruthless business insight on the burgeoning US railroad industry.

LEARNING ON THE JOB

Vanderbilt came from humble beginnings. His family, of Dutch stock, were farmers on Staten Island who ran a freight ferry service to New York to supplement their income. Although he had some education – he could read and write, albeit somewhat illegibly – the young Vanderbilt soon left school to work on steamships as they entered their heyday.

Paddle steamers like this one, named for owner Vanderbilt, were veterans of the often treacherous trans-Atlantic crossing.

With a loan from his mother he bought himself his own vessel and, in his twenties, ran a small fleet while also working for another successful steamship operator. During the 1812 war with Britain, he impressed people with his reliability and patriotism. Early on, he earned a nickname, 'The Commodore', which he relished his entire life.

From 1808 a government-granted monopoly existed on the route between New York and New Jersey. Vanderbilt watched from the sidelines as his employer at the time dismantled an opponent in possession of that business exclusivity. Later, Vanderbilt used hard-nosed techniques to lay waste to the company that had employed him.

Among his ventures were the Dispatch Line, started in 1826 and, later, the People's Line, offering cheap fares for all.

OVERSEAS VENTURE

With fortuitous timing, he began a sea-and-land route in 1851 from New York to San Francisco, as the Californian gold rush got into full swing. With the Panama Canal still nothing more than a pipe dream, the only alternative was a 90-day trip via Cape Horn in a clipper or a combination of steamship and land journeys across the Panamanian Isthmus.

After studying maps, Vanderbilt realized he could shave two days off the travelling time by using a hitherto unexploited route through Nicaragua.

He set the ticket price at a tempting $200 below that offered by rivals, and took the US mail for free. It wasn't the end of the story. He tried and failed to build a canal and nearly lost his Latin American interests to an American

IN DEFENCE OF CAPITALISM

Commentator and author John Stossel disputes that Vanderbilt deserves the title of 'robber baron'.

Vanderbilt got rich by pleasing people. He invented ways to make travel and shipping things cheaper. He used bigger ships, faster ships, served food on board. People liked that. And the extra volume of business he attracted allowed him to lower costs. He cut the New York–Hartford fare from $8 to $1. That gave consumers more than any 'consumer group' ever has.

adventurer. But, if Vanderbilt lost some battles along the way, he had the resources and the appetite to win the war. Eventually, that adventurer and those companies he so grievously undercut could not sustain themselves, and once again Vanderbilt reaped the financial rewards.

CUT-THROAT METHODS

Brutal business dealings that encouraged rivals to either sell up or buy his operations at inflated prices became Vanderbilt's stock in trade. 'There is no friendship in trade', he reminded rivals.

As his wealth expanded, he inevitably became a feature of US society – which found him vulgar and profane. But he was little deterred, eschewing ostentation and maintaining faith in his values of hard work and a simple lifestyle.

RIGHT ON TRACK

At the age of 70, when retirement beckons for most men, Cornelius Vanderbilt switched his interests from steamships to railroads.

It was a curious move in more ways than one. As a young man, Vanderbilt had suffered a broken leg in the Hightstown accident, the first in the country's railroad history in which there were fatalities. Although the engine on the Camden & Amboy line was travelling at a sedate 20 mph (32 km/h), a broken axle caused a carriage to flip over and two people perished.

Fellow passenger, 66-year-old former president John Quincy Adams called it 'the most dreadful catastrophe that ever my eyes beheld'. As for Vanderbilt, he had vowed never to travel by railroad again.

It was not a promise he would keep. His sharp business brain could see how railroads had transformed the country and its industry, outshining the steamships that once pre-occupied him. When railroads began to reach from coast to coast, he knew a change of tack

Unflattering cartoons were one of the few means by which new tycoons of the era could be humbled.

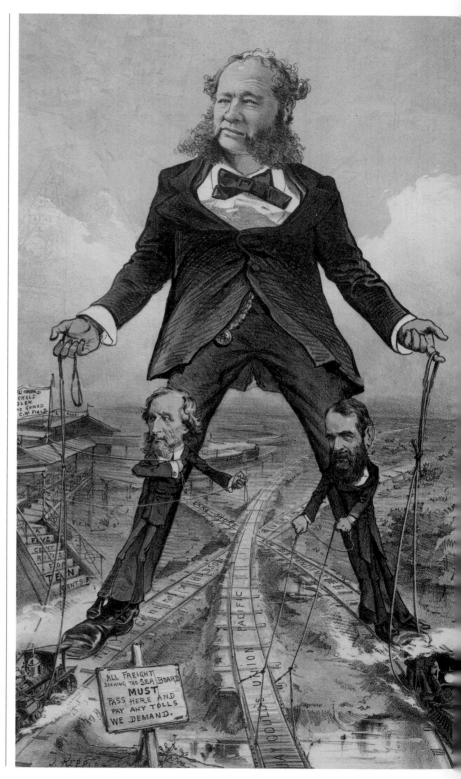

was required. His first foray involved buying stock in the New York & Harlem Railroad.

It was his son William who was an unexpected inspiration. William was one of 13 children born to Vanderbilt and his first wife Sophia. While his father was physically imposing, William was frail and was initially written off by his father. But, in reversing the ailing fortunes of Staten Island's railroad, William proved an adept businessman, who brought his father's focus to the possibilities of railroads.

BUYING INTO RAILROADS

In 1857, Vanderbilt took control of the New York & Harlem line, the only railroad to enter Manhattan from the north and east.

Soon, he had the Hudson River Railroad in his stable, and was targeting the New York Central. One of his old adversaries, Daniel Drew (1797–1879), tried to foil his ambitions by offering cheap freight deals on his steamships between Albany and New York. But when the Hudson River froze, Vanderbilt refused Drew access to his lines, leaving customers no alternative but to use Vanderbilt's trains.

His brusque manner and unyielding support of capitalism won him few friends. During the Civil War, he had declined to donate to a hospital for wounded soldiers, believing such public displays of generosity unseemly. In 1869, he came under attack from writer Mark Twain, who felt the materialism displayed by Vanderbilt, paired with the noticeable absence of philanthropy, marked him out as selfish. Twain declared him 'the idol of only a crawling swarm of small souls'.

Yet, in the same year, Vanderbilt released sufficient capital to foil a speculators' plot to bring down Wall Street by cornering the gold supply, thus averting an economic depression.

BACK TO BLACK

Vanderbilt is also thought to have influenced how trains looked. Early locomotive builders took immense pride in the appearance of the engines, indulging themselves with bright paint, shiny brass and ornamental scrollwork. Sometimes, pictures were painted on tenders to make them more distinctive still. But the fashion soon passed when Vanderbilt insisted all the locomotives plying his lines were painted black, so that his employees saved the time it took to clean and polish them. Soon, this was the standard followed by other railroads.

PHILANTHROPIC GESTURES

Ultimately, Vanderbilt did bequeath nearly $1 million to start a university that took his name, part of a personally devised plan to rejuvenate the south after the Civil War. There were also some cash donations to a church favoured by his second wife – a woman from the south curiously named Frank, who was 45 years his junior – although both amounts represented a small fraction of his fortune.

Later generations of his family made many more notable donations, although they soon dropped out of the ranks of the super-rich.

Yet, it was his railroad legacy that was impressive. By 1912, Vanderbilt's companies were operating 70,000 carriages a day along 12,000 miles (19,300 km) of track. More than half of the people in the US lived in territory covered by Vanderbilt lines.

TERMINAL TRIBUTE

Even rich men are mortal and know they can't take the trappings of wealth beyond the grave. So, many like to see a monument to their worldly achievements erected before death claims them.

Cornelius Vanderbilt was no different. His enduring memorial was to be Grand Central Depot, the New York station built on 23 acres (9 hectares), which opened in 1871, six years before his death.

It wasn't just a practical solution for a railroad magnate with lines criss-crossing New York City – although Grand Central Depot did become the single terminal for New York Central & Hudson

Grand Central replaced the station built by Vanderbilt to emphasise his worldly wealth.

River, the New York & Harlem and the New York & New Haven railroads, when previously three had been needed.

The splendid building was a shout-out statement to passengers and rival railroad men that business was booming.

UPSIDES AND DOWNSIDES

Travellers noticed some changes, too. They admired the design of the train shed, with its domed roof spanning the tracks. Platforms were brought up to the height of the carriages, a blessing for those who had previously struggled with the drop from train step to ground level.

But only those with tickets were permitted on to the platforms, with ticket examiners employed to enforce the new rule.

Pedestrians in the city also noticed the noxious fumes that emanated from the station, compromising their health.

Such was the growth in New York's railroad industry that Vanderbilt's masterpiece was soon too cramped for the number of trains. As early as 1899, the station was re-modelled to help tackle congestion and re-named Grand Central Station.

ELECTRIFYING CHANGE

A train crash in 1902 in the Park Avenue tunnel inspired an even bigger overhaul. Fifteen people were killed when one train ploughed into the back of another on the approach to the station, the driver having been blinded by clouds of smoke.

It was time to replace wheezing steam engines with clean electric trains.

New York Central engineer William J. Wilgus conceived the design, claiming the extraordinary vision came to him 'in a flash of light'. In its new incarnation it would be known as Grand Central Terminal.

A vast construction project began, at the expense of the original building, which took a decade to complete. Nearly 3.2 million cubic yards (2.4 million cubic metres) of earth were excavated for the construction of the terminal, as well as rock to an average depth of 45 feet (14 m) – enough to fill almost 300 railroad wagons every day.

About 25 miles (40 km) of water pipes and sewers had to be removed or re-routed. In a crescendo of construction, 10,000 people were working at the site, sometimes around the clock. At the time, the terminal cost $43 million to build, the equivalent of about $1 billion today.

ART AND CRAFTS

Grand Central Terminal is now cherished for being a monument to the Beaux Arts era. Fittingly, one of the design team, Whitney Warren, who spent ten years studying art in Paris, was a cousin of the Vanderbilt family.

Hallmarks are still apparent, like the magnificent clock at the information booth. Each of the four clock faces is made from opal, with an estimated value of more than $10 million. Another clock outside is shielded by Tiffany glass. The roof of the main concourse is embellished with a celestial scene, including 2,500 stars. The first all-electric station, it was awash with lightbulbs.

Passengers who rode on the luxury express between New York and Chicago used a walkway at Grand Central Terminal defined by a crimson carpet to get to their train. It's thought this might be where the phrase 'red-carpet treatment' emerged.

A cast-iron eagle with a 13-foot (4-m) wingspan, once a familiar sight at Grand Central Depot, was returned to Grand Central Terminal in 1997, after being located at a house in Bronxville. The owners were keen for it to become part of railroad heritage again.

The first train to leave one of its platforms, using one of the 46 tracks, was the *Boston Express No. 2*, which departed at 12.01 am on 2 February 1913.

JAY GOULD

Men bought railroads for power, fame and – above all – profits. It's the reason some of the era's most notorious businessmen would go to any lengths to secure pole position on the board.

Their aim was not to serve a travelling public or enhance the country's future prospects but to get rich – or richer – as quickly as possible.

Often, businesses that had had every last cent wrung out by their owners would suffer a drawn-out demise. One such example is the Erie Railroad, which withered during a commercial tussle that spanned nearly half a century.

The architect of many of its misfortunes was Jay Gould, a determined, curmudgeonly, ruthless go-getter who had form when it came to financial chicanery.

Gould was one of the new breed of businessmen willing to sacrifice integrity for hard cash.

His self-confessed raison d'être was to make money, and his recipe for doing so was simple: 'Keep doubling all your money and the result will be satisfactory.'

By 1880, he had governance of about 10,000 miles (16,000 km) or one-ninth of the nation's tracks.

And, to achieve his ends, he strayed into dubious areas – although the prevailing lack of regulation meant that few of his exploits were downright illegal.

Opposite: Jay Gould enjoyed great wealth generated through owning and operating railroads.

PANIC BUYING

Railroads were an expensive business, especially when it came to construction.

In the early days, the number of railroads in operation was vastly outnumbered by plans for railroads that never amounted to more than a well-intentioned blueprint. Most failed for want of money.

At the time, Federal assistance was virtually unheard of, but the national government sought to help with favourable legislation and even engineering expertise from West Point.

Individual states offered aid to an early clutch of projects, but consortium cash was favoured above the use of taxpayers' money. Inevitably, Vanderbilt was not alone in using his immense and expanding wealth to become a major player on the scene. His adversary, Jay Gould, followed that example.

Gould was the son of a farming family who, after schooling, became a map maker and surveyor. He later bought himself into a tannery business, becoming the sole proprietor after the Panic of 1857. It was this international glitch in trading that gave him an insight into how fortunes could be made on the money markets.

Until then, America's economy had been booming. But, suddenly, Californian gold appeared to be declining in supply. The 'bubble' that surrounded railroad construction burst when too many plans and not enough action proved the industry was not the trustworthy cash cow many had hoped. A major bank also failed, although that was due to corrupt management. But banks were trying to shore themselves up with gold reserves.

The effects of this economic wobble were exacerbated with the sinking of the SS *Central America*, en route to New York from Panama with 30,000 lbs (14,000 kgs) of gold aboard, freshly prospected from California. The disaster claimed the lives of 425 people. Confidence in the ability of the American economy to withstand the loss was sorely shaken.

As a result, numerous railroad companies went bankrupt, grain prices fell, the demand for manufactured goods slumped and unemployment levels soared.

Sympathetic mayors set about providing public works to help workers who would otherwise be destitute. Significantly, it was the northeast that was badly hit by the crisis, while the economy in the south – underpinned by cotton that had largely held its value – remained steady. This indicated to southern businessmen that their business model, with its use of slaves, was far superior.

SPECULATE TO ACCUMULATE

Gould was by now working on Wall Street and was soon tempted to speculate with struggling railroad companies. Like Vanderbilt, Gould was not one for getting his hands dirty. It was ownership rather than engineering that inspired him, and he bought off-the-peg networks so he didn't have to foot a considerable bill for railroad construction.

Later he explained:

The Panic of 1857 came on and everything was very much disturbed. Railroad values after this time went down very low and the first mortgage bonds of the Rutland & Washington Railroad were selling at 10 cents on the dollar. I bought all the bonds at that price, borrowing the money to pay for them.
I took the entire charge of this road and learned the business, as I may say.
I was president, secretary, treasurer and superintendent, had sole control...

Soon, he turned his attentions to the Rensselaer & Saratoga line, one of the earliest to be chartered.

Since October 1835, a service had been running between Troy and Ballston, a distance of some 25 miles (40 km). Like many conceived in haste, the line had its shortcomings and had to agree terms with the Schenectady & Saratoga Railroad so its passengers could travel onwards.

After the three-masted, wooden-hulled SS Central America sank off the South Carolina coast in 1857, the loss of its gold cargo helped de-stabilize the national economy.

When Gould became involved with the railroad he seized on the possibilities of leasing nearby lines to make better sense of routes.

'INTRIGUE AND DECEIT'

The saga of the Erie Railroad falls between comic farce and high tragedy.

In 1911, historian Edward Hungerford summed it up like this: 'It is a story of intrigue and deceit, of trickery and of scheming ... the monumental tragedy of the wrecking of a great railroad property – a property with possibilities that probably will never now be realized.'

The miserable fate of the Erie Railroad contrasted starkly with the hopes that surrounded its inception. It was one of the earliest projected, proposed in 1832 as the New York & Erie Railroad.

Public money flooded in to the enterprise, with the State of New York putting up $3 million. A further million came from private investors. However, despite the opening of the first section between Piermont and Goshen in 1841, the company went into bankruptcy.

Erie RR locomotives like this one from the 1890s were once a familiar sight on this busy and economically vital line.

So vital was the artery, that the mortgage agreement was shelved on condition that the line reached Lake Erie within six years.

However, it wasn't until 1851 that the broad-gauge track to Dunkirk was finally laid and the line fully opened for business.

WHISTLE-STOP OPENING

This landmark event was marked by President Millard Fillmore (1800–1874) taking a trip from New York City to Dunkirk in the company of many significant government figures, including secretary of state Daniel Webster (1782–1852).

A lawyer and seasoned political campaigner, Webster insisted on sitting on a rocking chair attached to a flat wagon, to take in the scenery. (A renowned orator, it was Webster's speeches that drew the crowds, rather than the presence of president Fillmore.)

Also on the outside of the train, a railroad employee gathered flags made by women living along the route to mark the auspicious occasion. Rather than buck the timetable, the train merely slowed down while the employee scooped up the pennants thrust at him by the makers, who stood on the platform.

'At the end of the journey the Erie Railroad had a collection of flags that would have done credit to a victorious army,' one observer noted.

The locomotive did stop long enough for the passengers to admire the impressive Starrucca Viaduct, 1,000 ft (305 m) long and 100 ft (30.5 m) high, which had taken a year to complete.

DASTARDLY DREW

Despite its uncertain history, the line still seemed an attractive investment to steamboat owner and Wall Street speculator Daniel Drew. He won a seat on the board after threatening to undercut the Erie on freight rates.

From the inside, he plotted to take control, loaning the company money which it could not repay. Then he began manipulating shares in order to line his own pockets. Today, the methods he used, like short-selling stocks and insider trading, would be unlawful. At the time, there was little to stop rampant speculation.

Vanderbilt was among many who were horrified at the religiously devout Drew's antics, but he knew Drew of old, from when the pair both invested in steamships, and inexplicably maintained a soft spot for him. As a consequence, Vanderbilt became a major Erie stakeholder, and Drew kept a place on the railroad's board, introducing Jay Gould and his associate Jim Fisk into the operation.

THE POWERS OF THE PRINTING PRESS

Even before the malevolent attentions of Gould, Fisk and Drew, the Erie Railroad was struggling after years of underinvestment. By 1868 it was being popularly described as 'two streaks of rust'. And the future seemed bleaker still.

Bonds were issued to raise money for steel rails. But Drew, Fisk and Gould saw a chance to siphon off this new capital, so those plans were abandoned and the existing iron rails were turned to help counter wear and tear. Worse was to come.

With no thought to its commercial wellbeing, Gould and Fisk sapped its strength when they milked the Erie RR of cash.

MILKING THE ERIE COW.

By now, Vanderbilt had decided to take full control of the Erie, not least to consolidate the New York network he was building, and he began purchasing stock.

In response, Drew, Gould and Fisk printed 100,000 counterfeit stock certificates with the intention of 'stock watering'. In essence, no matter how many stocks Vanderbilt bought on Wall Street, there were always more left outside his control.

KICKING A SKUNK

Although he was still substantially out of pocket, Vanderbilt conceded defeat in 1868, saying he had sufficient money to buy them all 'body and breeches' but that the printing press they used was priceless. Recognizing that the doubtful tactics employed were not outlawed, Vanderbilt said: 'In the present state of our country's jurisprudence there doesn't seem to be any limit to the amount of stock certificates that you fellows can manufacture out of white paper.'

Vanderbilt was left to ponder one of his favourite adages: 'It never pays to kick a skunk.'

An outraged Vanderbilt used a 'tame' judge to issue a warrant for the arrest of the three, who departed New York in haste, clutching the account books relating to the Erie.

The colourful story continued with threats by thugs and corruption of the legislature, as the trio sought to retrospectively legalize their exploits. Gould visited politicians in Albany with a satchel containing half a million dollars. Writs were met with counter writs and bribes to legislators topped by even more excessive amounts of money.

Even before Gould, Fisk and Drew fled the city for the safe jurisdiction of neighbouring New Jersey, the public was galvanized.

In their eyes it wasn't a case of heroes versus villains; the businessmen, politicians and judges were all bad guys. While Gould and his cronies were considered unscrupulous frauds, there was no appetite for Vanderbilt either, who was perceived to be seeking a monopoly that would mean price rises for freight and passengers.

Holed up in a hotel, the three men fuelled headlines with incendiary statements casting Vanderbilt as a menace.

After some months 'in exile', Drew wanted to return home, and he met up with Vanderbilt to hammer out an agreement. There were cash payments to Vanderbilt, who also insisted that some of the dud stock he'd bought was purchased by the railroad.

THE RISE AND FALL OF BOSS TWEED

The agreement hammered out with Vanderbilt meant Drew was removed from the board of the Erie Railroad. But Gould and Fisk were still very much in evidence, and were soon up to their old tricks. Emboldened by their previous successes, and by the amounts of cash they had furnished to local law makers, they made sure laws were passed to protect their positions.

Gould, now president of the railroad, also found a place for William Tweed (1823–78) on the Erie Board, starting a potent friendship.

Also known as 'Boss Tweed', he was a larger-than-life figure in the Democratic Party political machine – known as Tammany Hall. He was behind a brazen and widespread corruption ring in New York City.

Tweed had begun his political career as a volunteer fireman with a reputation for using violence to achieve his ends.

From 1851, when he won the first of numerous political posts, he embezzled millions of dollars from the city's coffers. To extend his influence, he bribed dozens of people and posed as a lawyer, although he'd received no training. With largesse, he distributed political favours, receiving large sums for the privilege. 'I don't care who does the electing, so long as I get to do the nominating,' he once said.

At the peak of his success, through the power of kickbacks, he ensured that only he and his cronies had access to the municipal accounts, thus shielding his crimes from censorious eyes.

That's not to say that poorer people living in New York didn't benefit. There were plenty of new developments and schemes, including a library, during his tenure. But the cost to the public purse was an eye-watering $30 million, even by the most conservative estimates. Other, far higher, figures are credible, as Tweed bought properties, estates and yachts and ostentatiously wore a 10.5 carat diamond tie pin. He dined on luxury foods such as oysters, although he didn't smoke or drink to excess. Some critics have put the cost of Tweed's exploits at $200 million, a staggering $2.4 billion in today's terms.

For a while Tweed's colleagues – mostly implicated by one shady deal or another – protected him. When Tweed was arrested in 1871, it was Gould who put up the $1 million bail that freed him so he could continue campaigning in an election, which he duly won.

Eventually, the edifice of Tweed's empire came tumbling down, after a campaign by a New York newspaper. He was jailed for two years in 1873 and re-arrested after being freed. Tweed was destined to die in jail, vilified for generations as the embodiment of municipal duplicity.

THE DEMISE OF FISK

The departure of Tweed from public life was not the only loss Gould had to contend with at the time. In January 1872, his long-time colleague James Fisk was shot after a scandalous relationship with actress Josie Mansfield.

Gould and Fisk were equally unethical in their approach to business. Together they had swindled their one-time partner Daniel Drew out of $1.5 million in a stocks scam even after he was ousted from the railroad. But Fisk was a counterpoint to the dour Gould – a colourful character with a handlebar moustache and a love of high living – who rejoiced in the nickname 'Jubilee Jim'.

Fisk was gunned down in a Manhattan hotel lobby, and both Gould and Tweed were at his bedside when he died. By 1873, with his greatest allies gone, Gould would have to continue as something of a lone wolf.

*Boss Tweed used
intimidation and
enticements to keep
himself at the pinnacle
of power in New York.*

HARPOONED BY A CARTOON

Although most of his enemies could be
bought, Tweed found that German-born
cartoonist Thomas Nast (1840–1902)
– the man who later popularized Santa
Claus – could not be paid off. Typically,
Nast, who worked for *Harper's Weekly* and
was a Republican sympathizer, depicted
an engorged Tweed with a bag of cash
as a head. While Tweed knew most of his
supporters could not read or write, they
would understand the pictures.

*Growing fat on
the city's coffers,
Tweed feared
popular cartoons
like this one for its
power to reach
illitorate voters.*

THE FRAUDULENT LORD

As if the Erie Railroad had not had enough to contend with in a troubled history, there was still more double dealing to come.

It occurred when a British imposter, who went by the name of Lord Gordon Gordon, cropped up in New York. He cut an impressive figure, in traditional Scottish dress and with an eloquent turn of phrase and stately manner.

Unknown to New Yorkers, he was a swindler on the run after making off with £25,000-worth of items from a London jeweller. Initially, he had fetched up in Minneapolis, fooling the bosses of the Northern Pacific Railroad into hosting him for months by telling them he was a potential investor.

Then he moved to New York without having parted with a penny, to execute his next fraud. In Jay Gould he saw his perfect victim.

Gordon claimed to be a representative of British bond holders on the Erie Railroad sent to

So many were caught up in the web of scandal surrounding the Erie RR that the cry 'stop thief' could spark a stampede of guilty men.

"STOP THIEF!"

"They no sooner heard the cry, than, guessing how the matter stood, they issued forth with great promptitude; and, shouting 'Stop Thief!' too, joined in the pursuit like *Good Citizens*."—"OLIVER TWIST."

replace Gould. Although British investors did have sizeable interests across the board in American railroads, Gould was unnecessarily impressed by Gordon's manner and immediately tried to buy his co-operation. Together, Gould and Gordon discussed plans to fleece those mythical British investors and, as a sign of good faith, Gould parted with $140,000 in cash and shares worth $360,000.

Rather than abscond with the money, Gordon started selling the shares, sparking suspicion and outrage in Gould, who watched tell-tale movements on the market. Gordon was duly arrested and tried. When it became clear to everyone he had lied about his ancestry, Gordon absconded to Canada.

A furious Gould set off in pursuit, accompanied by some powerful associates.

Without any sense of irony, the outraged and unscrupulous Gould tried to kidnap Gordon and bring him back to the US to face fraud charges. The plan was thwarted by Canadian police, who jailed the would-be kidnappers, causing some outraged US politicians to call for an attack on Canada.

Eventually, the kidnappers were released, but Gordon was free as well, and for a while his whereabouts were unknown. When he was found in Manitoba and police arrived to arrest him Gordon shot himself, casting Gould in the role of sinister stalker. Despite the notoriety he had won, Gordon's real identity was never discovered.

GOULD'S LAST STAND

Gould was finally removed from the board of the Erie Railroad in 1872 by a well-organized coup begun by genuine British stock holders.

Gould orchestrated a last stand at the Grand Opera House, where the Erie offices were based, barricaded in and defended by 40 policemen. But a phalanx of US marshals arrived, broke into his office and liberated the accounts books, which revealed Gould's sorry activities.

Compelled to pay back millions, Gould still managed to buy stock cheaply and sell it at a high price to help cover his costs.

At the end of the episode, it was estimated that Gould had milked at least $12 million from the Erie Railroad. The company's debts were hiked by some $64 million while Gould was in charge. Nor was there evidence of investment in rails or rolling stock to show for this. Instead, unseemly amounts had been paid to politicians and judges – and were corralled in Gould's private fortune.

The railroad struggled to relieve itself of debt. In 1895, it was paying more than $5 million in annual interest charges.

It would eventually be re-financed and reorganized on several occasions to ensure its survival well into the twentieth century.

A ROGUES' GALLERY

Vanderbilt and Gould knew every ruse in the book when it came to making money.

It's tempting to believe their modest beginnings fired in them a deep desire for wealth and influence. But they were just two of numerous tricky entrepreneurs in an unwieldy and predatory pack. And, according to Howard Zinn in *A People's History of the United States*: 'While some multimillionaire robber barons started in poverty, most did not. A study of the origins of 303 textile, railroad and steel executives of the 1870s showed that 90 per cent came from middle- or upper-class families.'

So, what defined a 'robber baron'? Well, there was a rich combination of traits that most revealed during their careers. Exploiting workers was a given at the time. Yet they not only kept a stranglehold on workers' rights but also put their tentacles into politics, to cast undue influence over policymakers. The aim was to fashion monopolies – and this sometimes meant taking control of a national resource. To do so, it usually involved manipulation of the stock market, which was bread-and-butter to men who abhorred regulation. And none was above looting the assets of the companies they bought and sold.

It was the era of blank-canvas industries – railroads, oil and steel – which were overwhelmed with money by men wishing to make their mark. Economies of scale were on their side as they drew on mighty cash reserves. For a while, they seemed untouchable, and their behaviour could not be redeemed by grand financial gestures made later in life.

Opposite: Railroad capitalists helped to spread a viable network across American states, but always sought large profits in doing so.

RAILROAD KINGS.

A WOLF OF WALL STREET

At first sight, Edward H. Harriman (1848–1909) was far removed from any common caricature of a robber baron.

He was small and thin, with rimless spectacles perched in front of melancholy eyes. A bushy moustache graced his top lip, but nonetheless he looked more bank clerk than railroad tycoon.

However, the fiercely determined Harriman proved to be a wolf in sheep's clothing when

When overground railroads came into the city, like this one in Union Square, New York, in 1893, it caused chaos on existing thoroughfares.

it came to acquiring and running railroads.

Born in New York, the young Harriman felt no desire to remain in formal education or to follow his father into the clergy. Rather, he looked for inspiration to an uncle who worked on Wall Street.

He was just 14 when he became a broker's boy, soon learning the wrinkles of Wall Street trading and revealing an uncanny aptitude.

Early on, he decided it was 'never safe to look into the future with eyes of fear'. No surprise, then, that he purchased his own seat at the New York Stock Exchange aged just 22.

CASEY JONES

A turn-of-the-century crash on an Illinois Central line turned one engineer into a folk hero. Casey Jones (1863–1900) was the sole victim of the accident, which happened when the passenger train he was driving ploughed into stationary carriages at a station.

Jones was a life-long railroad man who'd started with the Mobile & Ohio aged 15. He transferred to IC in 1891, where he became known for issuing a distinctive train whistle and for strict adherence to the timetable.

On his last journey, Jones began more than an hour and a half behind schedule and reached speeds of 100 mph (161 km/h) to make time. He was back on target when he approached Vaughan, Mississippi, in darkness.

Alerted by fireman Sam Webb, who saw the red rear lights of coaches on the line, Jones grabbed the whistle and the brake – and ordered Webb to jump.

When rescuers pulled his body from the wreckage, they discovered Jones' watch had stopped at the moment of impact: 3:52 am on 30 April 1900.

Although Jones died, his actions ensured his passengers were saved. Afterwards, an inquiry found Jones – notorious as a risk-taker – was responsible after ignoring warnings. Doubt has since been cast over the inquiry findings, as Webb consistently claimed there were no warnings in place.

Jones was later immortalized in a folk song written by a fellow railroad worker, Wallace Saunders, and in an American TV series.

His interest in railroad companies was piqued after his marriage in 1879 to Mary Williamson Averell, whose father, William, was president of the Ogdensburg & Lake Champlain Railroad, founded in 1849 and stretching for 118 miles (190 km).

For Harriman, it wasn't just a matter of financial rewards. Every aspect of railroad organization held a fascination for him, including steam technology, rail maintenance and congestion issues.

His first direct experience of running a railroad came when he bought the almost defunct Lake Ontario Southern Railroad and transformed its fortunes. Refurbished and re-branded as the Sodus Bay & Southern, he sold it to the Pennsylvania Railroad, which gave him sufficient capital to buy the Illinois Central.

HARRIMAN & THE UNION PACIFIC

Two facts mark out the Illinois Central from other railroads of the era. It came into being in 1851 after the US Congress made the first ever land grant for a railroad, a decade before they became commonplace. Land grants were a controversial carrot-and-stick device to encourage the spread of railroads. Illinois Central investors received a 2.5 million-acre (1 million-hectare) land grant for construction of the route between Chicago and Cairo.

And when it was completed in 1856, it was the world's longest railroad, at 705 miles (1,134 km). This all happened when Harriman was a child.

By the time he expressed an interest in it, the railroad was longer still, with an extension built to New Orleans. Remarkably, the 550-mile (885-km) stretch from Cairo to the Gulf of Mexico was converted from a 5 ft (1.5 m) width to standard gauge (4 ft 8½ in (1.435 m)) in a single day, 29 July 1881. It also consolidated with other lines, covering multiple states.

Once he was in charge, Harriman looked west for further expansion but, thanks to his careful management, the Illinois Central did not follow other companies in falling victim to the Panic of 1893.

According to Edward Hungerford, Harriman was 'a railroader with the intuitive sense that gives genius to a great statesman or to a great general'.

In 1897, the Union Pacific was taken into Harriman's corporate embrace. Once a key piece in America's railroad puzzle, it had suffered from years of underinvestment.

The failure of railroads was nothing new. During the Panic of 1893, no fewer than 156 railroad companies folded, with only the few most

Although he looked mild-mannered, Edward Harriman was a ruthless businessman who proved adept at running railroads.

promising examples being bailed out by investors. But Harriman believed the line had sufficient promise to warrant salvation and, typically, he swiftly turned its fortunes around.

With this line now thriving, Harriman looked elsewhere for rail links to expand, with his sights set on lines run by a rival, James Jerome Hill (1838–1916).

HARRIMAN VS HILL

Hill was a one-eyed, muscular rail magnate nicknamed 'the empire builder', who was just as happy swinging a pick during track building as he was glad-handing fellow businessmen.

He numbered among the railroad moguls who grew up in dire straits, in his case in Canada.

His first job in the US was as an 18-year-old book keeper for a steamship company. His first railroad purchase was in 1873, of the bruised Saint Paul & Pacific Railroad.

To further his railroad network, Hill had devised a $10 transportation policy that brought large numbers of Scandinavian immigrants to the Pacific northwest. He also established industries along new railroad lines to provide work. He wasn't minded to give any quarter to Harriman. Crucially, Hill was an ally of J. P. Morgan, whose pockets were deep.

Throughout his career, Morgan was disdainful of Harriman, whom he contemptuously called 'that little man'. Now, the rivalry between the two camps sparked such a frenzy of stock purchases that it was partly responsible for a stock market panic in 1901.

Eventually, they called a truce, forming the Northern Securities Company to share the spoils.

No one foresaw a collapse in its fortunes when the Union Pacific was forging through Utah in 1869.

IN COLD WATER

In 1899, Harriman financed a scientific cruise to Alaska, perhaps to indulge his passion for shooting grizzly bears. However, when a small inlet was spotted close by a glacier Harriman countermanded the captain of the steamer he had chartered, who feared the ship would be grounded or holed. 'Full speed, rocks or no rocks,' barked Harriman. As it happened, the inlet led to a hitherto unknown fjord that later took Harriman's name.

REBATES & DRAWBACKS

John D. Rockefeller dealt in oil and its by-products rather than in railroads. But, at the time, oil travelled in tankers on rails rather than down pipelines. Thus, railroads helped him become the richest man in the world.

Today, he is best remembered as a philanthropist, distributing his mighty wealth in jaw-dropping amounts to funds of his choice. However, he also presided over one of the most outrageous schemes to bleed money from railroad companies and their customers.

Diligent from childhood, Rockefeller, armed with his extraordinary numeracy skills, headed some successful businesses even before he created Standard Oil (SO) in 1870.

But it was this oil refining company that would seal his fortune. At the time, kerosene was its most significant product, used for domestic and industrial lighting prior to the invention of electricity.

Rockefeller's desire to keep the industry on an even keel was laudable enough. Indeed, he saw competition as 'ruinous'. But he chose to pursue that aim by squeezing the commercial life out of rival companies.

Looking for unwitting allies, his gaze fell upon the railroads that he used for regular shipments. There were three major railroad lines linking his refineries in Cleveland to outside markets: the Erie, the New York Central and the Pennsylvania.

John Davison Rockefeller (1839–1937) hobbled competitors by commanding special rates on railroads.

ROCKEFELLER'S REBATES

Standard Oil began demanding discounts of up to 50 per cent, swiftly agreed to by railroad companies who didn't wish to lose the business.

But more than that, Rockefeller proposed the railroad should pay him 'drawbacks'. This was effectively a rebate on the rates paid by producers using the line at a full or even inflated price – about which they knew nothing. Thus, SO was profiting at the expense of potential rivals, to the tune of hundreds of thousands of dollars.

For the railroads, there was some economic sense in limiting the way prices were driven down by competition, thereby keeping freight as profitable as possible. Freight companies were enjoying the benefits of the railroad tanker, which, in 1869, had replaced the flatbed wagons carrying barrels.

To disguise this double dealing, the South Improvement Company was formed, its title purposefully vague so as not to arouse suspicions.

Seeing profits perpetually leaking away towards SO and allied companies, the railroad companies felt compelled to hike rates regularly. It was an unprecedented price rise that finally forced the cosy collusion to unravel.

Oil men suspected they were being played, but they didn't know who by. When they heard news of a raise in rates they rioted in what became known as 'the Oil War'.

According to Ida M. Tarbell in *McClure's Magazine*:

On the morning of 26 February 1872, the oil men read in their morning papers that the rise which had been threatening had come; moreover, that all members of the South Improvement Company were exempt from the advance. At the news all Oildom rushed into the streets. Nobody waited to find out his neighbor's opinion. On every lip there was but one word, and that was 'conspiracy'.

Three thousand men marched against the South Improvement Company, branding it 'the great Anaconda' for its attempt to strangle trade.

'ETHICALLY INDEFENSIBLE'

Rockefeller's biographer Allun Nevins was, in general terms, an admirer of the billionaire, but he criticized a continued abuse of power in dealings with the railroads as 'ethically indefensible'. Although he was writing 70 years after the worst excesses, he said: 'We must condemn the misuse of power not only as a crushing blow to the company's competitors but as an indirect tax on the public.'

Oil producers were so furious they then mounted a boycott of both railroads and refiners. By April 1872, the railroads and SO decided to end rebates and drawbacks, replacing them with non-preferential rates. But Rockefeller's ambitions remained the same, and rebates for SO were soon back on the table.

Even after new railroad systems grew, old-style restrictive practices such as rebates and drawbacks persisted.

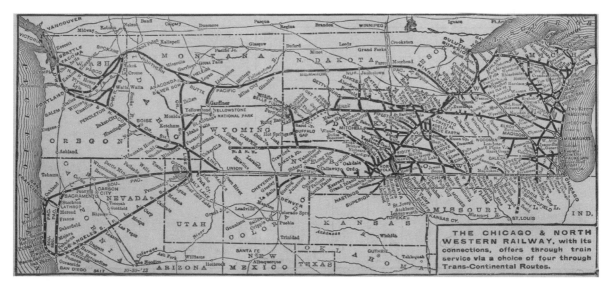

THE CHICAGO & NORTH WESTERN RAILWAY, with its connections, offers through train service via a choice of four through Trans-Continental Routes.

THE TIDE TURNS

After buying out competitors in Cleveland, Rockefeller set his sights on independent refineries in Pittsburgh, Philadelphia, Baltimore and New York.

But a few men were willing to stand out against him. The most courageous was Byron D. Benson (1832–88), who wooed other businessmen and engineers to join a new pipeline venture that would break Rockefeller's iron grip on the industry, and bypass the subservient train companies too. Short in stature but bold by

The inequality of the battle between Tidewater and Rockefeller's SO was apparent to everyone.

inclination, Byron was something of a Napoleonic figure in his native Titusville. He needed every ounce of personal charm to persuade people to back this audacious feat of engineering.

Pipelines had long been a feature of the oil industry and were used to break the monopoly of the teamsters (mule drivers) established early on in the oil industry. But all had been short and straight, with the contents carried by gravity.

The Tidewater Pipeline was to be 109 miles (175 km) long and laid atop the ground across the Allegheny Mountains in Pennsylvania, with two pumps sending oil from Coryville to Williamsport, from where it would be taken forward by railroads outside Rockefeller's sphere of influence.

TIDEWATER WINS THROUGH

When planning for the pipeline began in 1878 it was cloaked in secrecy. But Standard Oil had its own intelligence and espionage service, which soon picked up whispers about the project. Rockefeller, with his millions, vied to purchase the land needed for pipeline construction. He also persuaded railroad lines into being uncooperative.

The tycoon was so determined to scupper the scheme he had one man dress as a tramp, to squat outside relevant telegraph offices, noting the messages being sent on behalf of pipeline planners. Also, he sent imposters to the construction sites to gather more details.

Despite Rockefeller's attentions, the pipeline went into service on 28 May 1879. Although it carried an impressive 250 barrels of crude oil every hour, the speed at which it travelled was just half a mile an hour. On 4 June the oil appeared in Williamsport for the first time.

According to the Williamsport *Daily Gazette and Bulletin*, 'the oil had been heard pushing the air ahead of it two or three days prior to the arrival' and 'the oil came out of the pipe in strong volume'.

SAVED BY THE CAR

Rockefeller had bigger business battles ahead. Soon, oil fields in Russia and Asia were being drilled, and pipelines and newly developed oil tankers were being used to ship the produce around the world. The invention of electricity made kerosene old hat. As luck would have it, cars were invented, so the rising currency of petrol, previously a by-product in the oil industry, secured his future.

A spur was added to the Reading railroad to help get the first batch of oil to a refinery in New Jersey. While Rockefeller may have nursed a wounded pride, the Erie and Pennsylvania railroads were hit with a shortfall in revenue.

ROCKEFELLER'S RESPONSE

Standard Oil responded by trying to outdo the new venture, building four new pipelines of its own: to Cleveland, New York, Philadelphia and Buffalo.

Railroads were left floundering after his oil, accounting for 40 per cent of rail cargo at the time, found a new route to its various destinations. The crash that followed bankrupted about a third of the country's railroads.

Nor was it plain sailing for Tidewater: its iron pipe buckled in the summer sun, the price of crude oil dropped and there was a shortage of wooden barrels. The company was compelled to extend its pipeline to New Jersey.

Despite the on-going feud, Tidewater agreed to sell a third of its stock to SO in June 1882. The following year, both sides came to a market-share agreement, giving Tidewater 11.5 per cent of the oil business.

MONEY & MORALITY

Rockefeller saw little amiss with the cash-yielding cartel involving railroads.

His argument in its favour was simple: 'Who is entitled to better rebates from a railroad, those who give it for transportation 5,000 barrels a day, or those who give 500 barrels – or 50 barrels?'

Teamsters who once shifted Pennsylvania's oil in whisky barrels on carts had operated a monopoly. And Rockefeller didn't see a problem with buying up competitors, having manoeuvred them into a disadvantaged position. In what became known as 'the Cleveland massacre', he'd bought out three-quarters of his rivals by 1872. Some then posed as independents to muddy the waters for the rest.

But not everyone thought the same way. True, many sharp business practices were excused at the time, so lauded was the entrepreneur in America, but, Rockefeller was beginning to make some influential enemies.

One of them was Thomas A. Scott (1823–81), president of the Pennsylvania Railroad. He'd played a large part in designing the South Improvement Company, but in 1877, when SO began building pipelines that would leave the railroad bereft of business, Scott decided to play the same game and began buying refineries and pipelines.

Faced with a backlash from SO, which threatened to withhold business on a grand scale, Scott acquiesced and sold off the new subsidiary. But the episode – coupled with SO's command of the market now standing at 90 per cent – ultimately prompted Pennsylvania's state authorities to charge Rockefeller with orchestrating a monopoly. For the first time, but not the last, Rockefeller was placed on the radar by authorities with growing concerns for morality rather than money.

IN JUDGEMENT

Rockefeller's activities also stuck in the craw of a woman who was just 14 at the time of the 1872 'oil wars'. As a child, Ida M. Tarbell (1857–1944) watched her oil producer father Franklin only narrowly fend off financial ruin, while his partner committed suicide.

Her horror at the 'hate, suspicion and fear' that engulfed the community after the antics of the South Improvement Company never left her.

Much later, she became a journalist and wrote a carefully researched exposé of Rockefeller's tactics, helped by author and campaigner Mark Twain, revealing for the first time the extent of the tycoon's trickery.

Tarbell's findings were published in excerpts in *McClure's Magazine* and in 1904 as a book, *The History of the Standard Oil Company*:

When [Rockefeller] went into the South Improvement Company it was not to save his own business, but to destroy others. When he worked so persistently to secure rebates after the breaking up of the South Improvement Company, it was in the face of an industry united against them …

Every great campaign against rival interests which the Standard Oil Company has carried on has been inaugurated, not to save its life, but to build up and sustain a monopoly in the oil industry …

When the business man who fights to secure special privileges, to crowd his competitor off the track by other than fair competitive methods, receives the same summary disdainful ostracism by his fellows that the doctor or lawyer who is 'unprofessional', the athlete who abuses the rules, receives, we shall have gone a long way toward making commerce a fit pursuit for our young men.

Right: Tarbell's book – loathed by Rockefeller – exposed SO's dodgy dealings.

Below: For tackling big business, journalist and author Ida Minerva Tarbell was branded a 'muckraker' – a term for investigative writers of the era.

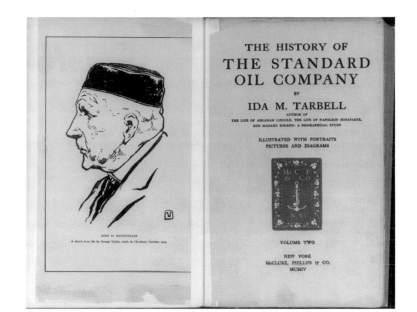

THE HISTORY OF
**THE STANDARD
OIL COMPANY**
BY
IDA M. TARBELL

J. P. MORGAN

One characteristic that links the robber barons is an agile mind, with the ability to see windows of opportunity where others see only brick walls.

This was especially true of John Pierpont Morgan (1837–1913), who specialized in amalgamating railroads. In his view, bigger was generally better – and always cheaper.

He mounted deft operations to secure the lines he had targeted for consolidation in the belief that controlled prices and profits were best for railroad bosses. Meanwhile, the promises of modernization, shorter trips and a more dependable service were dangled for customers.

But by eliminating competition, as he was fond of doing, he began fostering monopolies which went against the interests of the travelling public.

Initially, it seemed J. P. Morgan, as he was commonly known, would follow in the footsteps of his father, Junius, who was a banker. But while the over-bearing Junius was risk-averse, his son enjoyed the thrill of a swashbuckling commercial conquest.

Until the older man's death in 1890, this impetus was stifled, although J. P. Morgan had already started the business of re-organizing railroads in 1885, when he arbitrated between the New York Central Railroad and the Pennsylvania Railroad to bring an end to a damaging rate war that cast the future of both companies in doubt.

It was a role he adopted several more times before the 1893 Panic, when his involvement went up a gear, finally taking in the New York, New Haven & Hartford and the Northern Pacific railroads.

Morgan was certainly frustrated by what he saw as the fruitless skirmishes between railroad operators that endangered their profitability. And for some, Morgan was a captain of industry rather than a robber baron. After all, it was his intervention with hard cash that saved America's face during two economic crises, in 1893 and 1907.

But others pointed to the way his personal fortune was enhanced with every new involvement.

MORGAN'S METHODS

He was notoriously pitiless in his approach to companies and their workers in a quest to maximize profits. With every acquisition, there was a gruelling process of economies that usually involved job losses and short cuts, afterwards known as 'Morganization'. No matter that families risked destitution and the rate of accidents rose for want of proper maintenance.

Had it not been for his adventuring with the New York, New Haven & Hartford railroad after 1903 he might have avoided being bracketed with other robber barons. But his frontman, Charles S. Mellen (1852–1927), rode roughshod over newly wrought controls and employed dubious methods to secure railroad stocks. Also, the official rules of engagement had begun to change following government interventions, with a volley of new regulations.

Morgan ended up controlling an estimated one-sixth of the national railroad stock – but one of his railroad companies was deemed illegal under new laws.

Shortly before his death, Morgan was accused outright of bad management of the New York, New Haven & Hartford by the Interstate Commerce Commission, which characterized him as 'loose, extravagant and improvident'.

Opposite: Financier J.P. Morgan specialised in combining railroad companies, scaling back competition that would drive prices down.

LAST OF A KIND

J. P. Morgan died in Rome in his sleep, nine months before the Federal Reserve was established so that no single wealthy individual would enjoy the same dominance and influence over a democratically elected government again.

CURRENT INTERESTS

Although he is best known as a financier, J. P. Morgan sought a more radiant legacy. Consequently, he poured his money into the fledgling electricity industry in the hope of stealing kerosene king Rockefeller's soubriquet of 'the man who lit America'.

At first he backed Thomas Edison (1847–1931), a self-taught scientist who'd invented an 'automatic repeater', which dispatched telegraph messages to unmanned stations, aged just 16.

After a spell working at Western Union as a telegrapher, Edison moved to New York, where he began work on a series of inventions including a machine to record sound.

But it was his work perfecting the electric lightbulb that brought him public prominence. It was unveiled in his laboratory in 1879, using a wiring system designed by employee Nikola Tesla (1856–1943).

Edison's work attracted Morgan's backing. Indeed, the millionaire's New York home was illuminated by one of the 121 power stations delivering Direct Current (DC) that Edison had installed around New York by 1887, although Morgan's aged father did not approve.

A more inhibiting, technical problem was that DC could not travel more than a mile without dissipating.

Meanwhile, Tesla had gone his own way, teaming up with George Westinghouse (1846–1914), both of whom saw a brighter future in the stronger Alternating Current (AC). As each side lobbied for its current of choice, there began a war of words peppered with scare stories. To garner publicity, Edison killed dogs using AC, and even ensured that the newly created electric chair, used for capital punishment, was powered by AC electricity in the belief that it would turn the public against it.

MORGAN TAKES CONTROL

Ultimately, Morgan lost patience with Edison and stepped in to end the wrangle and protect his investment. Using his financial heft, he united Edison's various companies into a new firm, the Edison General Electric Company, in 1889.

Typically, Morgan then sought to consolidate further still, joining this business with leading rival Thomson-Houston Electric Company, cutting Edison adrift as he did so. The new business was called General Electric.

One significant electrical company remained outside Morgan's control. Westinghouse's business, responsible for lighting up the 1893 Chicago World's Fair, won the contract to build the hydroelectric plant at Niagara Falls.

There was a volley of bad-tempered legal spats between the two, ending in a patent-sharing agreement, which was signed in 1896.

SHADY DEALS

Morgan was a hard-headed and heartless businessman from the outset, making cash during the Civil War by selling defective guns to the Union. Later, he denied knowing the guns were faulty, but it's hard to exonerate him from charges of profiteering.

As a financier, he manipulated the price of gold, used insider knowledge to secure trade deals and encouraged cartels to rid his companies of competition.

However, all of these were lawful loopholes at the time which took him close to, but not across, legal boundaries.

Opposite: Thomas Edison was a brilliant scientist and had an innovative mind, but wasn't blessed with business acumen.

PATENT RECORD

Before his death, Edison secured more patents than any other inventor, registering more than 1,000 new ideas. Apart from the electric lightbulb, he is also remembered for the phonograph, the Kinetoscope – a forerunner of movie cameras – and a battery that was robust enough to power cars.

THE AGE OF STEEL

At a time when men yearned for a railroad ownership, Andrew Carnegie (1835–1919) had an eye for infrastructure.

Having spent formative years working on the railroad, he saw how the nation was changing and where he might play a part.

When he emigrated from Scotland aged 13, with parents William and Margaret, he was entrenched in the eighteenth-century industries.

Both he and his father worked in a cotton mill in Pittsburgh until he secured a job in a telegraph office as a messenger boy.

From this unlikely platform he made good, impressing Thomas A. Scott of the Pennsylvania

For a while, steel tracks were the hallmark of a modern railroad network and implied a smoother, safer trip.

Railroad sufficiently to be employed as a personal assistant at $35 a month.

'I couldn't imagine what I could ever do with so much money,' he later recalled.

By 1854, the diligent and able Carnegie had worked his way up to being superintendent at the railroad company, and was elevated to a role in running military railroads when Scott joined the government during the Civil War.

The conflict touched everybody's life. But for Carnegie it opened his eyes to the importance, not only of the railroad, but of the materials it needed to stay on track.

After dabbling in the Woodruff Sleeping Car Company, an iron works and the new oil industry, he left the railroad company in 1865 to found the Keystone Bridge Company, with Scott and J. Edgar Thomson, both at one time president of the Pennsylvania Railroad, as investors. Benefitting from the era of reconstruction, the company replaced wooden bridges with iron ones so successfully that Carnegie enjoyed an annual salary of $50,000 within three years.

Still, he didn't sit back to enjoy the trappings of wealth. Despite fondly held plans to retire early, he visited England to see the work of Henry Bessemer (1813–98), who had discovered a one-step way of producing abundant cheap steel from iron when previously the process had been slow and laborious, and relatively unproductive.

BOTH ENDS MEETING IN THE MIDDLE

Scott and Thomson benefitted so greatly from the association with the Keystone Bridge Company that they steered all Pennsylvania RR business its way. With an interest in both the railroad and the construction company, they profited twice over in deals. Although both strove to keep their association with the bridge company a secret Scott's shares were in his wife's name – it was largely recognized as a Pennsylvania RR company.

Carnegie installed Bessemer converters at the Freedom Iron Company, which he had formed in 1861. When they proved successful, he determined to expand the steel industry in America, beckoning in a new age of construction with steel, which was needed for skyscrapers, bridges and, of course, rails.

In 1875, the $1.2-million Edgar Thomson works opened in Pittsburgh, capable of producing 225 tons of steel rails each day. The plant is named after the president of the Pennsylvania Railroad, which in turn placed the first order for 2,000 steel rails.

DELUGE AT JOHNSTOWN

At the South Fork Fishing and Hunting Club, the industrial gentry of Pittsburgh could relax away from the grime and noise of the factories they owned.

After its opening in 1879, wealthy men, including Carnegie, might sit on the charming club-house porch enjoying a cigar and a whisky, while being serenaded by musicians. The more energetic of this elite would sail, row or fish on the Conemaugh Lake, previously known as the Western Reservoir, built in 1852 to provide water for the Pennsylvania Canal. By the time it was completed, the canal had been made obsolete by the arrival of railroads and the reservoir was abandoned.

The Johnstown floodwater scoured a broad pathway through homes and businesses.

Eight miles (13 km) long and 3 miles (5 km) wide, the lake became a magnet for the captains of industry for the purposes of recreation – but the 61 members of the club were demonstrably less keen on the costs of maintenance.

However, they found the money to lower the dam wall in order to have a road wide enough for two carriages to pass. Along with installing fish screens that blocked the overflow system, that served to put increasing pressure on the reservoir's structure.

DISASTER STRIKES

On a wet day at the end of May 1889, the dam finally gave way as water lapped over the containing wall, unleashing 14 million tons of water down the valley to Johnstown

and its 25,000 residents, some 8 miles (13 km) distant.

A decade previously, *Appleton's* had described Johnstown as 'a busy manufacturing borough at the confluence of the Conemaugh and Stony Creeks. The Cambria Iron-works ... are among the most extensive in America.'

A warning had already been dispatched to the city at lunchtime about the threat of a dam burst. But this had happened previously and no one took action other than to retire to the first floors of their homes.

By 4.00 pm, a tsunami 30 ft (9 m) high was heading towards the city, gathering pace as it cascaded downhill. Houses, trees, factories, railroads, bridges and telegraph poles joined the debris already churning in the water, and residents were quickly swallowed up in a torrent that was half a mile (800 m) wide. A report in the *New York Times* likened it to the rapids at Niagara Falls.

During the ten minutes it took for the tidal wave to pass through the northern part of the

RED CROSS RESCUE

Strenuous relief efforts were made at Johnstown, not least by the recently instituted American Red Cross. At its helm was Civil War nurse Clara Barton (1821–1912), who'd formed the organization in 1881 in Washington, having encountered the work of the International Red Cross while she visited Europe during the Franco-Prussian War.

city, 2,209 people lost their lives. The dead included labourers desperately trying to shore up the dam wall as it crumbled, under the supervision of club officials.

RESPONSIBILITY DENIED

In the uproar that followed the disaster, the club was frequently blamed for the neglect that caused it.

'Manslaughter or Murder?' raged the *Chicago Herald*. 'Our misery is the work of man,' claimed the *Johnstown Tribune*.

The club donated 1,000 blankets, while Carnegie proffered $10,000. But all the members stayed tight-lipped about its circumstances. Although a few legal cases were brought, none was successful. It seemed symptomatic of the era that wealthy men could err in terms of responsibility and evade the consequences. Thus, public tolerance of the robber barons diminished.

Raging torrents caused unprecedented destruction.

HOMESTEAD STRIKE

Hailing from a family of Scottish Radicals, Carnegie was, on the face of it, a supporter of worker's rights. However, his actions didn't always live up to the enlightened principles he professed to hold.

There's no doubt his views were shaped by his experiences. He'd grown up in poverty and watched his factory-worker father William die at the age of 51.

But his mentor, Thomas A. Scott, also died in humbled circumstances, brought low by Rockefeller and the intrigues he conducted against the Pennsylvania Railroad – as well as the 1877 strike that resulted (see page 158).

Pinkerton guards were escorted away by armed union men, unable to defeat the unhappy workers.

Perhaps as a consequence of this 'unacceptable' face of union action, Carnegie employed Henry Clay Frick (1849–1919) as his manager. Frick was already a successful businessman, manufacturing the coke used to fuel blast furnaces.

At first, the contrasting duo seemed to complement one another. From 1881, Frick expanded his business using Carnegie's money. Eight years later, Carnegie handed over the irksome daily running of his steel company to the hard-headed Frick.

But on labour relations, Frick was combative, while Carnegie – at least publicly – was peaceable, having declared a perceptive understanding of how industrial hostilities arose.

We assemble thousands of operatives in the factory, and in the mine, of whom the employer can know little or nothing, and to whom he is little better than a myth. All intercourse between them is at an end. Rigid castes are formed, and, as usual, mutual ignorance breeds mutual distrust. Each caste is without sympathy with the other, and ready to credit anything disparaging in regard to it.

Nonetheless, it was on his watch that the notorious Homestead strike occurred.

AT LOGGERHEADS

Feeling the effects of a national economic downturn, Frick went into negotiations at the Homestead steel mill in 1892, determined to break the burgeoning power of the Amalgamated Association of Iron and Steel Workers.

For their part, the workers believed themselves locked out by a belligerent management. Those workers who weren't part of the union quickly sided with the strikers.

GUNS FOR HIRE

Pinkerton's National Detective Agency was formed in 1850 by Scottish-born Chicago cop Allan Pinkerton. One of its early specialities was protecting railroad shipments, but Pinkerton's men also gained a reputation for pursuing outlaws. By the 1890s, it had 2,000 detectives on its books plus 30,000 reservists.

Frick called in Pinkerton guards to impose the corporation's will. But when 300 armed men arrived, they were faced with 10,000 strikers and a fierce battle ensued. The guards withdrew later the same day, but only after the deaths of nine men.

Ten days after the start of the strike, state militia men arrived to seize the plant. Strike breakers arrived on locked trains to bring the steelworks back to life.

The strikers enjoyed public sympathy until anarchist Alexander Berkman shot and stabbed Frick, who was lucky to escape with his life.

Finally, Carnegie Steel negotiated longer working hours and lower pay from an exhausted union and, by November, work had resumed after 143 days.

Frick had been at the front line, earning the enmity of working people everywhere. Carnegie absented himself in Scotland, but there was no doubt in everyone's mind that he was equally culpable. Yet he saw himself as another victim. To British statesman William Gladstone, Carnegie wrote: 'The pain I suffer increases daily. The Works are not worth one drop of human blood.' Behind the scenes he had written to Frick: 'We are with you to the end.'

With his reputation tarnished, Carnegie resolved to blame Frick and end their relationship

'WISE DISTRIBUTION'

By 1900, Carnegie Steel had hit production levels that were greater than those of Great Britain. But the industrial juggernaut he had created no longer gave unmitigated pleasure to Carnegie.

He continued a bitter feud with Frick after they parted company in 1899. 'You are being outgeneralled all along the line, and your management of the Company has already become the subject of jest,' Frick told him in a telegram.

The sniping with Rockefeller continued, and in 1900 he squared up to J. P. Morgan, who wanted to buy the steelworks to amalgamate with his own.

Suddenly, he paused for thought. After the death of his mother Margaret and brother Tom he had married and had a daughter. Was it time to spend more time in his native Scotland with wife Louise?

For him, a love of learning had always competed with the joys of unfettered capitalism. Moreover, he saw the peril of idolizing the dollar. At the age of just 33, he had written a note to himself:

To continue much longer overwhelmed by business cares and with most of my thoughts wholly upon the way to make more money in the shortest time, must degrade me beyond hope of permanent recovery. I will resign business at thirty-five, but during the ensuing two years I wish to spend the afternoons in receiving instruction and in reading systematically.

He had not resigned then, but had continued in business for three more decades, until the philosophical conflict of how to best spend his millions began to vex him. With relatively little warning he 'resolved to stop accumulating and begin the infinitely more serious and difficult task of wise distribution'.

GRAND-SCALE PHILANTHROPY

After accepting Morgan's offer for Carnegie Steel – which made him the richest man in the world – Carnegie set about spending for the public good.

He wasn't interested in charity so much as helping people to help themselves. As a consequence, it was libraries and schools that stood to benefit to the tune of hundreds of millions of dollars, both in Britain and America.

The largest sum went to the Carnegie Corporation of New York, founded in 1911 for 'the advancement and diffusion of knowledge and understanding among the people of the United States'.

His money also paid for a 'Peace Palace' at The Hague in Holland, in the forlorn hope of fostering a unity among European nations after centuries of conflict. It opened in 1913, just a

GREAT GIFTS

If he harboured hopes of donating more to charity than his nemesis Rockefeller, Carnegie would have been disappointed. Before his death, the oil tycoon had dispatched $1 billion to good causes. In 1913, the Rockefeller Foundation was incorporated, with Rockefeller giving $100 million in its first year, 'to promote the wellbeing of mankind throughout the world'. And that was just one of a string of grand gestures. However, the Rockefeller Centre in New York, although conceived in John D. Rockefeller's lifetime, was primarily the work of his son.

year before the outbreak of the First World War – a distressing event for Carnegie that compelled him to leave his beloved Scotland for the last time.

It's thought that in terms of bricks and mortar and charitable foundations, Carnegie offloaded some $350 million before his death. Even given this, he still died a rich man, with Forbes magazine estimating his wealth equivalent to $281 billion in 2006 values.

Carnegie pictured in 1913 shortly before he was devastated by the outbreak of war in Europe.

CREDIT MOBILIER

In the history of railroads there are two institutions that share the name Credit Mobilier, both privately run but publicly subscribed.

One, established in France in 1852 by brothers Isaac and Emile Péreire, used investors' money to pay for railroad projects around Europe and helped to finance France's second empire. The second gave title to an infamous episode in American railroad history, related these days to illustrate the worst excesses of the nation's railroad mania.

A sorry tale of exploitation by businessmen and politicians, it serves to show how development in America was pegged back by those whose first intention was to line their own pockets, no matter what the cost to the nation.

Those involved in the Credit Mobilier scandal are here depicted as modern Pharisees, declaring: 'Thank God we are not as other men are; we never lie, bear false witness against our neighbours, commit perjury or take bribes.'

THOMAS 'THE DOC' DURANT

The Credit Mobilier scandal was a defining and shameful episode in a country still reeling from civil war. Taxpayers and rail investors were fleeced by snouts-in-the-trough tycoons and politicians. Yet, amid all this corrupt profiteering, the Press remained woefully compliant.

Scamsters-in-chief were Thomas 'Doc' Durant, a rapacious tycoon, and Oakes Ames, a shovel-maker turned Congressman. Although eventually bitter enemies, they shared a similar overall philosophy: risk other people's money, reward powerful friends, cook the books and keep everything opaque. On the back of a respectable company (Union Pacific) and an exciting plan (the transcontinental rail link) they made vast fortunes while somehow staying a sliver within the law.

Durant was the initial driving force behind both Union Pacific (UP) and its main contractor – the construction company Credit Mobilier of America.

Born in 1820, in Massachusetts, Durant qualified as a surgeon but soon switched to his uncle's grain export business in New York City. He realized that railroads could transform inland transport connections and by 1853, using the fortune he'd amassed running contraband cotton from Confederate states, he founded the Mississippi & Missouri Railroad. He also made an influential contact.

The M&M linked Davenport, on the Mississippi River, to Council Bluffs on the Missouri. It provided both Iowa's first railroad and the first bridge across the Mississippi. But although the venture gave Durant valuable kudos, there was an early hitch. When a steamboat crashed into the bridge in 1856, the vessel's owner began legal action, declaring it a dangerous hazard. Durant and his partners defended the suit –

known as the Rock Island Bridge Case (see page 74–5) – and hired a brilliant young attorney to represent them. His name: Abraham Lincoln.

Lincoln's defence strategy helped ensure the case was eventually dropped, and Durant began looking for further opportunities in railroad finance. His juicy target was the Union Pacific Railroad Company, which, along with the Central (later Southern) Pacific, was set to build a transcontinental line. Given the huge risks involved for investors, lucrative government loans and land grants had sweetened the deal.

INSIDER DEALING

Durant was a master in the dark arts of insider-dealing. One of his most profitable early coups was to announce that the new Union Pacific line would connect to his very own Missouri & Mississippi Railroad. Seeing that M&M's business would be boosted, investors clamoured to buy shares, increasing their value. Meanwhile, Thomas Durant became a discreet seller of M&M – preferring instead to buy stock in a rival operator, the Cedar Rapids & Missouri line.

But not for long. A change of plan was announced. UP now wanted to connect its track to the CR&M rather than the M&M. Investors duly sold M&M stock, driving its price back down, and piled in to CR&M instead. All except The Doc. His CR&M shares had shot up in value, providing a tidy profit to buy back his old M&M holding at bargain price.

AND THEY'RE OFF

On 1 July 1862, President Lincoln signed into law an 'Act to aid in the construction of a railroad and telegraph line from the Missouri river to the Pacific ocean, and to secure to the government the use of the same for postal, military, and other purpose'.

By now, Durant was perfectly positioned. He'd invested heavily in UP via various stock-purchase shenanigans and as vice president had secured himself the role of general agent for its Eastern Division. That made him responsible for raising finance, sourcing materials and labour and lobbying Congress for the best possible terms. The seeds of the Credit Mobilier scandal had been sown.

Doc Durant worked behind the scenes to maximise his personal profits, frequently at the expense of the American government.

THE GAMBLE THAT NEVER WAS

The Credit Mobilier scandal was born from a simple truth: the US government badly wanted a transcontinental railroad.

But such a vast engineering project had to attract private investors. Many were unconvinced that eye-watering construction costs could be converted to long-term profit from train services.

Chief amongst these sceptics was Thomas Durant, vice president of Union Pacific. Unlike other robber barons, he believed that the big dollars lay in building, rather than operating, the railroad – especially given the lucrative government subsidies, cheap loans, land grants and mineral rights a desperate Congress was throwing at its Big Idea. Much of this state largesse had, incidentally, been secured by Durant himself through bribes to influential politicians.

Durant suspected that if the state money-tree was shaken still harder, more dollars would cascade down. But he needed full control. Having won the transcontinental contract for Union Pacific, why let outside construction companies get a slice of the action? Why not, instead, form his own 'construction' firm with fellow UP financiers? And so, in 1864, Credit Mobilier of America – cunningly trading on the name of a well-known French bank – was launched.

CROOKED DEALINGS

The first commercial act of Credit Mobilier of America was to submit a quote to Union Pacific for 667 miles (1,073 km) worth of line work. No one else got the invitation to bid and, unsurprisingly – as Durant was hiring himself – Credit Mobilier was successful.

Money from taxpayers and private investors, handed to Union Pacific, could now be paid directly to Credit Mobilier, based on the estimates and invoices it submitted. If everyone involved had been straightforward and honest, this arrangement might still have worked fairly. But they weren't. And it didn't.

Credit Mobilier had taken advantage of new limited liability laws, which meant its stockholders were liable only for the extent of their investment rather than their entire personal wealth. So who cared how quickly the line was built or the supposed financial risks? Durant and his pals at Credit Mobilier were guaranteed payment because over at UP they were signing the cheques.

The money-tree quickly produced its first crop of dollars. Credit Mobilier was being paid by the mile, so it was in the interests of Durant and his fellow promoters to avoid straight lines where possible. Enough twists and bends were

RAISING RAILROAD CASH

Thomas Durant's first hurdle at Union Pacific was to properly capitalize the company – in other words, ensure enough money flowed in from private investors to secure taxpayer-funded grants and subsidies. The 1862 Pacific Railroad Act limited the number of shares in UP to 200 per person, with a 10 per cent down-payment. This underwhelmed potential investors, so Durant told brokers he'd pay the advance himself on the promise of later reimbursement. The plan worked. Several prominent politicians signed up and word got round that the deal was sound. More than $2.1 million worth of UP stock was issued.

incorporated into the track out of Omaha that nine unnecessary miles were built. And that was just the start. Invoices to UP were inflated way above the true costs of construction, while genuine sub-contractors had their estimates racked up. In theory, Union Pacific should have been questioning Credit Mobilier's spending to protect the interests of its investors and the government. But that would just have meant Durant interrogating himself.

The stakeholders who could have asked tough questions were the politicians who so badly wanted a transcontinental line. But the Civil War was still raging and the Federal government's attention was elsewhere. Besides, Oakes Ames was taking care of awkward congressmen.

Oakes Ames (1804–73) was a major player in the Credit Mobilier scandal.

THE KING OF SPADES

Although Thomas Durant effectively won control of both Union Pacific and its main contractor, Credit Mobilier, his position was not unassailable. The Ames brothers, Oliver and Oakes, also had wealth and political clout. As UP investors and canny businessmen they could see Durant's game plan and wanted to play.

The brothers' money stemmed from a successful shovel-making business set up in Massachusetts by their blacksmith father, Oliver Ames Senior, nicknamed the King of Spades.

Their manufacturing company benefitted from the treble-jackpot of civil war, railroad construction and the California gold-rush and, as demand for shovels, swords and tools grew, so did their fortunes. By 1863, Oakes was a Republican congressman and a member of the Committee on Railroads. The transcontinental line had landed in his in-tray.

Within two years the project was in crisis. Under Durant's stewardship the track had been meandering around the Midwest, behind

Ultimately, the scandal left participants dead, dying or crippled in the view of one cartoonist. However, no punishments were meted out in its wake.

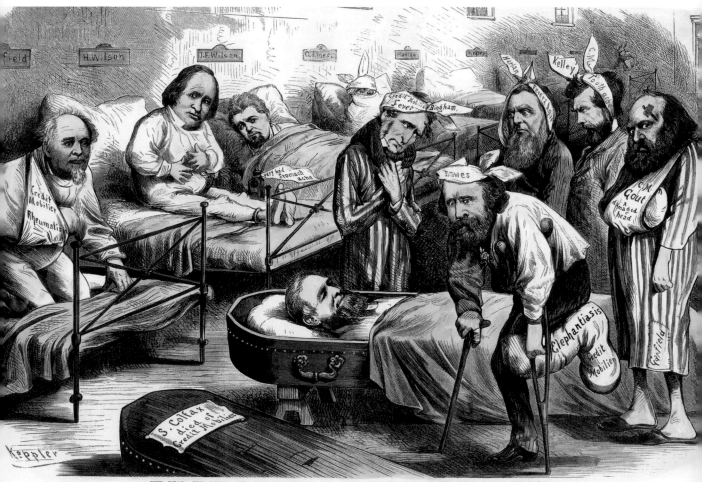

THE DEAD, THE DYING AND THE CRIPPLED IN THE CREDIT MOBILIER WARD OF THE UNION PACIFIC HOSPITAL.

schedule and mired in burgeoning costs. True, the Civil War had slowed progress – just 12 miles (19 km) had been built – but the underlying problem was Union Pacific's cash reserves, ruthlessly diverted into the pockets of Durant and his cronies via the semi-fictional accounts of Credit Mobilier. Something had to change. President Lincoln appealed to Ames Oakes to take personal control.

OAKES TAKES ON DURANT

Oakes recapitalized UP by using his position to obtain rail-construction contracts for his family business. He then invested a large chunk of the brothers' personal wealth into the floundering giant, allowing Oliver, as a major shareholder, to take over the presidency of Union Pacific. This marginalized Durant's influence, but Oakes then went further and ousted him from the Credit Mobilier board.

Durant responded with a wave of legal injunctions, the board split into squabbling factions and out on the track labourers sat idle.

Eventually, in October 1867, a grudging truce was declared. Durant would be restored to the Credit Mobilier board and, in return, a valuable construction contract would be awarded to the Ames brothers. This was the stuff of mafia business. And it was about to get a whole lot more complicated.

SHADY STOCK DEALS

Over on Capitol Hill, Oakes Ames was trying to head off mutterings about a congressional investigation into the cosy relationship between

FRIENDS IN CONGRESS

Ames must have known his actions were corrupt. Yet he convinced himself that he'd broken no laws. 'We want more friends in this Congress,' he wrote, 'and if a man will look into the law (and it is difficult to get them to do it unless they have an interest to do so) he cannot help being convinced that we should not be interfered with.'

It is thought Ames handed around $9 million worth of heavily discounted stock to his political friends.

Union Pacific and Credit Mobilier. Oakes knew exactly how things worked, but could hardly spill the beans publicly.

Instead, he upped the ante by distributing what might now be called 'virtual gifts' of cut-price Credit Mobilier stock. This was booming in value on the back of improved profits and a decent dividend, and two senators and nine representatives were fortunate beneficiaries (although some later returned the 'gift').

Ames dutifully recorded the transactions in a 'black book'. He generally kept the stock in his own name, distributing dividends as they became due, so avoiding embarrassment to politicians with direct influence over railroad laws and subsidies. In any courtroom in the world, such payments would be called bribes. Yet, bizarrely, none of Ames' Capitol Hill cronies saw a conflict of interest.

SCANDAL & AFTERMATH

In 1872, President Ulysses S. Grant was up for his second term. A long-time ally of the Union Pacific Railroad, his handling of the company's troubled financial past was now a big political issue. With rumours of secret sweeteners for congressmen gathering traction, the anti-Grant press smelt blood.

On 4 September, the *New York Sun* finally broke the story. One angry Credit Mobilier shareholder handed the newspaper incriminating letters from Oakes Ames appearing to implicate him in a corruption scandal. An incomplete list of Ames' congressional contacts emerged, amounting to political dynamite.

The list included incumbent vice president Schuyler Colfax, vice presidential nominee Henry Wilson, future president James Garfield, Iowa congressmen William Allison and James Wilson, Pennsylvania's William Kelley and Glenni Scofield, Ohio's John Bingham, Illinois's John Logan, James Patterson of New Hampshire and Henry Dawes of Massachusetts. Speaker of the House, James G. Blaine, had actually declined the offer of Credit Mobilier shares, but because his name was on Ames' list he was labelled corrupt anyway.

The *Sun* called it 'the most damaging exhibition of official and private villainy and corruption ever laid bare to the gaze of the world'.

UNCOVERING THE TRUTH

Blaine took the only real option he had. He instigated a full congressional investigation which, although it tainted Grant's new administration, reported too late to influence the election. It also exonerated Blaine, while casting light on how bribes were paid. Scofield, Patterson, Dawes, Bingham and Henry Wilson all bought discounted stock up front. Allison and Colfax waited for 'bonuses' before settling (at almost 70 per cent discount). Garfield, Logan, Kelley and James Wilson paid nothing but still got dividend income.

When questioned, Oakes insisted he'd done nothing wrong. 'We wanted capital and influence,' he said. 'Influence not on legislation alone but on credit good, wide, and a general favourable feeling [sic]. If the community had confidence in our ultimate success, that success was ensured.'

This all cut little ice with the press, especially those editors scathing of President Grant's administration. On 19 February 1873, the *New-York Tribune* fumed:

> *Well, the wickedness of all of it is not that these men were bribed or corruptly influenced but that they betrayed the trust of the people, deceived their constituents and by their evasions and falsehoods confessed the transaction to be disgraceful.*

But there were also hard questions for the press. Having failed to expose the scandal for years, some commentators suspected editors were now using it to undermine Grant. Artist Thomas Nast, a strong supporter of the president, produced a famous cartoon for *Harper's Weekly* a month after the *Tribune*'s rant. It shows shifty-looking congressmen, lined up on Capitol Hill, confronted by editors (including one preparing to throw a rock). Between them the mythical figure of Justice points at the politicians while addressing the journalists. Paraphrasing the Bible, the caption reads: 'Let him that has not betrayed the trust of the people, and is without stain, cast the first stone.'

END OF THE AFFAIR

Despite the corrupt and fraudulent acts instigated by Thomas Durant and Oakes Ames, neither man faced serious punishment. Durant later claimed to have made $2.4 million out of Union Pacific and Credit Mobilier (although he later lost $3 million building the Adirondack Railroad). After kissing goodbye to $1.5 million in the 1873 Wall Street Panic, Doc Durant spent the last 12 years of his life battling lawsuits from former associates.

As for Ames, he escaped with a congressional censure. No criminal charges were ever brought against any railroad company director or manager and, in 1883 – 14 years after the transcontinental line was finished – the Massachusetts state legislature even passed a motion exonerating Ames from blame.

Headlines about the web of corruption like these in the New York Sun in 1872 made compelling reading.

THE KING OF FRAUDS.

How the Credit Mobilier Bought its Way Through Congress.

COLOSSAL BRIBERY.

Congressmen who Have Robbed the People, and who now Support the National Robber.

HOW SOME MEN GET FORTUNES.

Princely Gifts to the Chairmen of Committees in Congress.

From 2,000 to 3,000 Shares Each to Henry Wilson, Schuyler Colfax, George S. Boutwell, John A. Bingham, James A. Garfield, the Pattersons, Eliot, Brooks, Dawes and James G. Blaine.

Correspondence of The Sun.

PHILADELPHIA, Sept. 3.—The revelations contained in the sworn testimony accompanying this need no explanatory introduction. It is the most damaging exhibition of official and private villainy and corruption ever laid bare to the gaze of the world. The Vice-President of the United States, the Speaker of the House of

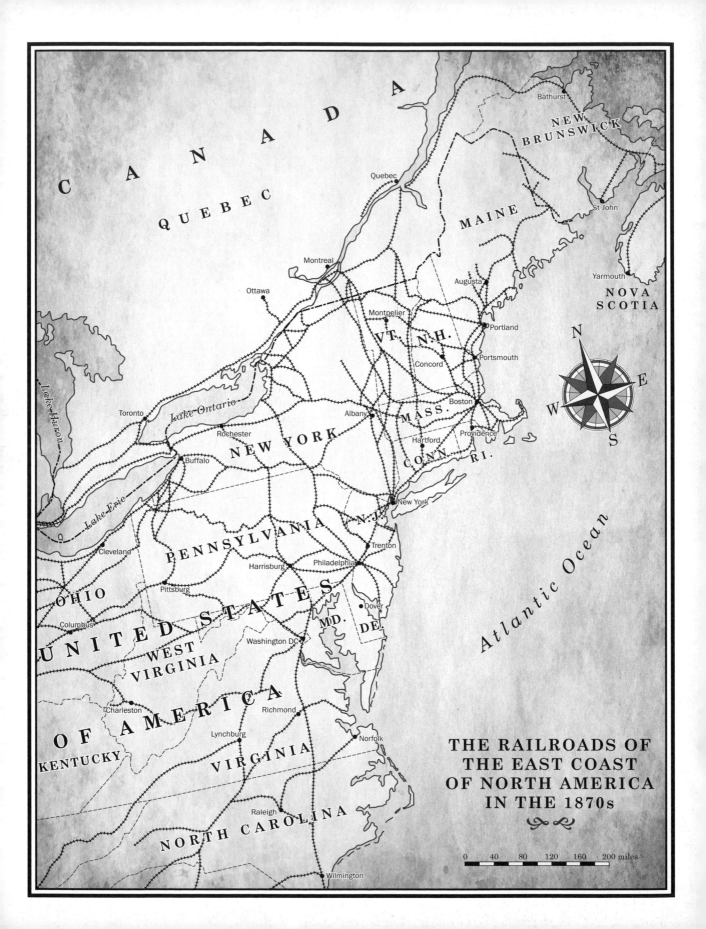

THE RAILROADS OF
THE EAST COAST
OF NORTH AMERICA
IN THE 1870s

Mormons, Irishmen and the Chinese were sometimes joined by Native Americans, such as these men from the Navajo tribe, when they were track building.

RECONSTRUCTION & THE GILDED AGE

In the half century that followed the Civil War, America was booming. First, came a period of reconstruction, in which the physical scars of the damaging domestic conflict would prove quicker to heal than those in the national psyche.

Then came the gilded age, a title borrowed from writer Mark Twain who, in his 1873 novel *The Gilded Age: A Tale of Today*, satirized the way serious social difficulties were masked by a shiny veneer.

The term clearly refers to the immense wealth of a few and the poverty that afflicted many. But behind it lies a deeper-rooted philosophy that drove the nation forward. This was the time when America became seriously ambitious for itself, with a mindset and a motto known as 'manifest destiny'.

The phrase was coined in 1845 by newspaper editor John O'Sullivan in connection with the annexation of Texas, and was used as a justification for the Mexican War.

But the concept didn't go up in smoke during the Civil War. Rather, the expansion of Federal America into its interior and overseas was afterwards considered a right, even an obligation, bestowed on the US thanks to its Anglo Saxon heritage. Underlying it was a belief that this was as God intended.

Initially, at its nucleus was the coveted notion that 'every man is equal'. But the idea veered off at a tangent until it was a tangle of faith, nationalism, patriotism and a feeling of cultural superiority.

Clearly, it struck a chord with settlers, traders, farmers, Democratic politicians and railroad-company owners.

Not everyone subscribed to the notion of a 'manifest destiny' for the US, however, and opposed to it were Native Americans, African Americans, Abolitionists and a number of politicians.

When expansion overseas beckoned, the Republicans justified it in terms of the 'new manifest destiny', once again relating to America's national identity and a feeling it was doing right by the world.

With the population mushrooming – a national figure of 35,700,000 in 1865 nearly tripled before the outbreak of the First World War – there was enough support for America's 'manifest destiny' to make it visible in history as it unfolded.

A new age of prosperity was ushered in when two locomotives met at the completion of the single track transcontinental railroad in 1869. The event also served to heighten a national sense of entitlement that shadowed the country's future conduct.

THE TRANSCONTINENTAL RAILROAD

Opening a railroad that linked America's east and west coasts would inevitably yield new wealth.

The idea was nothing new. A cross-continental railroad was suggested as early as 1836 at a time when it took six months to make the journey. Almost a decade later, wealthy entrepreneur Asa Whitney preached: 'It will bring the world together as one nation; allow us to traverse the globe in thirty days, civilize and Christianize mankind and place us in the centre of the world, compelling Europe on one side and Asia and Africa on the other to pass through us.'

After it opened in 1869, it didn't disappoint. In 1866, the estimated value of precious metals mined in the Pacific states and territories topped $100 million, a quarter of which came from California. The railroad would now bring those metals direct to eastern seaboard markets.

And in the first shipment of freight on the railroad heading east was a consignment from Japan.

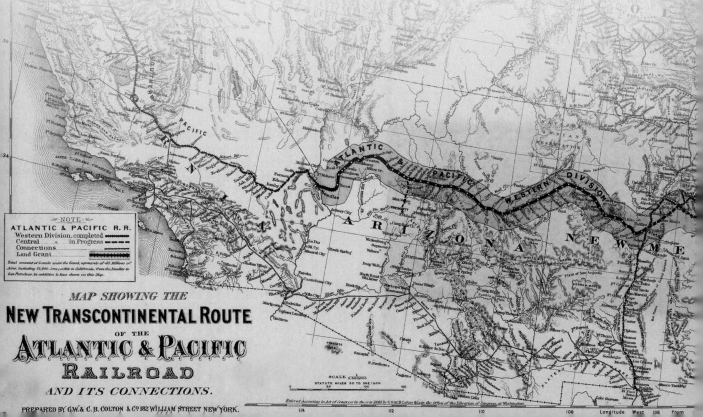

This had been the dream when Leland Stanford dug the first earth at the western end of the Central Pacific on a drizzly 8 January 1863. The Union Pacific, working from east to west, started track laying in 1865.

German and Italian immigrants may well have sat in their European homes reading about the opportunities linked to railroad construction before deciding to make the trip across the Atlantic.

But it was the Chinese, or 'celestials' as they were known, who in great numbers endured high winds, rain, drifting snow, unmitigated sunshine and dust storms whipping across treeless plains during the construction.

Thanks in great part to their labours, the US outstripped Britain in industrial production during the 1880s. Soon after, the US could boast a railroad network rather than a series of disjointed lines.

The successful transcontinental line spawned other projects, like this plan which was agreed by Congress in 1866. However, blighted by financial difficulties, the central portion was never built and the company operated in two segments.

LAND GRANTS

Crossing the continent with multiple railroad lines was top of the political agenda even while the Civil War raged.

When hostilities ended, there was still enthusiasm for the endeavour among those who theorized about the benefits it would bring, usually from the safety of Washington. However, among potential investors there were doubts.

The routes scythed through Native American territory, and some of the tribes posed a threat. Meanwhile, vast tracts of land were virtually empty, so where would paying passengers for the railroad come from?

Previously inert on infrastructure projects, the Federal government led by Republicans had already responded to this dilemma by instituting a scheme of land grants back in 1850, when the Illinois Central was given assistance. Prior to that, land grants had been given to help canals and wagon roads get established.

Before the Civil War, Iowa, Mississippi, Michigan, Wisconsin and Florida took advantage of the land-grant deal. Afterwards, it was primarily states that straddled the proposed transcontinental lines. There's no doubt it was an incentive to railroad builders – who also received loans for laying tracks – and for settlers.

LAND GRANTS

Before the land grants scheme was halted in 1871, it's believed 180 million acres (73 million hectares) were distributed, although not all would be used. Initially worth about one dollar an acre, the value of the land was hiked by the proposal to lay tracks to $2.81. By selling the land to settlers at its new value, railroads helped to raise capital for construction costs. For their part, settlers felt more confident when they saw rail links to the rest of the country hammered into the earth.

The biggest allocations went to Montana, which received 14.7 million acres, while California benefitted from 11.5 million acres. It wasn't given in strips but in squares, so the map

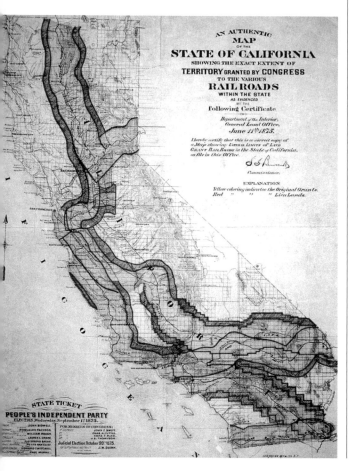

California benefitted from land grants, with new railroad tracks encouraging greater numbers of settlers to the under-developed region.

THINKING BIG

In the 1884 election, the Democrats hoped to skewer Republican chances with the accusation that the public domain had been 'squandered' through land grants. To make the point, Democrats drew up a map that exaggerated the amount of land distributed by a factor of four. Inadvertently, the map became a teaching tool in American schools for 60 years, and during that time pupils were taught that the better part of Iowa had been gifted to railroad companies. The error was only discovered and rectified in the 1940s.

Democratic party propaganda was taught in schools as fact for years before someone realized there was a significant problem with the maths.

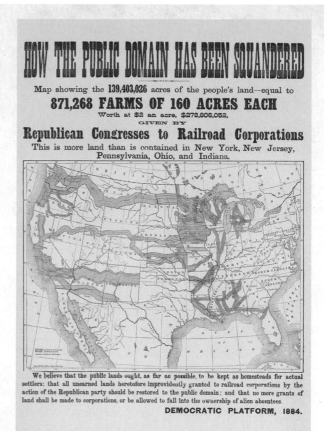

HOW THE PUBLIC DOMAIN HAS BEEN SQUANDERED

Map showing the 139,403,026 acres of the people's land—equal to

871,268 FARMS OF 160 ACRES EACH

Worth at $2 an acre, $278,806,052.

GIVEN BY

Republican Congresses to Railroad Corporations

This is more land than is contained in New York, New Jersey, Pennsylvania, Ohio, and Indiana.

We believe that the public lands ought, as far as possible, to be kept as homesteads for actual settlers; that all unearned lands heretofore improvidently granted to railroad corporations by the action of the Republican party should be restored to the public domain; and that no more grants of land shall be made to corporations, or be allowed to fall into the ownership of alien absentees.

DEMOCRATIC PLATFORM, 1884.

of ownership around railroad lines resembled a chessboard. The government could still cash in on further sales as neighbourhoods expanded.

In addition to Federal land, known as 'the public domain', the railroad companies also received allocations from the individual states, to build stations and interconnecting lines.

The terms were undoubtedly generous – though they hardly represented a bonanza for railroad companies, whose building costs through mountainous regions were high – and sufficient to entice the Central Pacific Railroad and the Union Pacific Railroad to build the first transcontinental railroad.

Later analysis points to the fact that only 18,500 miles (29,800 km) of railroad track was built as a result of land grants and loans – just

8 per cent of the total constructed between 1860 and 1920.

The scheme came in for criticism, especially when corruption linked to railroad companies became public, like the Credit Mobilier scandal. But it did succeed in stimulating settlement.

Conditions attached to the loans usually resulted in repayment, as the track acted as collateral. And when they were up and running, the railroads had to carry mail, government passengers and freight at special rates. If the proposed railroad line didn't appear, well, the land was simply returned to the government. It's thought the final total that went to railroad companies amounted to 131 million acres (53 million hectares), representing 7 per cent of the US at that time.

CRAZY JUDAH & THE BIG FOUR

In the absence of a railroad, travelling across America was a strenuous affair. It involved taking a ship around the treacherous southern tip of South America, with its attendant hazards, or cutting through Panama's swamps to reach the Pacific from the Atlantic, partially crossed by rail in 1855. A last alternative was the least popular: lumbering along in a wagon train for six months across the largely deserted interior.

This fired the zeal of Theodore Judah (1826–63), an engineer from Connecticut who easily visualized all the positives after he arrived in California in 1854. The state, newly aligned to the US, was full of opportunity, not least with the on-going gold rush.

He was so evangelical in recruiting support for the notion of a railroad that he was nicknamed 'Crazy Judah'. But he amounted to more than just big talk. It was he who built the Sacramento Valley Line in 1856, the first west of the Missouri.

When he wasn't lobbying government, he sought private investment. Together with a friend, Dr Daniel Strong, he mapped out the best route through the Sierra Nevada and began planning the Central Pacific Railroad of California.

Attracting the necessary pledges of cash to be incorporated under California law seemed an insurmountable hurdle until Judah met four men at a hardware store in Sacramento in June 1861.

FOUR STOREKEEPERS SPOT AN OPENING

Leland Stanford (1824–93), Charles Crocker (1822–88), Mark Hopkins (1813–78) and Collis P. Huntington (1821–1900) were men of modest means but became known as 'the big four', thanks to their association with the Central Pacific (CP).

All had been born on the east coast but migrated to California, ending up as successful storekeepers. Indeed, Stanford was elected as governor of (sparsely populated) California, the same year the Central Pacific was named by Lincoln as the company building the railroad east out of Sacramento.

Availing themselves of government land grants and loans, they also sought extra capital from a bonds issue. Mimicking the shenanigans that marked Doc Durant's leadership of the Union Pacific, Crocker left the group to start a contractor's business, which was awarded all the work generated.

The four stayed loyal to one another – for the duration of the project at least. Huntington said: 'We were successful, we four, because of our teamwork. Each complemented the other in something the other lacked.'

JUDAH JETTISONED

Alas, that teamwork did not extend to Judah, who vocalized his concerns about the way

'UNSEEN AND UNHEARD'

After his death, Judah's widow Anna complained that afterwards he was 'unseen [and] unheard' when the story of the Central Pacific was related. However, the American Society of Civil Engineers paid tribute to his contribution. 'Judah was . . . [CP's] founder and most influential advocate and it was largely through his manifold talents apart from engineering that a transcontinental railroad was recognized of national importance by Congress.'

Leland Stanford was drawn to California by the gold rush and ended up as California's governor.

Store keeper Mark Hopkins was known for being thrifty and became the CP treasurer.

Charles Crocker ostensibly left the quartet that backed the CP to form a construction company.

Collis Potter Huntington, the most ruthless of the four, went on to establish the Southern Pacific.

the Big Four's scheme was being managed, having hoped for a more public-spirited approach. In the summer of 1863 he was eased out with a parting payment of $100,000 for the stock he owned.

Outraged, Judah vowed to take control of the company once more, leaving California to find new financiers. Unfortunately, on his trip back to the east coast through Panama he contracted yellow fever and died.

WORKING ON THE CENTRAL PACIFIC

Tracklayers were hard to find on America's west coast. Most men who headed in that direction sought the better opportunities that gold mining appeared to offer.

Having just 800 men at his disposal when he needed several thousand, Charles Crocker employed a gang of Chinese labourers. They didn't seem the most promising material as all were short and slight. But, reasoned Crocker, the Chinese had built a Great Wall so must have some aptitude for construction.

Previously, Chinese labourers had been used on the California Central Railroad when it was built in 1850. Even so, Central Pacific construction superintendent James H. Strobridge was reluctant to hire them – despite the ill-discipline of the Irish workforce.

But Chinese workers soon proved themselves energetic and reliable, so much so that Crocker went first to San Francisco and in 1865 to Guangdong (Canton) to recruit more.

When construction was at its busiest, the CP employed a workforce of 10,000 – and about 90 per cent were Chinese.

Symbolically, a golden spike was used to complete the transcontinental line.

TERMS OF EMPLOYMENT

Distinctive for their wide-brimmed basket hats, the Chinese labourers worked from sunrise to dusk, six days a week for $30 to $35 paid in gold every month.

They became renowned for precariously swinging against granite rock faces in canvas seats, chipping at the rock and planting explosives to make headway.

A superintendent later said: 'I never saw a better working gang of men than they are. They are a class of people that do not drink and you can depend on them every day unless they are sick.'

For refreshment, they had lukewarm tea from a 40-gallon whisky barrel – and the boiled water used to make it kept those who drank it safe from dysentery. It was one man's role to replenish the barrel regularly, carrying fresh tea in old powder kegs suspended on each end of a bamboo pole perched on his shoulders.

The company provided 1lb (450g) of fish or meat and 1lb of rice, 5 ounces (140g) of vegetables and half an ounce (14g) of tea a day to each man at cost price. Men were organized into gangs numbering about 30, and each gang had a cook whom they paid from their wages. The cook would transform dried ingredients bought in San Francisco into a traditional feast.

Chinese workers washed before dinner, even in the spartan conditions of the Sierra, and sometimes smoked opium on Saturday nights.

Although Chinese workers were unsung heroes, at least one journalist observed how they were treated like slaves. Other immigrants in similar roles received the same pay but were also given board.

SILENT STRIKE

In 1867, Chinese workers went on strike, demanding $40 a month and a shorter working day. There was silence rather than violence from the workforce who remained inside their camps. Crocker responded by cutting off supplies. Within a week, the starving workers agreed to return to work for the same money, paying a fine for their actions.

It's thought some 1,500 Chinese workers died during the construction of the transcontinental railroad through heat, illness, rock slides or avalanches, although exact records weren't kept. Buried in trackside graves, their bones were later taken back to China.

Construction camps, like this one for CP workers somewhere in America's interior, lacked comfort.

THANKLESS TASK

Vile prejudice dogged the Chinese both at railroad construction sites and in San Francisco, where white workers, who feared their jobs were being stolen, rioted. Abuse directed towards Chinese people in the street was commonplace. In 1869 – the year the railroad was finished – a Chinese man was stoned to death in San Francisco by 'a mob of half-grown boys and Christian schoolchildren', according to a local newspaper. Further immigration from China was finally halted by the 1882 Chinese Exclusion Act, which effectively remained in force until the Second World War.

SNOW SHEDS

The winter of 1866–67 was one of the worst. Armed with the latest meteorological instruments, the superintendent registered 44 separate storms, varying between a short squall and a two-week blizzard. On one occasion, snow fell for four and a half days, depositing 6-ft (1.8-m) drifts that were perpetually whipped up by harsh winds. Workers who didn't die of cold risked perishing in avalanches. Total snowfall recorded that winter was 40 ft (12 m).

With admirable dedication, the Central Pacific workers made tunnels under the snow between

their shanty settlements and work sites. But it was difficult to bring in supplies. Every man spent most of his eight-hour shift wielding a shovel to ease access.

If it was arduous for workers, the CP hierarchy knew it would be hazardous for locomotives when they were finally running. There followed a series of experiments in ways to keep the snow off the tracks.

The first permanent snow sheds, built in the Sierras between 1868 and 1869 to help protect the line from harsh weather conditions, were also used by workers for shelter.

The long, timbered corridors used more than 200,000 cubic yards (153,000 cubic metres) of timber and stretched for 37 miles (59 km). Dubbed 'the longest barn in the world', the snow sheds were so effective the idea was soon borrowed by European railroad designers as well as those in Canada and Japan struggling with the same climatic issue.

EARLY EXPLOSIVES

During these winter snows, railroad workers were also tackling the 1,660 ft (506 m) long Summit Tunnel, the most challenging of fifteen on the route.

From early 1867, progress improved markedly with the arrival of nitroglycerin, made on site by chemist James Howden. Trials in transporting the newly marketed erratic explosive had resulted in deaths on board ships bound for California, at shipping offices and en route

Opposite: Snow sheds straddling the tracks enabled train services to operate even in the harshest winter weather. This engraving is taken from an 1874 handbook for settlers.

PEACEFUL PASSES

CP workers had few difficulties with aggression from Native Americans. This may have been because they were encountering Shoshoni and Paiute tribes, typically less warlike than some others. Railroad management also distributed free travel passes to the Native Americans, enabling them to hitch a ride in freight wagons on passing services. Sometimes, there were also gifts of alcohol designed to nullify opposition.

to the construction site, and its carriage was finally banned. So, instead, Howden shipped its components to the tunnel, where he blended the necessary concoction.

Fearing for his own life in the face of the volatile substances, he took to drink and left obliging Chinese workers – adept at using gunpowder since childhood – to carry out the explosive procedures.

Nitroglycerin increased the progress 124 ft (38 m) below the surface by more than 50 per cent. The following year, the more stable dynamite was invented.

Although the Central Pacific had enjoyed a head start over the Union Pacific, the granite peaks of the Sierra Nevada pegged their construction back to 100 miles (161 km) by the end of 1867.

But, once through this mountainous hurdle, the Central Pacific track layers picked up the pace, crossing Nevada and reaching the Utah border in 1868.

BUFFALO KILL

While Central Pacific workers were battling the snows, for Union Pacific men there was jeopardy of a different kind. Irish immigrant workers and Civil War veterans grading its line grew to dread the yelp of aggressive Native Americans, galloping towards them with tomahawk in hand.

Railroad workers were armed and often guarded by small units of the US cavalry, and the number of attacks by Plains Indians was relatively small. But when these did occur they generated widespread fear by becoming headline news.

One of the most notorious incidents was on 6 August 1867, when a freight train heading to Lexington, Nebraska, was ambushed by a party of Cheyenne and several men were killed. Although he had been scalped, telegraph repairman William Thompson survived, and walked 4 miles (6.5 km) to raise the alarm, hair in hand.

When a surgeon couldn't re-attach his top knot, Englishman Thompson sailed home, where he charged people to view it, before sending the hairpiece back to America, where it became a museum piece.

US GOVERNMENT VS NATIVE AMERICANS

Native Americans had good reason to be hostile. A huge area of their extensive territories had already been swallowed up by the US government. Worse was to come.

To punish the tribes that would not fall into line, the government developed a policy of eradicating the buffalo herds upon which all Native Americans relied.

Without them, even the most belligerent were more likely to acquiesce to white man's rule. Consequently, the army was encouraged to kill buffalo, and all efforts at a Federal level to conserve the herds were rejected.

Before intrusion, herds were some 60 million strong. The number killed by tribesmen was relatively small and every bit of the buffalo was put to good use.

The skull became a religious altar, horns were carved into implements, bones became arrowheads and dice, stomachs were dried out for use as buckets, while sinews were bow strings. Buffalo hides were used for tepees. The tail was a brush or whip, and the teeth were used for ornamentation or ceremonial rattles. Buffalo meat was eaten and the dung was used to fuel fires.

Buffalo hunters accessed the vast herds by train, often firing from the comfort of the carriage.

Buffalo Bill is best remembered for his Wild West show, featuring Sitting Bull some 15 years after the bloody Battle of Little Big Horn.

SHARPSHOOTERS ON RAILS

With the coming of the railroad, the killing of buffalo dramatically escalated. Swathes of animals were killed for sport by white men wielding powerful rifles from carriage windows. To the horror of Native Americans, the carcasses were left to rot where they fell.

Buffalo were also slaughtered to provide food for railroad workers. Buffalo Bill Cody (1846–1917) was employed by the Kansas Pacific

LAST STAND

The most celebrated American Indian victory over the US Cavalry was the Battle of Little Big Horn in 1876, also known as Custer's Last Stand. It happened in Montana, six years before railroads reached the state.

George Custer (1839–76) pitched 600 soldiers into battle without realizing that 1,200 Sioux and Cheyenne warriors awaited them. The tribes, led by Crazy Horse (1840–77) and Sitting Bull (1831–90), had been ordered to a reservation by the US government but had refused to leave what they considered to be sacred ground.

The rout inflicted by the Native Americans inflamed the US Army, which redoubled efforts to contain Native Americans, who within five years were forced to surrender.

Railroad to do just this, and he killed more than 4,000 in just 18 months.

Railroad companies shared the government's ambition to substantially reduce numbers in free-ranging herds as the animals posed a threat to locomotives by blocking the line. Farmers, too, wanted the land clear of buffalo – properly called bison – so they could graze their own stock.

There's a theory that diseased Texan cattle driven forward to either feed railroad builders or heading for Chicago's meat packers played a part in the buffalo's demise.

By the turn of the twentieth century, buffalo numbers had declined to a few thousand.

HELL ON WHEELS

As railroad workers progressed into America's open spaces they were shadowed by a curious entourage.

Purveyors of drink, gambling and sex travelled in their wake to establish pop-up communities dubbed 'Hell on Wheels', primarily designed to relieve working men of their money.

There were, of course, few pre-existing settlements for the track layers to visit. Accordingly, those who initiated 'Hell on Wheels' took a 100 ft (30 m) long tent to the site of a new railroad town, as a portable saloon. Muddy streets invariably nicknamed 'Rat Row' soon filled with shacks or tents with wooden facades that offered dancing, prostitutes, food, alcohol and accommodation – all lucrative outlets.

Usually, railroad workers were also in the company of more upright citizens, including teachers and shopkeepers seizing the chance to begin a new community that would be

Bear River City in Wyoming was another 'Hell on Wheels' town, which had 200 inhabitants in 1867 when this photo was taken.

serviced by the railroad. Doctors and dentists also made the trip, confident of trade among men isolated from basic services for months at a time. There was even a newspaper tracking the railroad, *The Frontier Index*.

However, no trappings of respectability could stop a raft of criminal activity taking place, and general depravity became a hallmark of such colonies.

ROWDY RAILROAD TOWNS

The first such town to appear was Fort Kearny in Nebraska, in August 1866. As the rails passed Fort Kearny, the components of 'Hell of Wheels' moved on to North Platte, also Nebraska, and then to Julesburg in Colorado.

As Major Henry C. Parry made his way to a Colorado military post, he found that miners and frontier folk, driven back by Native Americans, had congregated at North Platte. 'They were having a good time gambling, drinking and shooting each other,' he observed.

A newspaper editor who saw the anarchy unfolding at North Platte came up with the label 'Hell on Wheels'.

Sometimes, there was a sense of permanency from the start. Grenville M. Dodge (1831–1916) picked the site of Cheyenne, today the capital of Wyoming, as a depot in July 1867. It was named for the Native American nation that loomed large in the making of the railroad.

Initially, it took on all the characteristics of a Wild West town, the *Cheyenne Leader* newspaper publishing a column headlined 'Last night's shootings'.

GRENVILLE M. DODGE

Dodge began his career with the Illinois Central Railroad in 1852, and spent some time on the Rock Island Railroad before being asked by Durant to survey a route from Council Bluffs in Iowa to the foot of the Rockies. By chance, having been pursued by Native Americans, he discovered the most promising path. During the Civil War he served in the Union Army with distinction before re-joining the Union Pacific, despite having grave doubts about its management.

BAD BEHAVIOUR OUTLAWED

However, Dodge was keenly aware of how the rate of murders was taking its toll on worker numbers – with one figure pointing to four murders for every accidental death among the construction team.

He told 'General' Jack Casement (1829–1909), a loyal and popular employee of the Union Pacific, to clean up the behaviour of railroad men at play. After a crackdown, behaviour in Cheyenne became tolerable.

It was a similar story in Laramie, which began as a tent city but rapidly developed after the first train service reached there in May 1868. Rogue elements were finally hanged by a newly appointed 'vigilance committee'. Improvement followed so rapidly that the following year five women in the town served on a jury for the first time in American history.

THE RACE TO PROMONTORY

A sledgehammer symphony rang out across the plains as the railroad builders inexorably moved towards one another, planning to meet at Promontory Summit in Utah.

Each spike was struck three times as the track layers hit a rhythm. Ten spikes were used for each section of rail and there were 400 rails to a mile (248 to a kilometre). It was a race to the finish.

On 28 April 1869, the Central Pacific labourers laid 10 miles (16 km) of track in a single day, working at walking pace to achieve the target.

After one railroad stretching across the US was completed in 1869, other equally ambitious construction projects followed in its wake.

Between 5 am and 7 pm, about 400 men in perpetual motion laid 3,520 rails held by 55,000 spikes.

One cavalry man who witnessed it remarked: 'It was like an army marching over the ground and leaving a track built behind them.'

Driving them on was Crocker, who'd made a $10,000 bet with Durant of the UP about rates of progress that he was not intending to lose.

TELEGRAPHED TRIUMPH

Ten days later the ceremony marking the completion of the project was held, with two locomotives strategically posed nose-to-nose for photographic purposes.

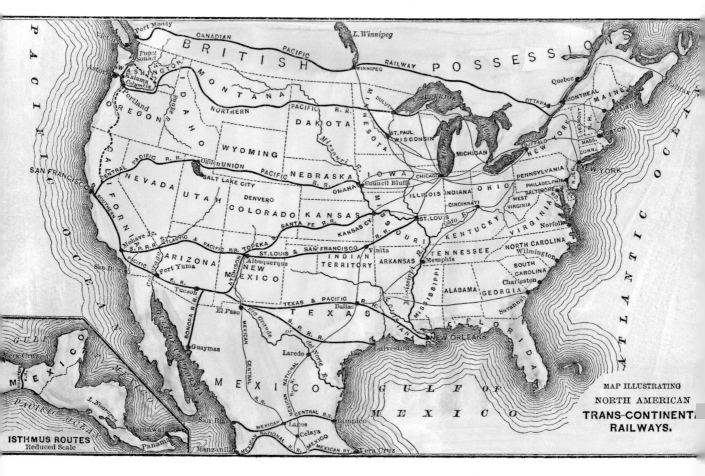

A silver hammer was wielded against a golden spike first by Stanford, who missed, then by Durant, who also missed. Grenville Dodge then stepped forward to complete the line.

Live news of the event was relayed across America by telegraph, a wire having been attached to both spike and hammer. It was rapidly followed by the word 'Done'. On the signal, cannons were fired simultaneously in New York and San Francisco as the nation celebrated what was sure to be a more economically buoyant future.

By any standards, it was a feat worthy of a national jamboree. In six years the railroad companies had covered some 2,000 miles (3,218 km) without the benefit of mechanical tools.

As far as the CP was concerned, all the materials had been shipped from the east coast via the tip of South America. Excavation rubble was carried away by hand until a stripped-down locomotive from Judah's Sacramento line was moved in to help. It was later joined by other engines as the single-track line grew. In addition, CP had to tunnel for a total of 6,213 ft (1,893 m).

As for the Union Pacific, its building schedule was mauled by the Civil War, with the conflict causing manpower shortages and crippling inflation. Only when the war finished were there sufficient labourers to put track on the ground. Both companies were virtually broken by the costs.

TEETHING TROUBLES

When the lines were linked, they immediately advertised a trip that took less than four days. The CP was charging $50 for a ticket from Sacramento to Council Bluffs. Travellers paid a further $123.50 to go on to New York. (The link between Sacramento and San Francisco was by ferry.)

The service was prone to breakdowns, with hastily laid track proving a weak point. Jay Gould took control of loss-making Union Pacific in

DEAL OR NO DEAL

Durant arrived late to the ceremony at Promontory Summit, held up by striking Irish workers who claimed they hadn't been paid.

It wasn't just this section of the workforce to which Durant owed money. A large number of Mormons had worked for the UP in Utah, in a deal brokered by their leader Brigham Young. Afterwards, he said he was owed $1 million by Durant and in the end he settled for $700,000-worth of railroad equipment, as Young remained determined to link his 60,000-strong settlement at Salt Lake City to the new network.

1873, admitting: 'Railroads had got to be a sort of hobby with me. I didn't care about the money I made, I took the road more as a plaything to see what I could do with it.'

In 1883, when the first locomotive to travel on the Northern Pacific Railroad got underway, there were more celebrations.

BIGGER, NOT BETTER

A single ribbon of rail laid across the continent was never going to be enough for this striving nation, but unravelling the stories of the remaining transcontinental railroads would not be straightforward. In an era of corporate railroad companies with a colossal sense of entitlement, the genesis of each became increasingly hard to discern as small railroads were swallowed up by bigger ones – which then amalgamated with others. Throw into the mix a series of line-leasing arrangements and the picture becomes hazier still.

The Northern Pacific's colourful story helps to illustrate the point. After the Philadelphia banking house run by Jay Cooke (1821–1905) sold bonds to help pay for track from Lake Superior to Puget Sound, the future looked bright. Cooke, who helped finance the Union during the Civil War, was on a personal quest to create better links for Duluth, Minnesota, which he felt had the makings of a major city.

Work had begun in earnest in 1873, when rumours emerged that Cooke had over-capitalized. As a result, the Northern Pacific collapsed, Cooke was made bankrupt and the 1873 Panic ensued. The ramifications were immense, with a 10-day closure of Wall Street and widespread loan foreclosures.

Still, the railroad was taken over and work on the 1,900-mile (3,058-km) line restarted, using imported steel rails. A second bankruptcy brought James J. Hill to the table of the Northern Pacific board.

The western section of the Northern Pacific was completed despite monumental boardroom disruption followed by bankruptcies.

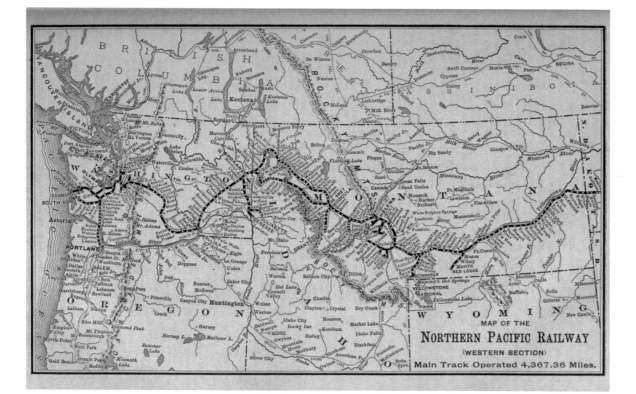

TRANSCONTINENTAL COOPERATION

Hill already had control of the Great Northern network of railroads, but neither that, nor the North Pacific, had a connection with the railroad hub at Chicago. Hill tried to take over the Chicago, Burlington & Quincy Railroad to remedy the omission – but so did Harriman, by now in charge of the Union Pacific (see page 152). Peace was brokered by J. P. Morgan in the usual way, in order to side-step another national financial blip and any undue competition. An era of cooperation coinciding with the start of the twentieth century and encompassing the Northern Pacific, the Great Northern and the Milwaukee Road began.

HUNTINGTON'S PRICE HIKE

Completion of the Central Pacific left 'the big four' (see page 190) thirsting for more. Further railroad building in California left them wealthy men, with more than enough means to take over the Southern Pacific, founded in San Francisco in 1865.

At Southern Pacific, Collis Huntington made few friends when he organized the purchase of numerous small lines in California then imposed a 100 per cent rate rise on its customers.

Similarly, Huntington promised settlers land in the SP curtilage for one price, then hiked it dramatically when they arrived. A Settlers' League was formed to sue the SP, which further antagonized the settlers by changing the course of a planned railroad line, leaving them isolated.

When railroad agents turned up on 11 May 1880, apparently to evict the settlers, there was a violent clash that left seven dead. The incident stoked anti-railroad feeling nationwide. Although the SP effectively won relevant court cases – with people on its land forced to buy it at premium rates – it lost public sympathy, with Huntington

FILLING UP FAST

When *Appleton's* was compiled at the end of the 1870s, the Northern Pacific Railroad had already completed the first leg of 'another great highway' across America, between Duluth and Bismarck, striking 'right across the centre of Minnesota and Dakota and [traversing] the richest portions which are fast filling up with settlers.'

En route, passengers were ideally placed to see the cascades and rapids of the St Louis River 'justly regarded as among the wonders of American scenery. Also worthy of notice ... are the lofty trestle bridges by which the railroad crosses several deep ravines.'

a focus for bile in newspapers for his apparent unfettered greed.

SP lines were etched on the map – including some narrow-gauge tracks in mining areas – until Union Pacific took control in 1900.

Wall Street panics linked to the railroad business became benchmarks of the nineteenth century. The one inspired by Jay Cooke's financial collapse was more far-reaching than most.

REGULATION & RAILROADS

Bribery, corruption, inducements and fraud were part and parcel of business during the gilded age.

As this era gave way to the twentieth century, there was a perceptible change in the ether as tolerance for big business and its self-serving ways began to wear thin.

Inequity in society was a powerful motivator for fresh thinking. For years, it seemed, political initiative to trim corporate greed was lacking. Although vast sums of public money had been swallowed up by the pugnacious railroad companies, no laws had been passed to keep their power in check.

Any small steps taken against railroad companies were soon thwarted by legal action in a sector of industry that, during the good times, appeared to be dripping with wealth.

By a quirk of fate, Theodore Roosevelt came to the presidency with the intention of making significant changes. He realized that his declared aims, to introduce laws that would protect ordinary people rather than fat cats, would find fertile ground among the electorate.

When his two terms in office came to an end in 1909, Roosevelt created the short-lived Progressive Party to continue a programme of reform. After an assassination attempt, he told reporters he felt 'as fit as a Bull Moose', and his party became known by that name.

In fact, the industrial landscape was changing, fast. Roosevelt's new party didn't last – but nor did the supremacy of the railroads.

Theodore Roosevelt was an unexpected resident of the White House, moving in after the assassination of William McKinley. A popular figure, he became the first American to win the Nobel Peace Prize for his mediation in the Russo-Japanese War in 1905.

THE CARPETBAGGERS

They were branded rogues from the north – profiteers set on exploiting post-Civil War reconstruction for personal gain. The prospect of building new railroads in defeated Confederate states, aided by fat government cheques, was a powerful lure. And with corruption endemic among lawmakers, fortunes were there for the taking.

'Carpetbaggers' earned their nickname from a cheap, distinctive style of luggage dubbed the 'carpet bag'. The term was initially coined to scorn political outsiders 'parachuted' into public office across the south by a Republican Congress determined to enforce the north's hard-won civil rights for slaves. Yet, it soon encompassed any stranger arriving at a southern railroad station with a suitcase.

To portray all these newcomers as ruthless entrepreneurs or political careerists would be a travesty; many were teachers or professionals with a genuine desire to export the north's prosperity. Indeed, some were former Unionist soldiers who, having 'discovered' the southern states, had fallen in love with them. But rogues there undoubtedly were.

In the rush to rebuild the south, Republican-controlled state governments had spent on a grand scale, incurring huge debts. The money was aimed at inducing corporate America to renew and extend the railroads, and it clearly worked: by 1877, the south's total railroad mileage had gone from just over 9,000 to almost 14,000 miles (14,500 km to 22,500 km).

Yet, it was an industry largely run by northern, often Republican, tycoons. In 1870, they owned 21 per cent of the network; within two decades the figure was 88 per cent. So frenzied was this dash-for-track that, when the voters of Arkansas were asked to decide on some railroad plans, detail was superfluous. Ballot papers were marked simply: 'For Railroads' and 'Against Railroads'.

BRIBERY AND CORRUPTION

The bribes that tainted American public life around this time were probably no worse in the southern states than anywhere else. But the financial crash of 1873, seeded in the north, and the prolonged depression that followed, allowed southern Democrats to portray corruption as a northern evil.

Carpetbagger Republican states began to fall to the Democrats and, indeed, the 1876 presidential election would have been won by Democrat Samuel Tilden but for some audacious vote-rigging by Republican governments in Louisiana and South Carolina.

RECONSTRUCTION ROGUE EXTRAORDINAIRE

So notorious a rogue was General Milton S. Littlefield, he became known as 'Prince of the Carpetbaggers'.

He was something of a Republican hero, having marshalled the political forces that helped get his friend Abraham Lincoln elected in 1860, and later serving with distinction for the Unionist cause. In 1863, he even set up Lincoln's 'Abolitionist Eden' on the Sea Islands off the Carolinas, training former slaves to be Unionist soldiers.

After the war, Littlefield made good money in the Philadelphia lumber business before arriving in North Carolina in 1867 with a tasty scam.

Having bought up pre-war state bonds (which had crashed in price), he persuaded the legislature to redeem them at face value. With the help of local banker George Swepson, he then took a controlling share in the Western North Carolina Railroad, doling out some $200,000 in political bribes to ensure a steady flow of state rail subsidies.

For two years, Littlefield played the state for cash. Basing himself in a bar, he connived with speculators to create grand and fraudulent railroad projects – securing an astonishing $28 million in public funds. He bought a newspaper to influence events, but was too canny to hold public office himself. Instead, his power flowed from the politicians – both Republican and Democrat – who had pocketed his bribes.

A RUINED RASCAL

Estimates vary, but Littlefield and his business partner Swepson are thought to have defrauded North Carolina of at least $4 million. They briefly expanded into Florida, but by the time of the Black Friday financial panic of 1869 the game was up. North Carolina put a price on Littlefield's head and indicted him for fraud.

Although he was never convicted, his reputation was shot and the 1873 stock-market meltdown finally destroyed his empire. In 1870, the Western North Carolina Railroad was bought by the state for $665,000.

By 1877, when this Thomas Nast cartoon was published, carpet baggers were derided figures for what were deemed faux attempts to rejuvenate the defeated south.

MORE "PACIFICATION."
THE "CARPET-BAGGERS" ARE PROTECTED: THAT'S A COMFORT.

GRANGER RAILROADS

Farmers were among the first to feel the chilling effects of the railroads' iron grip on pricing, and it was from the rural communities that the first call for controls was heard.

For most, there were no options to take their harvests to a marketplace other than by railroad. Only a few were placed to take advantage of canals or rivers.

Farmers started to organize as early as 1867, when Oliver Hudson Kelley from Minnesota launched the National Grange of the Order of Patrons of Husbandry.

At first, it was for social and educational purposes, with Kelley hoping to heal divisions caused by the Civil War. But it wasn't long before their ranks were more than three-quarters of a million strong, and the group adopted a more political stance. When farmers – and their wives – met at Grange halls, there was one topic that merited more complaint than most: the rates they were charged by railroads, which raised those prices at will and with impunity.

ELEVATED CHARGES

Wheat farmers were particularly hard hit, for railroads not only charged them for using the rails but also the elevators standing at the side of railroads, where grain was collected before being sold.

Elevators were immense structures, called 'prairie skyscrapers' or 'sentinels of the prairie', initially made from wood but later constructed in concrete. The distinctive design incorporated silos, a scale room, an office and room for a mechanized drive belt to take delivery of grain. At first, the drive belt was powered by horses, who gave way to steam engines, which were themselves made obsolete by gas and electric engines.

Elevators were placed strategically by railroad companies, which had sought to develop towns between 6 and 10 miles apart so farmers could unload their harvests and return home the same day. Despite being a fire risk, the elevators remained a familiar feature of farming life. By the 1880s, Kansas alone had 125 enormous structures dominating local skylines.

GRANGER VS RAILROAD COMPANIES

Between 1869 and 1875, the Granger movement flourished, and encouraged some states to pass laws that regulated train company activity. The Granger Cases were not only supported by farmers but also merchants and others affected. However, some farmers who were not well-served by existing lines opposed hostile action, hoping instead to induce the network to reach them sooner.

WHEAT FEAT

Farmers were witnessing a revolution in agriculture that industrialized their output. In 1855, at Paris's Universal Exhibition, an American threshing machine capable of processing 21 bushels (740 litres) of wheat in half an hour was on display. It bested a rival English machine that could only thresh 11.6 bushels (410 litres) in that time – but both were a considerable improvement on manpower, as a team of six could only manage 1.7 bushels (60 litres).

Flinching in the face of such restrictions, railroad companies, employing the services of expensive lawyers, sought legal redress.

The states involved had imposed restrictions that were, it was claimed, a violation of the American Constitution's 14th Amendment, designed in 1866 to ensure fairness for recently emancipated slaves. For their corporate clients, the lawyers insisted such

state regulation risked denying 'life, liberty or property' to the railroads.

In 1877, the Supreme Court ruled against the corporations, declaring it was a case of public interest rather than any kind of business infringement.

However, in 1886 there was a change of heart in the court room, following a sustained campaign by railroad companies. Powers used in Illinois to curb the Wabash, St Louis & Pacific Railway Company were declared unlawful and, three years later, the court said Federal judges should decide whether railroad rates were reasonable.

An elevator operated by the Union Railroad Elevator Company receiving a grain delivery by ship. On land there were railroad links that helped Ohio's farmers feed the rest of the nation.

OPERATED BY

UNION RAILROAD ELEVATOR COMPANY,

TOLEDO, OHIO.

1882.

Total Capacity, 875,000 bushels.
Receiving Capacity 350 Cars per day.
Shipping Capacity 350 Cars per day.

Marine Receiving and Shipping Capacity,
16,000 Bushels per hour.

RAILROAD RULES

According to railroad millionaire Jay Gould: 'People who think they can regulate all mankind... cause much trouble to both employers and employees by their interference.'

He wasn't alone in believing that big business was best left to its own devices. Government during the gilded age was notoriously ineffective in producing legislation that would either rein in the power of industrialists or improve the circumstances of the poor.

A cartoon marking the creation of the Interstate Commerce Commission, intended to root out punitive practices in the railroad industry, observes the erena was something of a circus.

That was reflected in the overarching 'laissez-faire' approach that politicians of the day adopted, believing that influential economist Adam Smith advocated an entirely 'hands off' style of government. In fact, Smith's economic theories were considerably more sophisticated than this.

Charles Darwin's theory of 'survival of the fittest', a phrase first used by him in 1869, was also taken by robber barons and others as endorsement that their talents at making money classed them as superior, and they expected to be treated as such. Then there was America's much vaunted 'manifest destiny', implying a divine pre-eminence, which happily chimed with railroad company goals.

MAKING FRIENDS AND ENEMIES

Meanwhile, the public at large, and small businesses in particular, were growing increasingly frustrated at the behaviour of railroads.

To curry favour with politicians or anyone else with influence, railroad companies dished out large quantities of free travel passes. Inevitably, this quiet bribery resulted in price rises being paid by ordinary customers. Before the end of the nineteenth century, those using such passes were dubbed 'deadheads' by irate fellow passengers.

James Walker (1820–81), a former railroad president, observed how 'the grant of a free pass to make one friend creates half a dozen enemies.'

SPECIAL RATES FOR THE BIG BOYS

Small businesses faced the inequity of paying more than larger rivals for the carriage of freight. Indeed, rates were so flexible that few railroad companies printed tariffs. There were also pooling agreements that favoured bigger companies.

Bankrupt railroads that continued to operate – of which there was an untold number – were no longer obliged to pay mortgages, and correspondingly lowered their rates. Competition like this was bad news for well-established large companies.

Pooling was intended to ensure an equal distribution of the available business, as companies got together to fix freight rates. It did help smaller railroads survive in turbulent economic times, but it was obviously anti-competitive and increased consumer costs. Large companies could afford to accommodate big shippers who demanded reductions or 'rebates', something a smaller railroad could not do.

FIRST STEPS

In 1887, the Interstate Commerce Commission was formed, the first faltering step towards railroad regulation. It was the earliest independent agency ever established in America, but was still a toothless dog as politicians tried to appease both the railroad companies and the public.

All these issues were fully aired by the 1879 Hepburn Committee report, which unveiled numerous abuses by New York's railroad companies. Giving evidence to the committee, William Vanderbilt admitted that his company granted 6,000 special rates in just six months to keep major shippers happy.

The official seal of the ICC, with its Latin motto which translates as: 'Out of many, there is one'.

THEODORE ROOSEVELT

When two shots rang out in Buffalo, New York, on 6 September 1901, the recently re-elected President William McKinley fell, mortally wounded by a trigger-happy anarchist. As a result, the face of Federal government began to turn a few degrees.

Into McKinley's shoes, as America's 26th president, stepped Theodore Roosevelt (1858–1919). History labels him a progressive politician rather than one rooted in the dubious political practices of the gilded age. And he is heralded for taking action against one of the railroad monopolies.

There's a certain irony in this, for McKinley had been financially backed by J. P. Morgan, Andrew Carnegie and John Rockefeller, who were confident that he would not rock their boats.

On the other hand, McKinley's Democratic rival, William Jennings Bryan (1860–1925), a gifted orator known as 'The Great Commoner', exhibited radical tendencies and exerted huge appeal. There was little doubt he had the appetite to tackle inequities in commerce.

In addition to providing money, the wealthy trio had ensured their workers would vote for McKinley, as company overseers observed which ballot box – one Democratic, one Republican – the employees used. They hadn't reckoned on a third candidate for power.

Roosevelt was uncomfortable with the way railroads were functioning and decided to break up the Northern Securities Company, the arrangement established between Harriman and Hill – who was backed by J. P. Morgan.

Legislation already existed enabling this to happen. The Sherman Antitrust Act of 1890 authorized the Federal government to take proceedings against monopolies that would lead to their dissolution. Until now, it had been used mostly against unions.

In fact, although the monopoly or trust was broken up, its stock didn't change hands so in effect little altered. But it was a warning shot across the bows of the railroads, and owners began to feel the wind of change.

With a new-found reputation as a 'trust-buster', Roosevelt passed laws to quicken the pace of cases mired in the Sherman Act and, with the Elkins Act of 1903, he made another attempt to stop railroad company collusion over prices. Anything that could be deemed a restraint of trade was now unlawful, and could mean a fine of $5,000 and a year in jail.

THE ICC GROWS SOME TEETH

But his most significant victory in pursuit of railroad regulation was the Hepburn Act of 1906, which finally gave substantial powers to the Interstate Commerce Commission to end rebates and free passes. Only railroad employees, the clergy and charity cases would now receive travel chits.

At last, the ICC could itself set maximum rates, so customers were no longer subject to the whims of railroad companies. The ICC was also given access to railroad company books to ensure the new rules were being kept.

The act was named for Republican William Hepburn, from Iowa, who was chair of the House Commerce Commission. It came the same year as the Meat Inspection Act and the Pure Food and Drug Act, both of which were also weighted towards the interests of consumers.

Roosevelt felt a halfway house had been reached, with wholesale exploitation by the railroad companies curbed, but government interference limited. However, shippers felt the act too vague, while railroad companies complained at the way the free market was being manipulated.

In 1910, the Elkins Act was further amended under Roosevelt's successor, William Taft, to permit the ICC to change rail rates on its own initiative. Plans proposed by Taft to permit pooling were dropped at the eleventh hour, after Southern Pacific raised its fares across the board, causing a public outcry. By now, lorries and cars were gaining popularity and the position of the railroads was for the first time coming under threat.

THE CASE FOR THE DEFENCE

Although now cast as villains by the public, railroad companies felt they had immense hurdles strewn in their path. Initially, the men behind the companies had been risk takers, investing time and money in ventures that were by no means guaranteed. Indeed, many men were ruined by their commitment to a railroad blueprint.

Railroad companies had no appetite for rebates and drawbacks, but had been drawn into punishing agreements by powerful corporations in order to maintain business. Income that remained after rebates were paid was split between shareholder dividends, loan repayments, the purchase of new equipment, a wages bill and enhanced safety measures. Profits, they argued, were not a given.

By 1910, when this picture dates from, Roosevelt was out of office and the head of the 'Bull Moose' party.

A SUMMER OF STRIKES

After the financial furore caused by Jay Cooke's bankruptcy in 1873, it took years for the economy to recover.

Railroad families endured pay cuts rather than the rises necessary to keep up with spiralling costs, while unemployment was rife.

Against this backdrop, B&O president John Garrett decided to further slash the wages bill, allegedly out of financial necessity, rather than reduce the dividend paid out to investors – with catastrophic consequences.

A directors' meeting approved a 10 per cent reduction for everyone earning more than a dollar a day, starting from 16 July 1877.

Previous wage cuts by the B&O and other railroads had been introduced without undue consequence. Unions were still in their infancy, and other disputes had been swiftly ended with the use of strike breakers.

But this time, workers were feeling altogether less compliant. They abandoned freight trains, first at Camden Junction then at Martinsburg, West Virginia. State militia men were called in, but failed to dislodge the striking railroadmen, who were by now being supported by a considerable number of townspeople, including women and children. Only when Federal troops were finally summoned to Martinsburg did some 600 blocked trains begin to move.

Strikers reacted angrily when so-called 'scabs' were brought in to drive locomotives, hauling them away. Despite widespread action only limited gains were recorded by the strike.

SUPPORT FOR STRIKERS

But this wasn't the end of it. The strike spread across America's railroad heartlands among 100,000 workers, and in turn found support among miners, mill workers, foundry workers, the jobless and others. Sometimes, it amounted to peaceful protest. In Harrisburg, the local militia gave up their weapons rather than shoot strikers who were friends and neighbours.

But the walkout in Philadelphia, involving men from the Pennsylvania Railroad, was marred by violence. In Pittsburgh, buildings burned as rioters fended off the National Guards, and the ensuing riot left 24 people dead. An already tense stand-off there had been aggravated when one man refused to drive an exceptionally long train, powered by two locomotives but poorly staffed, because he felt it was dangerous.

In Reading, where the railroad company was two months behind in paying its staff, 11 people died in riots. There were clashes in Cumberland, Baltimore, St Louis, Chicago, New York and elsewhere.

In total, more than 100 people died, 1,000 were jailed and up to half the nation's freight trains ground to a halt – although passenger trains weren't targeted.

Without food and money, men could not sustain themselves and their families, and strike action inevitably petered out. On 28 July that year, the *Chicago Times* announced: 'The fight with the Communists is at an end'. *Harper's Weekly* talked in terms of the striking men being 'savages'.

But a few precious concessions had been won. Some of the pay cuts were withdrawn or reduced. At the B&O, hours were shaved and pay improved

GOOD CAUSES?

Theories abounded about why strike fever enveloped America that summer, with most in authority blaming 'Internationalists' and Communists inspired by the Paris Commune, the radical Socialist government that ruled the French capital for a few months in 1871.

Catholic immigrants were also denounced as troublemakers by a largely Protestant establishment. However, welfare issues were at the heart of the issue.

Prior to the strike, the working week was often short, which resulted in skeleton crews manning services. Employers took hazardous shortcuts by economising on staffing levels while workers desperately needed a longer working week to make ends meet.

It's also likely that the unusually hot weather that year made homes more insanitary and caused epidemics of deadly diseases that claimed the lives of frail and infant family members.

in tiny increments. And the strike may have contributed to the 1880 creation of the welfare group, the B&O Employees Relief Association. To any neutral observer, it underscored the industrial muscle that the railroad companies possessed and, conversely, the lack of it enjoyed by working people.

THE PENNSYLVANIA RAILROAD EMPIRE

It wasn't among the first to get going, but the Pennsylvania Railroad became a national giant.

Incorporated in 1846 – a full 16 years after the nation's first locomotives took to the rails – it began as a modest 137-mile (220-km) link between Harrisburg and Philadelphia, with a branch line to Erie. Its first passenger service between Pittsburgh and Philadelphia was up and running in 1848, and Harrisburg was finally reached two years later.

Yet within a few decades the PRR was an institution. The railroad company was part of an industrial jigsaw in the state, interlocking with coal mines and the steel industry.

Tens of thousands of people depended on its success – not only those directly in the pay of the PRR, but others who built locomotives, carriages and signals, the timber businesses supplying sleepers and the foundries providing rails.

At first it was mostly men on the payroll. But, as the company extended, there were jobs for women as telegraphists, clerks and ticket agents. Options for African Americans remained limited. In addition to track laying, they worked as station janitors and dining-coach waiters.

PRR domination was challenged only by the New York Central, associated with the Vanderbilts, and to a lesser degree by the Baltimore & Ohio.

It is fondly remembered for running the Broadway Limited, a plush 16-hour service between New York and Chicago, which took travellers – often featuring A-list Hollywood stars – between the cities in considerable style.

In 1936, elegant corporate branding extended to the locomotives thanks to French-born designer Raymond Loewy (1893–1986), who designed distinctive shark-nosed and torpedo-shaped engines.

Despite its stature, the PRR has not survived, although its demise didn't occur until the 1960s.

A restored Pennsylvania Streamliner #5809, *parked along the railroad station at the North Carolina Transportation Museum.*

J. EDGAR THOMSON

The solid foundation upon which PRR success was built can be attributed to one man, J. Edgar Thomson (1808–74), who steered it to greatness with a prudent blend of investment and innovation.

At his death, 'the Pennsy', as it was affectionately known, had 6,000 miles (9,650 km) of track, paid a pleasing annual dividend after surviving numerous national financial meltdowns, and was the world's largest corporation. One testament |to his triumph was the upward trajectory of company profits. In 1852, when he took over following an ugly boardroom battle, the annual profits were $617,000. When he died, the figure was $8.6 million.

Born into a Pennsylvania Quaker family, Thomson gained a sound understanding of engineering expertise from his father, John, who helped build the Chesapeake & Delaware Canal. He visited England in 1832 to glean more knowledge about railroads, returning to work on Pennsylvania's first public transport system, a concoction of canals and railroads featuring steam engines that hauled carriages up hills, called the Main Line of Public Works.

Following a spell on the Camden & Amboy, he forged ambitious routes for the Georgia Railroad from 1834 before joining the PRR as chief engineer.

He had already begun planning the Horseshoe Curve in the Allegheny Mountains, which has served as his memorial, before being elevated to company president.

LUCKY HORSESHOE

Lauded for being a simple answer to a complex problem, the Horseshoe Curve is a closely drawn loop of 2,375 ft (724 m) of track, built to assist a mountain ascent, with help from Herman Haupt. It rises 1.8 ft in every 100 ft (a gradient of 1.8 per cent).

Its construction saved hours of travelling time. Pennsylvania's first railroads – the Portage Railroad and the Philadelphia & Columbia – had been state funded in 1834 so passengers and freight could travel between

The Horseshoe Curve reflected the style and innovation for which the PRR became renowned.

WILLING AND ABLE

Part of Thomson's legacy was to help daughters of railroad workers killed on duty. In his will, he left a trust to assist bereaved families, and the John Edgar Thomson girls' boarding school was opened in Philadelphia in 1882.

Philadelphia and Pittsburgh on a combination of railroads and canals in about four days, replacing the previous option of 20-day journey by wagon.

But a slick service depended on the canal being free of ice. Rails gradually replaced the canal section, but in 1852 the cumbersome Portage Railway, with its inclined planes, still didn't operate at night. Thomson finally found a swift route through the forested mountains and, after the emblematic Horseshoe Curve was opened in 1854, journey time was reduced to around 15 hours.

It was part of a $2.5 million route between Altoona and Johnstown. The 450, mostly Irish, workers who laboured there were paid $3 a day. At the start of the twentieth century, two extra tracks and an observation platform were added.

The Curve was so iconic that its destruction was planned by Nazi saboteurs in 1942, one of a dozen key sites earmarked.

THOMSON TAKES COMMAND

As company president, Thomson soon bought most of Pennsylvania's pre-existing railroad and canal interests, so he had control of the state's transport network. He then concerned himself with a sensible spread of the company that focused on speed and safety, achieved by way of expert engineering. It was a strategy that propelled profits upwards and took the PRR web into neighbouring states and beyond, until it reached between Chicago and St Louis and encompassed New York.

Thomson made other, less tangible, changes that also marked his tenure with greatness. With Haupt's help, he double-tracked lines to make train timetabling more efficient.

Iron rails were switched for steel. Locomotives were fuelled by coal rather than wood, with Thomson seeing advantages in the proximity of rich coal fields. He established a diverse chain of command that helped as the business rapidly expanded.

MAN OF ACTION

Quiet rather than charismatic, Thomson worked closely with Haupt and later with Thomas A. Scott, whom Haupt had once employed as a freight agent in 1850. A decade later, Scott was vice president.

After his death, Thomson was recalled by one contemporary as reticent and taciturn. 'Actions spoke for him, not words.'

THOMAS A. SCOTT

When Thomson died in 1874, and Thomas A. Scott (1823–81) took the reins at the Pennsylvania Railroad, it was a seamless switch, despite their contrasting characters. But Scott was destined for a roller-coaster term in office.

An 1881 obituary for Scott in the *New York Times* acknowledged that Thomson and Scott worked harmoniously, but drew distinctions between them:

Thomson was acute of intellect but slower in movement and inclined to be conservative. Scott, on the other hand, was quick, impulsive and fond of brilliant moves. The two minds formed an admirable counterpoise.

Thomson thought, weighed, planned and decided after mature deliberation schemes which Scott's impulsive nature grasped at once and when the word was given quickly carried out.

Although he favoured logistics above engineering, most thought Scott, the son of a Scottish-Irish bar owner, was an asset to the Pennsy, as well as being 'affable' and 'unassuming'.

CHEERY BUT CHALLENGING

According to Carnegie, he was the most personable man in America, while former colleague Col John W. Forney described Scott as 'genial, cheerful and buoyant'. Initially, Rockefeller thought him unscrupulous, but later revised his opinions, even when relations between Standard Oil and the Pennsy were strained, calling him 'a great railroad man'.

But that's only half the story. There's no doubt that when charm alone failed, Scott was willing to lobby hard for the interests of the railroad, even resorting to bribery. Abolitionist orator Wendell Phillips was certainly convinced Scott splashed company cash to get his way. 'There is no power in one state to resist such a giant as the Pennsylvania Railroad.'

If the PRR was guilty of bullying the state legislature, so was the steel industry run by Carnegie, the oil business ruled by Rockefeller and the coal kingdom of Frick.

Certainly, the policy of buying, leasing and combining railroads, begun by Thomson, was continued, to the detriment of passenger interests. Scott has since been dubbed the father of the modern corporation for his opaque organization of railroads through holding companies. His reputation has suffered, too, for being secretive about deals.

Scott managed to keep the PRR profitable – but only just. A year before he became president, Jay Cooke's banking and railroad empire collapsed, and its adverse ripple effect would continue throughout Scott's time in the post.

SCOTT THE INTRANSIGENT

Scott was also stung by the 1877 railroad strike, famously complaining that the discontented workers should try 'a rifle diet for a few days and see how they like that kind of bread'. Some years before, as a freight agent, he had worked alongside these workers, yet still chose to impose pay cuts and hazardous working conditions rather than invest in fundamental safety measures. Company losses of some $5 million during the turmoil might have been avoided if he had agreed to talks.

TRANSCONTINENTAL TRIAL

The PRR was not the only challenging railroad company Scott dealt with during the 1870s. Like Jay Gould, he quested for a transcontinental line and alighted on the southernmost option, the lowest and shortest between the oceans. Under his governorship it was known as the Texas & Pacific.

On paper it seemed as though it couldn't fail. Scott hoped to cash in on land grants. The experienced General Dodge was chief engineer. But the era of land grants was coming to an end and, despite a trip to England to seek fresh finance, he found himself in desperate financial difficulties in 1872 when Junius Morgan called in a loan guarantee. To his horror, former protégé Carnegie refused to help.

For a while, Scott clung on to his interests in the T&P at the expense of the Pennsy, although these were later taken over by Jay Gould.

In 1878, he suffered the first of three strokes and in 1880 was compelled to give up his interests in railroads altogether.

The Texas and Pacific Railway Company, chartered in 1871 to link Marshall in Texas to San Diego in California, was blighted by construction delays while Scott was involved.

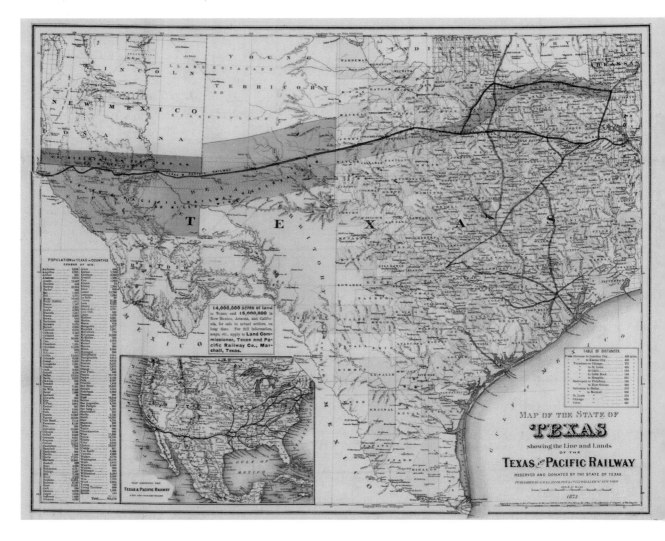

PENN STATION

The PRR continued to ride high for decades. By the turn of the twentieth century it was operating more than 10,000 miles (16,000 km) of track, had 100,000 employees and a budget which matched that of the Federal government. So familiar was its moniker and livery, it had been acclaimed as the 'standard railroad of the world'.

Visionary Alexander Cassatt (1839–1906) was in charge at the time, determined to produce some statement engineering to further define the company.

Thanks to him, the Rockville Bridge was opened in 1902, the product of two years of hard labour by 800, mainly Italian, workers. It comprised 48 elegant stone arches measuring 3,830 ft (1,165 m) and spanning the Susquehanna River near Harrisburg. Although the bridge was made from 220,000 tons of sandstone, it was filled with 600,000 barrels of cement to shoulder the burden of heavy modern locomotives.

TUNNELLING UNDER THE HUDSON

But his greatest legacy was the splendid Penn Station, a monumental terminal built atop a new underground hub for trains emerging from tunnels under the Hudson and East Rivers.

He was struck by the need for another approach to New York, after enduring the chaos of arriving in New Jersey by train and taking a ferry across the busy Hudson. Recent plans for a bridge had been shelved.

During its demolition Penn Station still revealed glimpses of its former glory.

When he later visited the Gare d'Orsay in Paris he realized that stations could be noble rather than workaday and that electric trains working underground were an untried option.

The first hurdle was buying the necessary land, some eight acres of it, in Tenderloin – at the time smothered by tenements and a functioning red light district. Three men went door-to-door offering cash for immediate property sales.

Then there was the extraordinary tunnelling project needed to get PRR trains into Manhattan, which, according to *Engineering News*, was 'the most extensive and difficult piece of submarine tunnel work ever undertaken'.

Tunnellers, known as sandhogs, died from 'the bends' brought about by underground pressure, and they drowned when tunnels flooded. Exaggerated press reports about fatalities began to tarnish PRR's public image.

CASSATT'S CLASSICAL MONUMENT

To cap off this immense undertaking, Cassatt had in mind something grand and classical, to bring a feel of Ancient Rome to the streets of a thoroughly modern metropolis.

He called in noted Beaux Arts architect Charles McKim (1847–1909), whose company was behind other mammoth and stylish projects, including Boston Public Library, Harvard School of Business and the National Museum of American History in Washington, D.C..

When it opened in 1910, the station had granite, marble, steel and glass fused together in a celebration of city and engineering, presented like a gift from PRR to New York's people. It was soon a beloved landmark. As art historian Hilary Ballon pointed out: 'Penn Station did not make you feel comfortable; it made you feel important.'

'ACT OF VANDALISM'

By the end of the Second World War, 109 million people passed through Penn Station each year. But numbers declined after the war, and the PRR faced cash-flow difficulties. In response, it proposed rebuilding the station. In 1963, a three-year demolition programme began, despite opposition. According to the *New York Times*: 'Until the first blow fell, no one was convinced that Penn Station really would be demolished, or that New York would permit this monumental act of vandalism against one of the largest and finest landmarks of its age.'

Madison Square Garden was built in its place. Recently, a further redevelopment has been announced, with New York state governor Andrew Cuomo saying that the present station was dark, constrained, ugly, dated and 'a lost opportunity'.

Despite the demolition, the PRR could not survive, filing for bankruptcy two years after a merger with New York Central.

Tenement living in New York was a grim reality for immigrants and, as this 1891 photo reveals, contrasted sharply with the city's monumental public buildings.

COMFORT & SAFETY

Today, the prospect of travelling by rarely seen steam trains inspires great excitement. While the ubiquitous chugging locomotive, its progress marked by the plume from its smoke stack, has disappeared, the romance attached to it remains vibrant.

But spare a thought for nineteenth-century travellers, who were assailed with smuts as they waited at stations. Inside carriages, the atmosphere was fuggy, with long-distance travellers unable to wash or change their clothes. Sanitary arrangements were at a minimum, as were hygiene standards. Sleeping was often done sitting up.

For locomotive crews there were different concerns, primarily focusing on safety. Despite the introduction of train orders – a telegraph sent between stations to establish the whereabouts of a service and thus eliminate the chance of collisions – the safety record on American railroads remained an anxiety.

A preference for single tracks was partly the cause, although fires, driver tiredness and inadequate rail maintenance all played their part.

Despite an alarming rate of crashes, people still chose to use the train and the burgeoning middle classes preferred to travel in something classy. George Pullman's luxury coaches transformed the travelling experience for those who could afford them. They were generally staffed by African American workers.

A Pullman carriage on one of the Pacific routes offered a measure of comfort, although engravings like this, which appeared in European newspapers, depicted unfeasibly wide dimensions.

BRAKES & COUPLERS

On an Illinois summer's night in 1887, an overnight train, packed with trippers for Niagara Falls, was heading down a slight incline at about 40 mph (64 km/h) when the driver noticed flames ahead, licking around a wooden trestle that supported the track.

His engine crossed the breach, but a second locomotive attached directly behind to haul the 15 coaches slammed into the bank.

According to the following week's *Harper's Weekly*, '[Carriages] came crashing with terrific force upon one another, telescoped throughout their length and piled in splinters over the broken and burning trestle.'

The Chatsworth crash was one of the worst in American railroad history, claiming the lives of 85 people and leaving many wounded – but it wasn't an isolated incident. There were plenty of hazards dogging the American rails at the time.

On this occasion the trestle caught fire after a crew had been sent by the railroad earlier in the day to burn undergrowth left tinder-dry by a drought. But the risk of sparks from steam locomotives igniting wooden structures was well known and there was an on-going campaign to replace timber in bridges with iron, steel or stone.

SHOCKING STATISTICS

The risk to passengers was not inconsiderable. In 1902, figures shows that 271 US rail passengers were killed and 6,323 injured. But that paled compared to the figures relating to railroad employees. Ten times as many railroadmen were killed that year, while the injury figures stood at 1,189,000.

Five years later the news was worse, with 571 passengers and 4,218 railroadmen killed.

The rates of death and injury in America stood at double those recorded in the UK. Only about half of the families involved received compensation, which never exceeded six months' pay.

SAFETY MEASURES SLOWLY ADOPTED

Changes were being made, albeit slowly. Recognizing the perils of a primitive block-braking system, George Westinghouse had patented an air brake as early as 1869, and he continually refined his design.

But Westinghouse had difficulty persuading railroad owners of its merits. Vanderbilt spluttered with indignation when Westinghouse tried to make a sale. Could Westinghouse really be suggesting that trains could be stopped by air?

Men were frequently injured linking railroad carriages together. As a consequence, brakemen became easily distinguishable for having missing digits or deformed hands.

FIGHTING FIRES

Passengers and crew both feared the consequences of a train blaze. However, these reduced in frequency during the 1880s when oil stoves, candles and gas lamps began to be replaced by steam heating directed from the locomotive, and electric lights. State laws centred on smoke abatement, drafted in the early years of the twentieth century, improved fire safety and hastened the electrification of the railroad system, which had begun just a few years before.

In 1873, Confederate veteran Eli Janney developed an automatic coupler that eliminated the need for human hands in the procedure.

Twenty years later, the Safety Appliances Act at last decreed that Westinghouse's air brake and Janney's coupler were mandatory. Although there was a generous grace period of seven years for railroads to come into line, it was the first Federal legislation on employee safety.

This was followed by other Federal laws to protect workers and passengers, including one that limited working hours and another that governed the way employees emptied locomotive ash pans, something that had previously caused widespread injury. Steel-bodied carriages, first introduced in 1907, and covered vestibules replacing the platforms that once existed at carriage ends also made train travel safer.

Although it took some time for results to become apparent, 1931 figures show that the number of railroad workers who died numbered 615, while only 30 passengers were killed.

Westinghouse's air brake enhanced passenger safety.

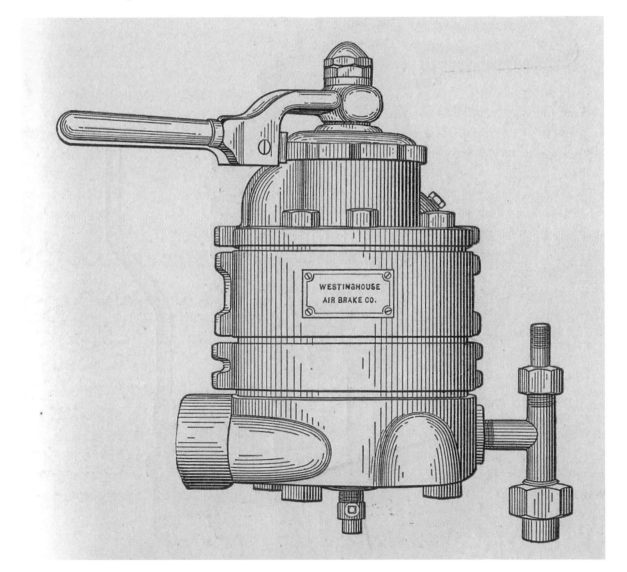

GEORGE PULLMAN'S PALACES

When George Pullman (1831–97) travelled on an overnight train between Buffalo and Westfield, New York, he learned just how uncomfortable rail travel could be.

Typically, carriages had inadequate suspension, hard seats, poor ventilation and if beds were provided, they were only boards.

He decided to change things by building luxury railroad accommodation for passengers who wanted to travel in style and were willing to pay for the privilege.

After some trials, his flagship coach, 'Pioneer', was ready at a cost of $18,000 – in time to be attached to Lincoln's funeral train at Chicago for Mrs Lincoln's comfort.

This lent Pullman huge kudos, and he committed his personal fortune to a new company, which from 1868 was known as the Pullman Palace Car Company.

Rather than sell the carriages, he leased them to train companies or even wealthy individuals, who revelled in the coil spring and rubber block suspension, the plush carpets, richly varnished wood and silver-trimmed lamps. There were sheets on the bed and curtains shielding the sleeping compartments. Before long, he added a restaurant, and by 1879 he had a pool of 464 coaches and an annual turnover of some $2.2 million.

Luxury carriages were popular. As actress Eleanor Robson Belmont pointed out: 'A private railroad [carriage] is not an acquired taste. One takes to it immediately.'

Pullman wasn't the first to produce sleepers. A rudimentary model was in service as early as 1836. Nor was he the only carriage builder to build well-appointed train accommodation. Webster Wagner (1817–82) was a ticket and freight agent on the Schenectady & Utica Railroad in 1843 when he came up with the notion. His first sleeper coaches ran on the New York Central in 1858, while his drawing-room coaches appeared in 1867. Wagner died when one caught fire. Eight years later his company was taken over by Pullman's.

But Pullman was the most well-known. He also became notorious for his autocratic ways.

PULLMAN THE PATRIARCH
In 1880 Pullman bought land outside Chicago to build a town named after him. He believed he could provide decent accommodation for workers in the locality of a new factory. So far, so benevolent.

Pullman succeeded in selling his coaches to British railway companies.

However, the homes were strictly hierarchical, reflecting a feudal society in this company town. And, after the Panic of 1893, when Pullman cut jobs and wages, he continued to charge the same rents to his workers, despite curbing their income.

On 11 May 1894, 4,000 workers went on strike under the banner of the American Railway Union. More than 30 people died as a result of sabotage and riots as the union organized a boycott of Pullman coaches nationwide. On 4 July, Federal troops took control of Pullman. The union leaders were jailed and Pullman's workers went back to the factory although they never forgave him for his treatment of them. After his death from a heart attack, Pullman was buried in a lead-lined coffin that was concreted into the grave for fear of his body being dug up by disgruntled employees.

George Pullman built a town for his workers, but its feudal organisation left them frustrated and angry.

STANDARD CLASS

In 1892, author Robert Louis Stevenson wrote about his rail journey across America, where he found superior accommodation on the Central Pacific line after travelling on the perpetually troubled Union Pacific.

The cars on the Central Pacific were nearly twice as high, and so proportionally airier; they were freshly varnished which gave us all a sense of cleanliness as though we had bathed. The seats drew out and joined in the centre so that there was no more need for bed boards and there was an upper tier of berths which could be closed by day and opened at night.

FLORIDA LIFE

For transforming a shabby backwater into a chic resort, Henry B. Plant (1819–99) was hailed as 'the king of Florida'.

Plant began his railroad empire after the Civil War by rebuilding the wrecked southern track system, which he then coupled with a steamship company.

He dubbed his network 'the Plant system', and it supplied the southern state's rich array of produce – including citrus, celery and cigars – to hungry markets on the eastern seaboard in quantity, swiftly and cheaply.

To this he added a chain of hotels, with each branch of his business promoting the others.

THE DELIGHTS OF TAMPA

It was with this joined-up thinking that he transformed Tampa from a village of a few hundred people to a first-class venue.

After picking it as the terminus of his Florida railroad and the home port of his steamships, he built a $3 million hotel with 511 rooms, the first in Florida to have a lift, electric lights and a phone in each room. (In 1898 it became the US military headquarters during the Spanish–American War, fought over Spanish colonies in the region.)

With its exotic appearance and sumptuous surroundings, the hotel dominated a town where pavements were new and the population still sparse. But before long Tampa began to blossom, with a golf course, swimming pool, casino and horse-racing track soon attached to the hotel.

One newspaper report in 1895 described Plant as 'one of those remarkable men who master all conditions and create environment. He is a builder – a creator. A whole state blossoms at the touch of his magic wand.'

With the development of Florida, his name is usually coupled with Henry Flagler (1830–1913), a friendly rival whose Florida East Coast Railroad led to the expansion of Miami and Palm Beach.

JIM CROW LAWS

However, not everyone in Florida was benefitting from the Plant system effect.

African Americans everywhere were freed from slavery following the Civil War. But wounded southern states immediately legislated to curb their rights with what's known as the Jim Crow Laws.

Plant's exotic and luxurious hotel in Tampa was visited by train and steamship passengers.

Under the much-vaunted 'separate but equal' rationale, trains had accommodation reserved for white people and Jim Crow cars, which had no luggage racks, smaller toilets and less comfortable seating, for African American passengers.

In Florida in 1865, an African American who was found in accommodation not designated for them risked being pilloried or whipped, with the number of strokes limited to 39. Admittedly, the same penalty applied to European Americans straying into cars earmarked for African Americans, but it is not clear why they would choose inferior carriages.

And an 1887 law insisted Jim Crow carriages were 'equally as good and provided with the same facilities for comfort as for white persons'. Railroad companies risked a $500 fine if they did not concur. But Jim Crow cars that have survived into the modern era do not tell a story of equality. And this was set against a host of other life-limiting laws. Segregation legislation continued to be passed in Florida until 1967.

STANDARD TIME

With each railroad company using 'sun' time, schedules fell between haphazard and nonsensical, with noon in Chicago and Washington coming one hour and 23 minutes apart. As early as 1870, the *Railway Gazette* had urged the US to mimic Britain's adoption of 'railroad time', advocated by railroad guide writer George Bradshaw, among others, and introduced from 1847. But the idea was opposed by many, including churchmen who felt it flew in the face of God's authority.

On 18 November 1883, the US was nominally divided into time zones, each with uniform times an hour apart from its neighbour. However, it wasn't until Congress acted in 1918 that standard time became compulsory.

Jim Crow cars were notoriously scruffy by comparison with white-only coaches running on the same trains.

BRIDGES & TUNNELS

As railroad momentum continued after the Civil War, so cities and towns were indelibly marked by their presence.

Take Boston as an example. *Appleton's* outlines just how railroads proliferated there by the 1880s.

The Lowell Railroad depot is one of the largest and finest in the country. It is of brick trimmed with Nova Scotia freestone, 700 ft long and 205 ft wide. Just beside it in Causeway St stands the depot of the Eastern Railway; and a few paces from the latter is the depot of the Fitchburg Railroad. The Boston & Albany depot is in Beach Street ... the depot of the Maine Central is on Haymarket Square ... the Providence Railroad is on Columbus Avenue ... the Old Colony Railroad is at the corner of Kneeland and South Streets and that of the New York and New England Railroad is at the foot of Summer Street.

There was a new enthusiasm for bridges and tunnels, not least to take railroad tracks underground in cities that were being choked with tracks.

By 1873, the Baltimore & Potomac Tunnel and the Union Tunnel both opened in Baltimore at a cost of $4.5 million.

Unfolding technology meant rivers and mountains that had previously been barriers to railroad extensions could be conquered. But triumphal arches and record-breaking burrows came at a cost for workers employed on the keynote projects. Some were killed and many more still were injured, as they worked in desperately claustrophobic conditions underground or underwater.

Brooklyn Bridge became emblematic of New York after its completion in 1883.

COPYRIGHT 1896.

J.S. JOHNSTON

THE EADS BRIDGE

Like a broad, blue vein, the Mississippi River runs for 2,300 miles (3,700 km) through the heart of America where, for decades, it proved an obstacle to railroad expansion.

While narrower rivers could be bridged, freight still had to be ferried across the Mississippi, known as the Father of Waters, at St Louis, costing time and money.

Chicago and St Louis, keen commercial rivals after the Civil War, eyed one another across Illinois with suspicion as they vied for dominance in the domestic market. The longer St Louis was saddled with this barrier the better, as far as Chicago was concerned.

Accordingly, Chicago businessmen sought exclusive rights to build a bridge in St Louis – one they knew they would never construct.

EADS THE INNOVATOR

The ruse may well have delayed the construction of a river crossing, with four river bridges being built in Chicago before one was opened at St Louis. But when James Eads (1820–87) produced a blueprint in 1867, it incorporated the latest technology to reach a third of a mile across the river, at a height of some 60 ft (18.2 m) in order to permit clearance for ships.

Eads proposed building the world's first steel-arch bridge, to the consternation of steel magnate Cornelius Vanderbilt.

Designer James Eads had no qualifications when it came to bridge design but his sound instincts led to a stunning river crossing.

FACTS AND STATS

The three spans of the bridge, two of 502 ft (152 m) and the central one measuring 520 ft (520 m) were braced with hollow steel tubes. The bridge had two storeys: the lower one for trains and the upper for horses, carriages and pedestrians. On the city side of the river, trains disappeared into a 4,800-ft (1,463-m) tunnel to avoid its busy centre.

As an ill-educated boy, Eads had sold apples on the streets of St Louis. Although he had since made a fortune in salvage, he was no expert in bridge design, as detractors were swift to point out. Even his supporters urged him to consult seasoned bridge builders.

Although Eads was confident in his design, Carnegie at first refused him use of his steel, fearing poor publicity for his prized product should the bridge fail.

A testy relationship existed between the two men from the first, although ultimately he and Eads came to an agreement.

SINKING THE FOUNDATIONS

But it wasn't the only difficulty faced by Eads. He built caissons – pressurized, watertight chambers – to create the foundations for the granite and limestone piers on the bedrock of the river. Although he'd seen them used in France, it was the first time caissons had been put through their paces in America.

As the depth increased to 100 ft (30 m) below the surface, and the pressure became greater, men started suffering from severe stomach ailments: what we now know to be 'the bends'. Fifteen men died as a result. Eads provided a floating hospital alongside the decompression chamber, but his doctor didn't fully understand the cause of the illness.

Builders were also inundated during spring floods and lashed by a tornado so powerful it lifted a locomotive from its rails. Would the steel bridge hold firm? Eads had sent several batches of steel back to Carnegie to be re-rolled, to fulfil the specification on metal intensity.

To dispel any doubts about the strength of steel, a circus elephant was led along the bridge before locomotives were sent across. When the Eads Bridge was officially opened on 4 July 1874, by General William Tecumseh Sherman, it was the largest bridge in the world.

Although Carnegie had sold his stock in the bridge before it was completed, he later described the bridge, tunnel and its approaches as 'magnificent'.

According to *Appleton's*, which put the cost at $10 million, the bridge 'is regarded as one of the greatest triumphs of American engineering.'

HOOSAC TUNNEL

When America's longest tunnel opened in 1875, a lengthy episode in engineering history came to a close. But any triumph felt by those involved was tempered by a few sobering statistics.

The 5-mile (8-km) long Hoosac Tunnel had taken 20 years to build and cost ten times the original estimate.

EASTERN ENTRANCE TO HOOSAC TUNNEL.

WESTERN ENTRANCE TO HOOSAC TUNNEL.

At one end of the tunnel there was tough granite while workers at the other dealt with crumbling rock.

An equivalent project in Europe, the Mount Cenis tunnel, opened in 1870, was three miles longer, took seven years less to complete and was consequently considerably cheaper.

SLOW PROGRESS FROM THE START

It had begun in 1854 with an optimistic refrain: 'On to Hoosac, on to the west.' Traders in and around Boston were delighted at the prospect of a direct link with the Erie Canal.

But some of the costs reflected long-running political opposition from those with different vested interests, who called it 'the Great Bore' or 'the Road to Ruin'.

Like the Alpine link, the Hoosac Tunnel took shape only slowly at the start, with men hammering on handheld drills, called steel drivers, making limited headway.

It wasn't until 1867, when Charles Burleigh (1824–83) invented a drill operated by compressed air and mounted on a frame, that better progress was made.

Three years later, *Scribner's Magazine* published an account of a journalist who had visited the tunnel under construction at its eastern end.

By the use of drilling machines, the progress of the work has been greatly accelerated. An average advance of one hundred and fifty feet a month is made at the heading at this end... The clamor which they make is absolutely terrific.

He reported that the 750 workers were mostly Irish but included some Cornish miners.

Using nitroglycerin in place of gunpowder also speeded up tunnelling work.

A different issue confronted men at the western side of the mountain, where progress was slower. They dug into the crumbling edifice of 'porridge' rock. A brick-built tube finally resolved the issue but added greatly to the bill.

HEAVY COST IN HUMAN LIFE

The human cost also gave pause.

The worst accident occurred in 1867 at the central shaft, which had to be sunk vertically from mountain top to track level, the height of the Empire State Building. When the shaft was half completed a fire knocked out the steam-driven air and water pumps, and the 13 men below were showered with tools and sparks. All died from suffocation or drowning.

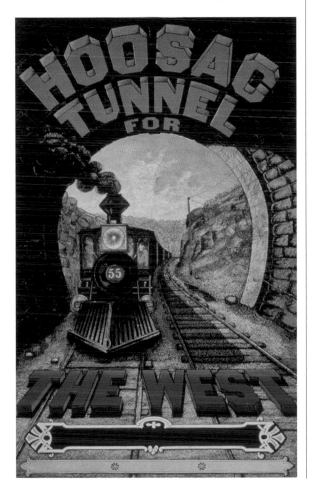

JOHN HENRY

In American folk lore, John Henry is a freed slave employed as a steel driver on a Chesapeake & Ohio Railroad Company tunnel who competes with a steam-driven drill. Although Henry wins the contest, he immediately collapses and dies. No one knows the exact identity of John Henry, but the episode features in folk songs used in workers and civil rights campaigns.

Afterwards, the shaft – re-opened a year later – was dubbed 'the bloody pit'.

In 1868, costs were already at more than $9 million. Now Irish-born Canadians Walter and Francis Shanly took over the project, and their policy of better treatment for workers helped accomplish the mammoth task.

ASPHYXIATING FUMES

By 1899, about 50 trains used the tunnel daily. But, despite the central shaft and a giant fan, the problem of noxious locomotive smoke blinding and choking drivers and passengers was immense.

One solution seemed to be the recent development of oil burners, steam trains fuelled by oil. But the toxic fumes from these were even worse.

Charles Mellen, of the New York, New Haven & Hartford Railroad, managed the tunnel when he took over the Boston & Maine Railroad, and had electric engines tow steam locomotives through the tunnel to alleviate the problem.

Hopes were high that the Hoosac Tunnel would bring new prosperity by opening a swift route to the west.

THE BROOKLYN BRIDGE

Brooklyn Bridge is an American icon, a triumph of foresight, design and engineering genius. In connecting the great population centres of Manhattan and Brooklyn, it became the beating heart of a great city. Yet, although it originally incorporated a railroad, it never quite embraced the age of steam.

Since the early nineteenth century, New York's city fathers had agonized over the need for a bridge over the East River. While Manhattan (population c.800,000) was overcrowded, Brooklyn, across the water, had barely half as many residents. Linking them would help spread the population and encourage Brooklyn's development.

But the river was tidal, turbulent and one of the busiest waterways in the world. Building bridge supports across it would be, it was claimed, a major hazard to shipping. Similar arguments were being trotted out by steamboat owners across

The opening of the Brooklyn Bridge helped alleviate traffic on the busy waterway beneath.

America, in a futile attempt to deter railroad competition. However, in the case of New York, the opposition had real merit, even when the loudest voices came from the host of ferry operators who would be affected.

NEW YORK IN SUSPENSE

A solution finally came from a German immigrant, John Roebling (1806–69). He had made a breakthrough in suspension-bridge technology by adding a stabilizing wire-rope framework on either side of the main span. Happily, he also started a seven strand wire-rope manufacturing business.

The wire rope had proved successful in his previous projects, across the rivers Delaware, Niagara and Ohio, and with the support of influential Brooklyn businessman William Kingsley, Roebling won permission from the New York State Legislature. A private company was formed with the City of Brooklyn (as main beneficiary) taking $3 million worth of shares, and the City of New York subscribing $1.5 million. The company would make money through tolls capped at 15 per cent profit per year.

In 1869, work started on what would, at 1,595 ft (486 m), be the longest suspension bridge in the world. It was also the first built of steel. Sadly, Roebling never lived to see it; a freak accident in which his foot was crushed by a ferry resulted in the amputation of some toes and a fatal tetanus infection.

His son Washington (1837–1926) took over as chief engineer, only to himself endure an unforeseen peril.

To ensure a solid foundation, construction workers dug the riverbed inside sunken wooden chambers. Pressurized air kept water out, but the return to the surface in iron carriages, known as airlocks, was too fast and caused 'the bends'.

NO FUTURE PROSPECTS

As elsewhere, the tracks across Brooklyn Bridge were doomed by successive transport revolutions. Initially, the BRT's aim was to consolidate surface and elevated railroads across Brooklyn and Queens. But the onset of the First World War hit the company badly. Raging inflation and the aftermath of the Malbone Street Wreck, in which 93 people were killed, left it financially strapped. In 1923, it was reconstituted as the Brooklyn–Manhattan Transit Corporation. The BMT fared little better. By 1944, when the car was king, the elevated railroad was converted to a trolley-car system and within a decade the tracks were removed completely.

Washington Roebling himself was affected and remained partially paralysed for life.

SUCCESSFUL OPENING

Despite these setbacks, Brooklyn Bridge opened to wild celebrations in May 1883. An estimated 250,000 people strolled over its elevated walkway in the first 24 hours, while below them horse-drawn traffic, trolleys and even livestock bustled along.

Roebling had provided for two elevated railroad tracks along the centre of the span, and these were initially used by the New York & Brooklyn Bridge Railway. It operated an odd hybrid arrangement involving cable cars and steam locomotives (which manoeuvred the cars in and out of each bridge terminal). However, when the Brooklyn Rapid Transit Company took over in 1896, the cables were converted to electric power.

TIMELINE

1825 Erie Canal opens

1826 John Stevens runs a steam locomotive on a test track at his home in Hoboken

1827 Granite Railway gets underway, using horsepower

1828 First shovelful turned on the Baltimore & Ohio Railroad

1829 Horatio Allen drives the British-made *Stourbridge Lion*, the first locomotive to run in the US

1829 Rainhill Trials in the UK settle issue of locomotive design, with George Stephenson's *Rocket* selected

1830 *Tom Thumb*, the first locomotive built in America, loses its race with a horse on a B&O line

1830 *Best Friend of Charleston*, built at West Point Foundry, begins a scheduled service

1831 Another West Point Foundry engine, *DeWitt Clinton*, becomes the first to run on northern rails

1831 First all-iron T-rails introduced to US, used in place of strap-iron rails

1832 Louisiana and Virginia open first railroads

1832 Jervis builds *Experiment* for the Mohawk & Hudson Railroad

1832 Cowcatchers are added to locomotives

1832 Alabama opens its first railroad

1833 The 136-mile (219-km) route between Charleston and Hamburg is completed – the longest in the world

1833 First two passengers to die in a train accident in America perish at Hightstown, New Jersey

1834 Kentucky opens its first railroad

1836 Florida, Michigan and Ohio open their first railroads

1837 Georgia and Mississippi open their first railroads

1838 Illinois and Indiana open their first railroads

1840 **2,818 miles (4,535 km) of track in operation**

1842 Tennessee opens its first railroad

1846 Mexican War breaks out

1848 First section of Pennsylvania Railroad opened, between Harrisburg and Philadelphia

1850 Illinois Central receives the first Federal land grant

1850 **9,000 miles (14,484 km) of track in operation**

1850 Wisconsin opens its first railroad

1851 Erie Railroad completed

1852 Missouri opens its first railroad

1853 Texas opens its first railroad

1854 Horseshoe Curve opens in Pennsylvania

1855 Iowa opens its first railroad

1856 California opens its first railroad

1857 Arkansas opens its first railroad

1858 **One estimate says there are 26,000 miles (41,843 km) of track in operation, meaning an average of one mile of railroad for every 38.5 square miles (99.7 square km) of territory**

1859 Abolitionist John Brown's ill-fated railroad attack

1859 First commercial oil well drilled at Titusville, Pennsylvania

1860 More than 30,000 miles (48,280 km) of track in operation

1861 US Civil War starts at Fort Sumter

1862 The Great Locomotive Chase

1862 Minnesota and Oregon open their first railroads

1864 Pacific Railroad Act increases land grants to 20 miles and allows railroad companies to sell bonds equalling the government loans they have received

1864 First steel rails used in the US, imported from England by the PRR

1865 US Civil War ends at Appomattox. Although the precise number isn't known it is thought about 700,000 men died during hostilities

1865 President Lincoln is assassinated

1865 Pullman's first coach in service

1866 First refrigerated shipment of fruit carried to Chicago on Illinois Central train

1867 'Thunderbolt Express', with its freight of only strawberries, operates between southern Illinois and Chicago

1867 Cambria Iron Works in Johnstown produce the first steel rails made in America

1869 Union Pacific and Central Pacific meet at Promontory, Utah, to complete the first transcontinental railroad link in the US

1869 George Westinghouse develops the air brake

1870 53,000 miles (85,295 km) of track in operation

1870 New signals help improve safety

1871 Vanderbilt's Grand Central Depot station opens in New York

1872 Oil War breaks out in Pennsylvania

1874 Eads Bridge opens in St Louis

1875 Hoosac Tunnel opens

1877 Widespread railroad strikes

1880 93,000 miles (149,668 km) of track in operation

1882 11,500 miles (18,507 km) of track built this year alone

1883 Standard time adopted by railroads

1883 Brooklyn Bridge opens

1887 Interstate Commerce Commission formed

1890 163,000 miles (262,323 km) of track in operation, half of which are made of steel

1893 Safety Appliances Act makes better brakes and couplers mandatory

1894 George Pullman's workers go on strike

1900 193,000 miles (310,603 km) of track in operation, 95 per cent of which are made of steel

1903 Elkins Act passed to stop restraint of trade by collusion on price

1906 Hepburn Act ends rebates and free passes

1907 In New Jersey alone, 45,810 people are recorded as being employed by the railroads

1910 Penn Station opens

1916 230,500 miles (370,149 km) of track in operation

CONCLUSION

Few in America remained untouched by the sight, sound and smoky reek of locomotives as networks sidling across the continent exerted their steely embrace.

Entire towns depended on them to survive and thrive – mining and steel towns especially so. But they weren't alone. Altoona, 100 miles (160 km) east of Pittsburgh, was established by the Pennsylvania Railroad Company in 1850 at the point where heavy-duty locomotives replaced less powerful models for the challenging ascent into the Alleghenies. An initial population of 2,000 was ten times bigger in 1880, and the town had some 82,000 residents by 1930 – a significant proportion of whom were involved in the railroad works. The expansion of railroads had created a way of life that directly affected millions.

Bound up with the railroads were numerous other businesses, including those that made shovels, picks and spiking mauls, conductors' watch fobs and ticket punches, staff uniforms, railroad cap badges and depot clocks. The railroads also had cutlery and teapots for dining cars, as well as calendars, match books, lighters, pens, paperweights, rulers, postcards and pictures to advertise their success.

Nor was *Appleton's* the only nineteenth-century guide to American railroads. *Poor's Manual of Railroads* and *The Official Railway Guide* were just two of the directories that offered insights into steam railroads and the companies that ran them.

Railroads were so entrenched in daily life that they became cultural icons – and spawned familiar offshoots. Phoebe Snow was one such early twentieth-century example: a make-believe socialite dressed in white who travelled on the Delaware, Lackawanna & Western Railroad and revelled in the cleanliness of her clothes, thanks to the anthracite fuel fed into that line's engines. Her serene smile and rhyming verse became more mascot than advertisement until First World War shortages ended her reign.

And, in retrospect, her disappearance seemed to herald the ebbing of the railroad era that had once been so dominant.

The appearance of the first motor cars at the turn of the century didn't unduly concern railroad companies, as excessive costs kept automobiles in the realm of the very rich.

But the bold decision in 1913 by manufacturer Henry Ford (1863–1947) to mass-produce Ford Model Ts on the world's first moving assembly line did make an impact. Before this model of automobile stopped being made in 1927, no fewer than 15 million had taken to the road.

The arrival of the car, which permitted its owner so much freedom in terms of timing and destination, came just ahead of passenger airlines, which began running after the First World War. Although scheduled services didn't become routinely used by many until the 1930s, in America, where there were vast distances to cover, aircraft were a natural substitute for locomotives. Thus, after the Second World War, the number of rail passengers plummeted by an estimated 84 per cent in 20 years.

By 1966, less than 2 per cent of all inter-city passenger travel was by rail.

Two years later, the doomed coupling of the Pennsylvania Rail Road and the New York Central to form Penn Central seemed to spell out the bleak future that awaited passenger railroads, always far less profitable than freight, even in the good times.

With the national network unravelling fast, the government stepped in to help form Amtrak in 1971, a quasi-state-run operation that would ensure the survival of passenger trains, despite associated financial implications.

Still, a quarter of the nation's routes, quested for and cherished in previous decades, fell into disuse.

It wasn't necessarily the end for derelict railroad lines, however. In New York, one urban railroad relic was transformed into a garden. The High Line in Manhattan was even planned to reflect the plants that grew at will around the tracks after it was finally abandoned in 1980. It is progress, though not the sort previously linked to railroads.

Their time in the sun may be over, but the epic dynamism and scale that railroads brought to America during 100 years that neatly straddled two centuries will never be put in the shade.

Although passenger trains are less popular than previously, the work schedule of locomotives that pull freight trains in America is still hectic, with their distinctive profiles lining up at yards like this one in Kansas.

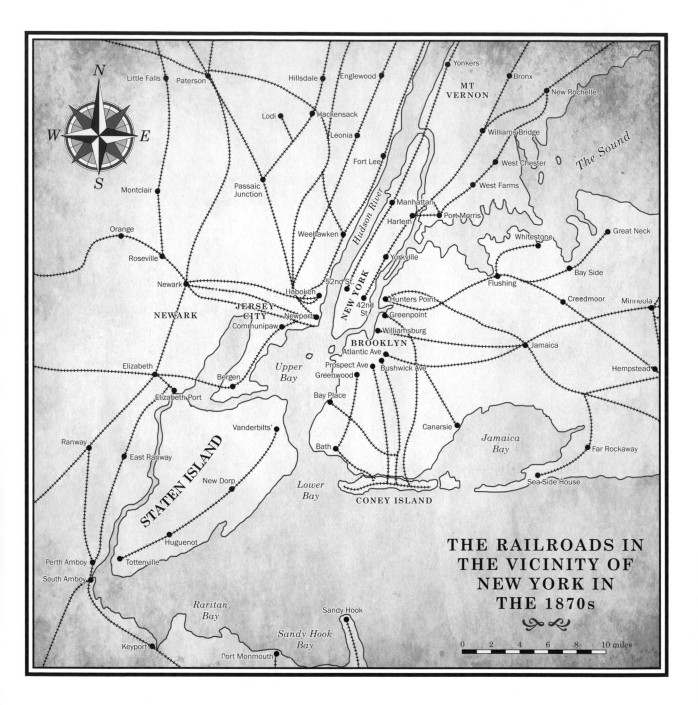

Opposite: A 1930's vintage American railroad poster.

The New EMPIRE STATE EXPRESS

NEW YORK CENTRAL SYSTEM

INDEX

PICTURE CREDITS

14–15 © AP/Press Association Images; 33 © The Geography and Map Division, Library of Congress; 40 source unknown; 49 source unknown; 70 © Putnam Museum, Davenport, Iowa; 72 © Rock Island County Historical Society; 107, bottom © The Library of Virginia; 159, top © Everett Collection/REX/Shutterstock; 188 © US Department of the Interior, General Land Office; 189 © Cornell University – PJ Mode Collection of Persuasive Cartography; 194 © The Art Archive/REX/Shutterstock; 203 © Everett Collection/ REX/Shutterstock; 221 © Texas State Library and Archives Commission; 227 © William Wallace Wood, The Westinghouse E-T Air Brake Instruction Pocket Book; 231 source unknown

Alamy: 11 (© Rick Pisio\RWP Photography); 16 (© gameover); 19, 22–23 (© Chronicle); 27, 42, 94, 132 (© Niday Picture Library); 30, 68, 80, 83, 90, 114, 142, 167, 181, 191 top right, 191 bottom right, 192, 210, 211, 228 (© Granger Historical Picture Archive); 35, 78–79, 104–105, 119, 186–187 (© The Protected Art Archive); 44–45, 137, 149, 172–173, 178, 200 (© North Wind Picture Archives); 52, 126–127, 159 bottom (© Photo Researchers, Inc.); 54 (© X3A Collection); 61 (© Ivy Close Images); 66 (© The Print Collector); 71, 85, 202 (© 916 collection); 82 (© Chris Pondy); 91 (© Edwin Remsberg); 97 (© 615 collection); 99 (© Joe King); 100 (© nsf); 106, 154, 161, 191 top left, 191 bottom left (© Everett Collection Historical); 107 top (© IanDagnall Computing); 108 (© Classic Image); 112 (© Collection PJ); 121 (© Alpha Historica); 123 (© Historical Art Collection (HAC)); 124 (© GL

Archive); 129 (© Old Paper Studios); 139 (© Oldtime); 155 (© A2Z Collection); 163 (© David Cole); 166 (© Heritage Image Partnership Ltd); 196, 224–225 (© INTERFOTO); 201 (© Anka Agency International); 216–217 (© Robert (Bob) Edmonson); 217 top (© Daniel Borzynski); 229 (© Christine Whitehead); 230 (© Brian Jannsen); 245 (© Shawshots)

Getty Images: 20, 38, 56, 84, 92–93, 101, 122, 164, 209, 218 (© Buyenlarge); 24 (© Fine Art); 28 (© Historic Map Works LLC); 31 (© Archive Photos / Stringer); 36 (© George Rinhart); 46, 146 (© Interim Archives); 50 (© Science & Society Picture Library); 59 (© George Skadding); 62, 110 (© Authenticated News / Staff); 64, 134 (© Universal History Archive); 74, 76–77, 86, 89, 152, 156, 168, 175, 177, 214, 223 (© Bettmann); 75, 116–117, 232–233, 237 (© Library of Congress); 125 (© Juan Camilo Bernal Photographer); 130 (© Roger Viollet Collection); 140 (© Museum of the City of New York/Byron Collection); 145 top (© Museum of the City of New York); 145 bottom, 236 (© Kean Collection); 153, 193 (© PhotoQuest); 150 (© FPG); 171, 184–185 (© Underwood Archives); 183 (© Leonard McCombe); 197 (© D. F. Barry / Stringer); 198 (© Fotosearch / Stringer); 204–205 (© Topical Press Agency / Stringer); 207, 213 (© Stock Montage); 222 (© Robert R. McElroy); 234 (© Print Collector); 238 (© De Agostini Picture Library); 243 (© Bloomberg)

Maps on endpapers and pages 182 and 244 by ML Design

PUBLISHER'S ACKNOWLEDGEMENTS

The publishers would like to thank everyone at Fremantle who has supported this book. For unlimited help and advice, with grateful thanks to John Comerford and Alison Kreps. To Cat Ledger, Esther Johnson, Judi O'Brien and Mark Chare for vital backup. And, of course, special thanks to Michael Portillo for his invaluable contribution. To Daniel Mirzoeff, Pam Cavanagh and Alex McLeod for their support.

Publishing Director: Iain MacGregor
Researcher and writer: Karen Farrington
Designer: Keith Williams, sprout.uk.com
Project Editor: Laura Nickoll
Editorial Assistant: Harriet Dobson

BIBLIOGRAPHY

Iron Road to the West: American Railroads in the 1850s by John F. Stover (New York: Columbia University Press, 1978)

American Railroads by John F. Stover (University of Chicago Press, 1961)

Rails Across America: A History of Railroads in North America edited by William L. Withuhn (Smithmark, 1993)

North American Railways by J. B. Hollingsworth and P. B. Whitehouse (Bison Books, 1977)

The American Heritage History of Railroads in America by Oliver Jensen (Random House Value Publishing, 1993)

Useful websites: http://www.jstor.org/ and http://www.american-rails.com/